# The Crucial Voice of the People, Past and Present

## *Education's Missing Ingredient, 2nd edition*

### Victoria M. Young

ROWMAN & LITTLEFIELD EDUCATION
A division of
ROWMAN & LITTLEFIELD PUBLISHERS, INC.
Lanham • New York • Toronto • Plymouth, UK

Published by Rowman & Littlefield Education
A division of Rowman & Littlefield Publishers, Inc.
A wholly owned subsidary of The Rowman & Littlefield Publishing Group, Inc.
4501 Forbes Boulevard, Suite 200, Lanham, Maryland 20706
www.rowman.com

10 Thornbury Road, Plymouth PL6 7PP, United Kingdom

British Library Cataloguing in Publication Information Available

**Library of Congress Cataloging-in-Publication Data**

Young, Victoria M., 1956-
The crucial voice of the people, past and present : a second edition of education's missing ingredient /
Victoria M. Young.
p. cm.
Includes bibliographical references and index.
ISBN 978-1-4758-0021-0 (pbk. : alk. paper) -- ISBN 978-1-4758-0022-7 (electronic)
1. Public schools--United States. 2. Education--Aims and objectives--United States. 3. Education--
Parent participation--United States. I. Title.
LA217.2.Y68 2012
371.010973--dc23
2012022263

Printed in the United States of America

*"No law or ordinance is mightier than understanding."*

—Plato

This book is dedicated to my mother,
Adeline Magnotta Young (August 15, 1926–November 15, 2009),
and to my father, James Nicolas Young, Jr.,
a teacher by profession and by example.

# Contents

# Foreword

## Gary M. Ratner

In this remarkable book, Idaho veterinarian, parent, school volunteer, and education advocate Dr. Victoria Young raises some of the most fundamental questions confronting the future of American public education. Do the American people genuinely believe in providing equal educational opportunity for our millions of children in low-performing schools? Do America's citizens understand that public policies have resulted in severely unequal and inadequate education, particularly for disadvantaged children? Since the No Child Left Behind Act (NCLB), high-stakes testing strategy has widely failed to turn around our low-achieving schools and is causing serious harm. Is there an alternative strategy that works? What will it take to profoundly redirect America's fundamentally flawed and destructive "tests and sanctions" laws and policies so that schools improve and provide all our children a good education?

At root, *The Crucial Voice of the People: Past and Present* is a call to action for America's citizens to stop being passive about the test and sanctions strategy that many politicians and the education establishment have imposed on our public schools nationwide over the last two decades. Young powerfully reminds us that we, America's citizens, are the ultimate source of political power and public policy in our democracy. We, the people, need to learn about what "reform" policies have been imposed, what's wrong with them, and how they need to be changed. Then, we must speak out publicly and work together to make sure that our lawmakers and the education establishment stop perpetuating our failed high-stakes testing strategy. Instead, they must concentrate on helping schools improve. The key is doing what works in school leadership, instruction, curriculum, school climate, and parent and community involvement and support.

How, you might ask, did an accomplished veterinary doctor from Idaho—whose profession involves diagnosing and treating cattle and horses—become knowledgeable about the history and policy of American public education and committed to trying to improve America's low-achieving public schools? After getting her bachelor of science and doctoral degrees at Michigan State University, Young and her husband moved west, ultimately to the city of Caldwell, Idaho. As a grateful beneficiary of a good education, Young was anxious that both of her children received a good education, too.

She chose to enroll her son and daughter in Caldwell's Title I, low income, public schools. Like American parents generally, Young wanted to have trust in her children's schools and teachers. But then the trouble started.

After getting her son on the bus for the first day of kindergarten, Young drove to the elementary school and discreetly watched to be sure he made it safely into the building. What she found were kindergarteners and first graders dropped off—by themselves—into a partially unfenced school yard, exposed to the street, without any adult supervision. Although she repeatedly raised concerns with the school's administration about the lack of security and supervision in the school yard, there was still no security fence eighteen years later.

While volunteering two days a week in her son's second grade class, Dr. Young noticed that about "20-30 percent of the kids were exhibiting various signs of having learning difficulties." When she mentioned this to the teacher, the teacher resignedly said: "I think you are looking at our future dropouts." Apparently, she did not realize that Young's son was in that group.

As a result of such experiences, Young spent eleven years volunteering in her children's schools. Concerned not just about her own children, but for all the children who were similarly being denied a high quality education, Vicki went further. She devoted eighteen years to her children's schools, school district, and the Idaho legislature, focused on improving school safety, curriculum and instruction, and the high-stakes testing strategies prevalent in Idaho schools.

Armed with extensive personal experience as a parent, volunteer, and advocate, and after extensive reading of important education and related texts, Young wrote the first edition of this book, published in 2009. The book's goal is to overcome our nation's longstanding denial of equal educational opportunity to millions of students, especially those in thousands of low-achieving schools and districts nationwide serving concentrations of disadvantaged children. Its approach combines the tradition of Biblical prophecy—to call upon Americans' deepest moral duty to "do unto others as we would have them do unto us"—with our deepest democratic principle—to provide equal rights for all citizens. Its message is directed to you and every individual American: our economic, political, and social strength and our well-being as a nation depend on *you* to overcome the blight of grossly inadequate public education for millions of our nation's children!

Continuing to read widely in the field after publishing the first edition, one of the things Young found was my own work critiquing NCLB and advocating dramatic shifts in its policies. Young initially contacted me in the spring of 2011 in her capacity as Chair of the Information Coordinating Committee of the national Save Our Schools (SOS) March and Rally. I was immediately intrigued by her unusual interest in, experience with, and knowledge about school improvement issues. Finding much common ground in our respective interests and concerns, in the summer of 2011 we co-led a workshop at the SOS Conference on how to lobby Congress to restructure NCLB. Working together highlighted the depth of Young's grassroots experience, her knowledge, enthusiasm, and dedication.

The second edition follows the basic structure of the first. The early chapters describe serious school problems that Vicki confronted involving school security and reading, math and science instruction, and her attempts to improve the situations. The middle chapters expand the inquiry nationwide by exploring basic deficiencies in the federal NCLB law and various states' high-stakes testing requirements. The last chapters focus directly on solutions: what policies should be adopted instead, and what must citizens do to change public policy?

The book provides a wide range of valuable information and insightful ideas and recommendations. Key themes include:

- The reasons unequal educational opportunity persists include the lack of transparency and exclusion of the people by America's political and educational leaders, the people's failure to hold the education system's leaders accountable, and the self-serving role of the "educational-industrial complex."
- Substantially improving low-achieving schools cannot be done just by adding discrete "programs," but requires a comprehensive "change process" or "theory of action."
- A lot is already known about the contents of what works to improve low-achieving schools, including the common elements of successful school turnarounds.
- "Community education organizers," housed in, and drawing on the expertise of, the Cooperative Extension System, should be employed in communities with "chronically low-performing schools" to help educate citizens about school improvement problems and solutions and to facilitate change.

- The federal role in elementary and secondary education needs to change profoundly: (i) from imposition of "tests and sanctions" to helping schools improve, returning toward the "community schools" concept of the original (1965) Elementary and Secondary Education Act (ESEA); (ii) from mandating tests and improvement goals for all public schools to restricting mandates to schools in "dysfunctional communities" and focusing especially on providing "experienced experts to assist them in evaluating their problems and their solutions"; and (iii) from holding schools accountable for continuously raising state standardized test scores to holding states and low-performing schools and districts accountable for implementing systemic educational improvements known to work.
- To enable such profound changes in American law and public policy to occur requires first changing public opinion to support the changes. (So far, politicians and the education establishment have not listened to urgings for the fundamental changes that are necessary.)
- To change public opinion, we, the citizens, must educate ourselves to gain knowledge about the real causes and solutions for low levels of student learning, especially in schools and school districts serving concentrations of disadvantaged children.
- Then, we, the people, must organize together and take democratic "social action" to demand that politicians and educators make the necessary profound policy and legal changes ("revolution") at the federal, state and local levels.

The book strengthens its case with powerful quotations from outstanding thinkers about American education and democracy over the last two hundred fifty years. For example, it highlights John Adams's insight that "knowledge alone . . . can preserve [the people] from tyranny" and Horace Mann's observation that "in this country . . . [i]t is only by enlightening and concentrating [public] opinion that powerful effects [in promoting education] can be produced."

I believe that *The Crucial Voice* is particularly timely right now for two major reasons. First, though NCLB's test and sanctions strategy has itself demonstrably failed, Congress has likewise failed for more than four years past the due date to replace it. While the Administration's "waivers" temporarily relieve participating states of some of NCLB's most egregious mandates, the waivers themselves are much too test-driven, fail to concentrate on helping schools improve, and leave some states still subject to NCLB in its entirety. Citizen action is desperately needed now to break the stalemate between Republicans and Democrats over reauthorizing ESEA and to direct both parties on what the proper federal role should be.

Instead, the people must come forward and finally say: this American "Emperor" of tests and sanctions—which has been dominating America's so-called school reform for the last twenty years—"has no clothes!" This is the critical time to do it: while the ESEA is still awaiting reauthorization and its direction can still be profoundly altered.

Second, from the "Orange Revolution" to the "Arab spring" and the "Tea Party," this is an extraordinary historical period in which citizens—in both democracies and autocracies around the world—have been organizing and speaking out to demand changes in leadership and public policy. Most relevantly, in mid-2012, a dramatic grassroots movement against high-stakes testing has begun in the United States, spearheaded by school boards in Texas and Florida. This citizens' movement should be seen as a significant step toward the bedrock reforms that *The Crucial Voice* is advocating.

This is a critical moment in the history of American public education. Will the United States perpetuate its demonstrably failed and harmful test and sanctions-driven "school reform" strategy, unknown to the leading "education" nations? Or will we instead shift our strategy to helping our low-achieving schools improve, and our students learn, by doing what works? Whether or not millions of our children will receive a good education—sufficient for them to successfully participate in, and contribute to, America in the 21st century—hangs in the balance.

If you'd like to learn first-hand about real problems encountered by one caring parent and her children in schools serving concentrations of poor students and difficulties encountered in trying to solve them, this book will give you valuable insights. If you'd like to learn what you could do to help greatly improve the education these children receive by transforming America's current test and sanctions school reform strategy, this book will give you valuable guidance. If you're willing to consider actually jumping in and working to redirect our school reform strategy to a successful one that works *with* the people—not *against* them—this book will give you invaluable support and motivation to get started.

Gary M. Ratner
July 2012

# Preface

If parents "do not understand," is it not, in part at least, because educators have been woefully negligent about seriously "educating" parents about classrooms, schools, roles, pressures, constraints?

—Seymour B. Sarason

As a parent, in addition to giving my unconditional love and support to my children, three major responsibilities are mine to bear. Those obligations are to keep my children healthy, keep them safe, and provide them with the best education possible. As a parent seeking quality in education, I have failed.

Making sure our children were rested, well fed, and respectful of others was not enough. Reading to them almost every night starting when they were very young, being involved in the classroom, participating in our parent teacher organization, keeping myself informed as much as possible about educational issues, and even going to school board meetings was not enough. I did everything I could to try to ensure the best opportunity for a good education for our children. I trusted the education professionals to do the rest. I trusted the schools.

My trust turned out to be misplaced. That trust is forever gone and in its place has grown a healthy skepticism. It is three years after the publication of this book's first edition. So much has "changed" but so little real progress has been made. Yet I remain optimistic that true, lasting improvement can occur in the public education system of the United States, and it must. When the National Commission on Excellence in Education published *A Nation at Risk: The Imperative for Educational Reform* in 1983, it was supposed to be a defining moment when the lights would go on in the minds of all Americans and the importance of the need to improve education in every classroom in the United States would be illuminated.

I now understand that the public remains ignorant of the findings and recommendations of that national commission. Yet, *A Nation at Risk* continues to be seen as marking the beginning of our modern day "education reform wars." And we don't understand what it was all about. We have always had "turf" wars and politically motivated power struggles, but this is different.

This war appears to have started over the question, is there a crisis in education? This war rages on while one fact remains certain; during the last three decades of attempted education "reform," children have fallen through the cracks while adults fight about who is right. For the approximately 30 percent of children that this nation fails to provide with the best education possible, it is a crisis. End this war!

We fight against a corporate reform model, against a business reform model, against outcome-based education, against standards, against standardized tests, against privatization, against public schools and their teachers. We argue about how our downfall began and who is to blame for our faltering schools. The fight becomes more about the side we are on, or the label we carry, and less about what we should be doing for children. Have we forgotten what we once *fought for*?

Did political and business leaders take over education policy and now dictate classroom practices because they found "the establishment" educators inept and unwilling to listen? Or did they take over as part of a plot to undermine our republic through standardization and privatization of our schools? I don't know—and frankly—I don't give a damn. I just want to see us stop the in-fighting long enough to do what is right for our kids, our communities, and our country.

If the public only knew what all was going on behind the scenes, they would be up in arms. And that would be a good thing, at least temporarily.

The truth is, too few people grasp the current situation and understand the deadweight of a poor education system; it can take us under. People aren't realizing education's influence on their top concerns: the economy, health care, and the environment. Others say, "If it's not broken, don't fix it." But at what point do we admit the education system is broken? Is it when workers can't fill out an application or make correct change or when the quality and essential quantity of our teachers and higher education personnel declines to an irreversible level?

Historically, there would have been no need for true equal educational opportunity in the United States if we were going to maintain a slave class. If our educational goal in the United States now is to maintain a subservient lower class, then don't change our system. If you feel satisfied with the idea that educational opportunity is for the "haves" and mediocrity in education is fine for the "have-nots," then let us do nothing but stage reforms that benefit a few and give some well-meaning people a warm fuzzy feeling while too many of our children, and our country, gets left behind in this now-global economy that we have created. Every day we are losing American talent that we don't even know exists; it is talent that is unrecognizable in the disinterested students being viewed as hopeless.

Why should you listen to me? Here is one really good reason; I put my own children through the very "type" of school that all the "experts" and "do-gooders" say they want to "reform." There is a difference between "do-gooders" looking for areas where they can "do" what *they* think is best versus "doers" that pitch in and do what is needed for children in need. In my schools, the poverty rate classifies them as "Title I, " and their indicators of educational quality have been alarmingly dismal. I learned the hard way the lessons I now want to share.

I was fortunate to have been raised in a family led by a World War II veteran who got ahead in life by using his GI Bill combined with income from our local iron factory, which no longer exists. My dad taught mathematics for thirty years and built his own little empire of small businesses in our town. He lives the American Dream. Education provided him that opportunity.

I am a common, middle-class American who worked hard to invest in my own education. The belief was that education would serve as a safety net for remaining in the middle class; it would keep me out of poverty. It was an investment that has served me well, to date.

My own path in education led to the much respected profession of veterinary medicine. Having practiced for over twenty-five years and having been actively involved in education reform for twenty years, I found my profession and the teaching profession remarkable similar. I hope the reader does not take offense at the comparison of teaching children to training and working with animals, for none is intended.

Within the traditional public school system, I am just a parent. I have no credentials in the field of education. But please consider that much of my time in veterinary medicine was spent on farms or in exam rooms using my knowledge and skills to draw conclusions and communicate to everyday people my findings concerning the problem identified, potential solutions, and future prevention of problems. Those processes in veterinary medicine I understand well. Those are the same processes that should be applied to the problems of our education system. Gaining insight into these issues through the education system's "school of hard knocks" gives a person a unique perspective of the solutions.

Please don't close your ears and minds to me because I lack educational credentials. Find the patience and respect to listen and consider my views because I am one parent who has behaved like the scientist within me. I have observed children learning, teachers teaching, administrators managing, and the actions of our school board along with some interaction with state and federal educational bureaucracies. I noted my observations, unconsciously at first and mainly mentally but sometimes in notes to myself or editorials in the newspaper. I reviewed, researched, and evaluated my beliefs against many others in the education field, both current and historical. I listened to others and reflected.

In the end, it seems we need to base development of a teaching philosophy on our beliefs and principles, observed correlations, knowledge of the developing brain, and common sense about how to best help children learn. We must become and remain vigilant to the constantly changing needs of our communities and the educational structures that are of integral importance to building and maintaining successful communities. Our goals must be based on the desires and needs of our people.

That is the combination of thoughts that led to the one idea presented within this book that I considered "mine" when I wrote the first edition. Since then I have discovered others who came before me with similar ideas. They serve to reaffirm my beliefs and justify the time spent in writing this second edition. Their ideas deserve to be heard.

My belief remains firm that the largest single problem with the so-called education system of the United States is its failure to listen to the people it was supposed to serve.

The ideas, suggestions, and solutions in this book are mainly taken from others. There are many in the past and the present with solutions for improving the K–12 American education system. Many speak the same phrases that we too often discount as clichés. So, I ask the reader not to think of the well-known phrases as clichés but rather to think of them as wise thoughts from the past that have been repeated so often they have become clichés. I ask the reader to hear those words anew as voices from the past trying to echo words of wisdom to us.

The major resolving principles and beliefs contained in this book correlate not only with the historical beliefs of many but also with modern research. This is not to insinuate that this book is research-based in the strict sense of the words. Rather, it should more appropriately be considered experience-based and research-backed, since much of what I found in my research over the years goes unnoted because I was reading for interest and not with the intent of writing a book.

Remember, my beliefs, from the perspective of a parent, were based first on observation and common sense about how children learn. But, when common sense and research do align, shouldn't we give those concepts our focused attention?

Writing the first edition, I convinced myself to be calm and analytical, as if the issue of educational improvement was no longer personal. You know what, it is personal; more so now than ever before because once you understand what is happening, you can see where "change" is leading us and even though my children didn't receive the best education, I still want a public system left standing in their future. Our republic is at risk.

"Statistics and their interpretation by experts show only the surface dimension of the difficulties we face. Beneath them lies a tension between hope and frustration that characterizes current attitudes about education at every level. . . . What lies behind this emerging national sense of frustration can be described as both a dimming of personal expectations and the fear of losing a shared vision for America" (on, 1983, 11–12). These are words from *A Nation at Risk*.

Nothing will change what has already occurred, so now becomes the time to learn from our past and from each other. I understand people's frustration and resultant unwillingness to put forth the time to listen. That's why parents like Bonnie C. ask me, "how *long* is your book?" Keeping regular people in mind, my first edition was short but left too many important concepts up to the reader to clarify. This time I've done my best to make the solutions simple, easy to understand, and useful. Really, this book is short, considering the gravity and complexity of the problems this country faces. My major point is that there are no excuses for shrugging and walking away thinking what is proposed can't be done. It can. It is being done in schools and communities across our country and around the world.

Individual chapters can be *used* by different people to suit their needs. For example, Chapter 8, "What's Next: Starting in the Trenches," can serve to give the reader some verbal ammunition to explain what school improvement looks like. It can be used as a discussion piece in your own community. Chapters 4 and 8 along with Addendum 1 should be a must read for those looking to change the No Child Left Behind law. You can write your own "briefs" of them for your congressman; it's called "citizen lobbying." Personally, I think everyone involved in the education system directly should read Chapters 6 and 7; my advice is to take small bites and digest well. And Chapter 10, "Democracy and Education: The Powerful Will Drive Progress," is written for all citizens. Read and share. I hope you decide to read the book cover to cover for the fullest understanding. The objective is that you do what you can.

To thoughtfully consider the current needs of our education system; we have to begin with understanding. I use brief stories in Chapters 1–4 and occasionally throughout to set the stage for understanding for those of you who have not experienced any difficulties. After all, successful school districts are the rule in this country. They have similar characteristics, which include personalized learning with effective teachers and an appropriate curriculum with instruction taking place in an inviting, caring environment.

These schools don't just happen. They are guided by leaders with the knowledge, skills, experience, desire, and motivation to overcome personal barriers to cooperation.

Most kids that make it through the public schools do so without any apparent problems. Many parents are aware of problems with public education but not in their school or with their child. Others are unaware of problems or don't associate their children's failures or societal problems with education. But is not the true test of education measured by *life indicators* of happiness?

Many will be able to use their own stories to illustrate my points. These are people that weren't so lucky in the great gamble for the best education for their children. These are people that experienced dysfunctional school districts where the governing structure and leadership are not asked by the community to provide transparency and accountability for the underperformance of their schools.

I many times heard myself asking, "Why me?" as I once again phoned or visited our school district's office. One has to consider walking away from the whole mess. Time and again you hear "you can't change the system"; "forgive and forget."

I wanted to forgive and forget the injustices I've seen and experienced in this "failing" school system. But the injustices are spreading and growing as the level of disrespect, incivility, and distrust is rising. There are things that should not be forgotten, and this is not the time for any Americans to look the other way. It is time for Americans to *make the choice* to improve our existing public schools.

Parents, educators, and students should not forget what they experienced and leave the next generation to experience the same problems. We know what mistakes have been made. Will we speak? Will others hear our crucial voices?

The demographics of Title I (low-income) schools like mine do present some unique troubles to solve, but the major problems are the same as for any other schools (urban, suburban, or rural), where maintaining a disciplined yet stimulating learning environment, quality educators and administration, and financial and community support in order to provide quality learning opportunities for all is the universal dilemma.

In reading the works of others, I was led to believe that the roots of these problems are also universal. One wrote about school boards and I wondered how I missed seeing him at mine; it sounded like our local board. Another wrote about her children in a public elementary school; it sounded like she was in our classrooms, but I never saw her either. Our stories are the same with different details and varying degrees of severity.

The problems are manifested in classrooms all over, not just in "failed" schools. But the encouraging thing is that we do have the answers to our problems, with each school and each classroom having its own unique solutions. The bigger problem is the systemic lack of support and guidance for local improvements. It is *a systemic problem, a national issue.* Just as a few disruptive, out-of-control kids can rot the learning environment of a classroom; areas of educational neglect can rot the whole of our society.

So at this time, it is very important that people understand their role in school improvement and the need for complete and thorough change of "the system."

Everywhere I go, I find the common people instinctively drawn toward the idea of "change," but specific changes in education that represent *real progress* have not been part of the talk. Now is the time. We must come together and admit that we, U.S. citizens, can do a better job educating all our citizenry than we are currently doing. As the National Commission on Excellence in Education stated, "This unity, however, can be achieved only if we avoid the unproductive tendency of some to search for scapegoats among the victims, such as the beleaguered teachers" (1983, 12). It's time to listen.

As a country, we all have a stake in education. If you can't or won't consider the country as a whole, think about your own schools. A government report in 1939 called *The Evaluation of Secondary Schools* summed up the situation well by stating, "In a democracy, a school should not be satisfied with being good; it should strive constantly to become better" (Cooperative Study of Secondary School Standards, 61). For our children's sake, we need to do better.

The reality is that we have ignored the views of parents, teachers, and students for far too long. And we do it to each other. We continue to battle over the "how" to reform while ignoring those that have already experienced "failed" reforms. We are talking at each other, not conversing or debating. Very few people are listening long enough to come to an understanding of where we have been with education reform, what the current truths are, and collectively and collaboratively decide where we need to go.

To collaborate means to work together, to cooperate with the enemy. There is a lot of talk about "democratic" schools and the importance of "teaching" about democracy, but shouldn't we first practice what we preach? Teach by example. Will we ever get the result we seek when we don't use the process we wish to promote?

The "education reform wars" have got to stop. They are a tug-of-war over opposing political agendas with teachers, students, and their families as the collateral damage. The fight will only be *about* the children if we make it so.

In a country founded on democratic ideals, we must constantly work at not making judgments without a fair hearing from the people. To keep our heads above water, to strive to stay one stroke ahead, we must act now to correct the mistakes of the past and prevent those in the future as best we can.

Our K–12 education system in the United States of America does not take the honor of being best in the world; it's not even second best. It is well below that using any measure. And being part of the public schools, at this moment in time, has left me feeling like I've fallen into a swiftly moving current, grasping at times for a handhold, but each time finding it out of reach.

What is there to grab hold of? In Idaho, there is *outcry* over a proposed law to put hunting tags up for sale to the *highest bidder* because the people here understand what "equal opportunity" means when it applies to their individual rights. They see the injustice of allowing the "haves" to have special privileges. But they fail, as most of the nation does, to see how dangerous it is to deny "educational opportunity" to any child.

Living in the beautiful state of Idaho with its narrow mountainous roads winding above treacherous white-water rivers along with dangerous irrigation ditches running through backyards, I warned my children repeatedly as they were growing up that if they fell into rapidly moving water: "Don't fight the current. Don't look back. Go with the flow and look for your chance to grab onto something to help you get out."

In some ways, life is like that swiftly moving stream. But it isn't identical. In life, we should look both forward and back. We must look back to learn from the mistakes and successes of the past yet always keep looking to the future with the hope of reaching our goals, fulfilling a vision. And there are times we must fight against the current.

Observation, research, and much trial and failure did produce in me a vision for the education system of the United States. That became agonizing, for sending your own children to school daily while recognizing and realizing what serious mistakes are being made is pure hell. On a regular basis, I wished I didn't know what I know; I wished I didn't care about the children, parents, and teachers suffering within this system. Facing the facts is hard to do.

*Dare You Face Facts?* by Muriel Lester served as my final inspiration to write about education. Through her book, she was appealing to the United States to lead Europe to peace, a peace based on *mutual understanding* with the help and unity of the spiritual and governmental leaders of America, a country in which she believed that "No other people has such initiative, such resourcefulness" (1940, 121). She felt that knowing firsthand "about the happenings" in Europe, in China, and in Africa in the 1930s and 1940s left her "shouldering the burden of caring." She was reaching out with the *hope of finding others* who would care and *hoped to move them to act*. Like her, I feel that knowing what I know, and caring, in my case about the public education system of the United States, has been my burden.

Thinking about the times she must have gone through, my anguish and frustration can't compare. That thought gives me the energy to once more relive my journey down the public education stream as just a parent who cares.

# Acknowledgments

Thank you to the National Science Resource Center for allowing use of their Theory of Action Model and for their contributions to science education. Their efforts to instruct teachers must reach beyond those borders, as I trust it will through expanded use of their model for action.

Many people are represented among the thoughts and between the lines of this book. Some have been near and dear to me while others were strangers passing the time while waiting in lines, traveling on airplanes, or in the Laundromat. As you read, many of you will recall hearing some familiar words; I thank you for listening.

My local library provided the access to the books necessary to make this writing possible. Thank you, ladies, for always being helpful without ever knowing what you were helping accomplish—just doing your jobs. Thank you to libraries, in general, for their cooperation in loaning items thus expanding learning opportunities through shared resources.

Special thanks to my publishers, Rowman & Littlefield, for giving an unknown, uncredentialed, obscure individual a voice and now a second chance. And thank you to Patricia Stevenson for her patient and reassuring manner during my first editing process, to Carly Peterson for her devotion to this second editing, and to Mary McMenamin for acting as my guardian on round two. Particular thanks to Tom Koerner for setting the stage for my final revision by reminding me of my former English teachers, who seemed to be looking over my shoulder as I worked. Thanks to those teachers.

Sincere appreciation to a very special educator, Dr. Seymour Sarason. He provided a seed for growth with his encouragement early in this endeavor. With what few words we exchanged, he made me believe I have something to say worth being said. His gentle goading made me question myself further and give more to my writing than I had originally anticipated, that being in keeping with what a true teacher does.

Thank you to all the education advocates and activists that I have been fortunate enough to have had contact with in cyberspace and to those whom I have actually met. You know who you are and you know that efforts big and small will produce a ripple effect. Without the efforts of many, I would not have had the honor, privilege, and enjoyment of working with Gary Ratner, founder and executive director of Citizens for Effective Schools. It is rare to find someone who finds value in the perspective "from the bottom." Finding Gary's work on No Child Left Behind was like finding a gem in the darkness.

And special thanks to Jack Minzey for endorsing my first edition while knowing I had not read his extensive work on community education concepts. There was no better introduction to those concepts than being able to meet and talk directly—impressive work from a noble man.

This book was enhanced through the efforts of Gina Ferguson, my former neighbor, fellow parent, and friend. Before knowing of the existence of this project, she was providing encouragement by sharing books, and her insight and experiences both of schools and life. She kept my feet to the fire at a crucial time and kept me in line with her uncanny ability to spot my human moments of laziness in my writing. From her timely enlightenment to her careful reading and questioning, she brought this book from a wish to a reality.

And we give recognition to her husband, Gary, and mine, Patrick— the men that stand behind us women but who themselves are strong parents and supporters for their children and their wives. And further acknowledgment goes to Gary and Gina's boys for unwittingly acting as little reminders as to why this effort is worthwhile.

To my own children, words can't do justice. This effort truly would not have come to being without you. I thank you both for the encouragement you unknowingly gave me through your support of my efforts to "stick up for kids" all these years. I learn so much both from you and through you. Through the sometimes turbulent waters we travel, because of you two, the journey is always amazing. Thanks for teaching me through your eyes. I hope I set a good example and will now humbly except your critique as we once again travel down this stream together.

## Chapter One

# Safe and Disciplined Schools: Civility Lost on Our Own Turf

> Government should actively promote good as well as repress evil. That is a free government where the people make their own laws; and that will be a good one where the people are wise and virtuous. But, virtue and wisdom do not come by inheritance; they must be propagated by education.
>
> —William Penn

Sending your first child off to kindergarten is a very memorable moment. We lived about six blocks from our elementary school, which was definitely within walking distance, but we sent our first child to kindergarten at a point in time when parents were questioning the safety of children everywhere. The memory of a twelve-year-old boy being abducted while biking with his brother in rural Minnesota was all too fresh in our minds. So we decided to have our child ride the school bus.

In a then-current parenting magazine, it was being suggested that if you were concerned about how your child might handle the bus ride to school and going on his or her way without you, you should find a spot at school where you could see him or her get off the bus but where they couldn't necessarily see you watching. For a "first-timer" looking for peace of mind, it sounded like a good idea.

1

## EXPECTING SAFE SCHOOLS

After seeing our son onto the bus, I hopped in the car and went over to the area where I knew kindergarteners would be gathering. From a distance, I saw him get off the bus and be directed around to the playground area. Shortly thereafter, he appeared in the area where kindergarten students were supposed to wait. Great! What a relief.

Unfortunately, that relief was short-lived. It began to dawn on me that from where I was standing I was looking out over a group of kindergarteners and first graders with no adult in sight. This area was around the side of the building, so it was out of sight of the main playground. I was standing by a fence that only partially enclosed the area; it was open to the street. Surely, I must be mistaken. I looked and looked for that potentially really short adult. Waiting until the teachers came out to bring in the kids and they were safely inside, I left for home and the telephone.

According to the school staff, they didn't have the playground duty schedule completed. My assumption at the time was that they took my comments to heart, about the area being open to the street and potentially dangerous in various ways, and were giving the resolution of this matter immediate attention. The next day, we repeated the pattern of the first day and once again that area was not supervised. Again, the school staff gave their assurance that they were working on the problem. The third day, same thing, only this time the complaint was left until the following morning.

That morning at the bus stop, I asked another mother if she was aware that no supervision was provided near the area open to the street. She was not. She also had a kindergartener and wanted to see for herself if it was a problem. She joined me at the spot where, once again, no adult was in sight. She was mad. And she had something that was apparently effective in changing the situation. She was tall, robust, and vocal in a commanding sort of way. It could have been a coincidence, but the next day adequate supervision was apparent.

Eighteen years have passed. I can't say for sure that proper supervision in that area continued. What is known is that the physical condition of the area, which makes it a safety hazard, still exists and is recognized by others, including the administration. It is clearly noted in a recent school district facilities report. You would think someone would have put up a secure fence by now.

Of course, being just parents, our views are often taken as being based more on sentimentality than substance. Or the administration may treat a problem as though it was the only time that particular problem has been brought to their attention and you, of course, are the only one having the problem; if only that were always true.

Anecdotal is the word I've most often heard school administrators use to refer to parents' stories. It means they view this type of testimony as "entertaining accounts of some single happening" (*Webster's*, 1976). It implies that our stories are not necessarily fully truthful. They usually aren't confirmed by statistics; they many times can't be proved or disproved. Apparently, that justifies inaction even on what would appear to be a commonsense issue, like proper fencing.

## REQUIRING DISCIPLINED CLASSROOMS

Three years after the fence incident, our second child entered kindergarten (different school, same district). The grounds were exceptional. It felt very safe. She loved going to school. All was wonderful until about two months into the school year, when she got slammed from behind onto the blacktop. It was the result of standing in line waiting to go to music in a different building. She didn't have a scratch on her hands. She took it totally on the face. The unruly boy's father did call to somewhat apologize by saying "Boys will be boys."

The disciplinary consequences of this boy's action were never revealed to us by the school, leaving us to assume none occurred. At that point, we took a deep breath, didn't pursue the matter any further, and watched as our daughter suffered some major discomfort. Fortunately, time does heal wounds, and she only has some minor scarring. This same boy, however, persisted in being a major disturbance to every one of the classrooms he shared with our daughter.

But he was of minor consequence compared to the boy labeled as "severely emotionally disturbed" who moved into this school and our daughter's classroom in the third grade. As a classroom volunteer it was obvious this new boy was very smart and seemed to know right from wrong. He was very likable. He was never a problem when I or anyone from the education department was in the room. But the reports from our daughter, confirmed by the teacher, were that he was being really destructive to school property, and disrespectful to the teacher and the assistant who had been assigned to supervise him.

This boy was disrupting the whole class. Upon asking the teacher if she had a problem with my going over her head to address this issue with the administration, her response was "Please do." That was the defining moment when the unconscious decision on my part was made to take on what would become a battle for safe and disciplined schools in our district.

Before anything was done to correct the disruptions in this classroom, this boy hit the teacher. That action did not get him kicked out of school. It only got him into the detention room where he hit that supervisor, which then got him placed in a special program in a neighboring city. The situation might have improved if he had been "handled" differently. If at the very least the one-on-one aid assigned to him had developed a relationship rather than "shadow" him, things may have worked out better. He was smart and needed expert help—help that he didn't get in this public school system. Unfortunately for the teacher and the other students in the class, the year was almost over when he was removed.

## PRODUCING SAFE AND DISCIPLINED SCHOOLS

During this conflict, the decision to address the administration meant looking at our district policies, procedures, and state laws concerning discipline. In the course of these developments, various discussions occurred with the administration at all local levels. It appeared that policies were in place that could have helped before this classroom situation had escalated. Wasted instructional time could have been saved. The students' and teachers' year could have been much different. Obviously, misunderstandings had occurred.

In Idaho, we have a law establishing the basic assumptions governing the state responsibility to provide a *Thorough System of Public Schools*, as do most states. In Idaho Code 33-1612, the first three of these assumptions deal with safe and disciplined school issues. The wise writers of this law may have put safety and discipline issues at the beginning of the list signifying their importance to any further educational goals being realized. Those expectations are: "1) a safe environment conducive to learning is provided, 2) educators are empowered to maintain classroom discipline, and 3) the basic values of honesty, self-discipline, unselfishness, respect for authority, and the central importance of work are emphasized."

During this period of research and discovery, it became obvious through discussions with teachers that many didn't feel they were empowered to maintain discipline. In this law, it clearly states that they are empowered. Empowered means they are "permitted to, authorized, enabled, or given authority" (*Webster's*, 1976). Yet somehow we had gotten to the point where either we didn't understand the concept of discipline, we no longer were teaching teachers how to maintain discipline, or the teachers weren't getting the administrative, legal, or parental support to maintain discipline, or a combination thereof.

Feeling so strongly that we must get to the bottom of this issue, attending Safe and Drug-Free Schools Advisory Subcommittee and District Committee meetings were the next step in seeing what approach our district was taking. These committees had been required of our district as part of the settlement of a lawsuit. Their discussions seemed to point to the need for consistent procedures for discipline, on a district-wide basis.

After a December 17, 1998, meeting, the following was recorded: "Considerable discussion took place related to the importance of appropriate levels of continuity between buildings (middle to junior high to high school) relating to school rules, consequences, and procedures." It was decided that, through handbook revisions, this issue be addressed by building administration. This is how our system intended to fix itself—through handbooks.

Between December 1998 and April 1999, the situation was escalating in our daughter's classroom and other ongoing safety and discipline issues had surfaced in this school and other schools in the district. A small group of parents were growing impatient with the ongoing meetings and discussions and felt that the administration was only seeking input from a very limited, select group of patrons. It was decided that the best thing to do would be to call a town-hall type meeting to open the lines of discussion with more parents. The plan was to collect a wide variety of opinions on the issue of discipline and present a written summary to the school board that would include written anonymous comments to be collected after the meeting. The date of the meeting was set for April 20.

Before the meeting, issues were discussed with each principal, all of whom seemed to be very receptive to the proposal of an open exchange of ideas. Some of their comments were used anonymously on the overheads that were prepared as talking points for the evening. The answers to our school's discipline problems had not been predetermined by this group as evident by the question marks that surrounded the solutions section. The overheads looked like this:

### Mutual Goals
Ensure that no student prevents a teacher from doing his/her job
Ensure that our students' right to learn is not interfered with
Ensure a safe place to learn and work

### Our Needs
Establish respect
Establish consistency in policy and its implementation
Establish enforceable consequences that are enforced

### Solutions
District discipline policy that is consistent from building to building
Social skills curriculum

Clear and concise parent and student information
Clear and concise teacher instruction
Safety devices
Keep It Simple
Respect, Consequences, Consistent
Discipline is the process of training a child so that the desired character traits
and habits can be developed

On April 20, 1999, the meeting took place as scheduled. The next morning, the *Idaho Press Tribune* (our local paper) wrote that the meeting had been called by parents to discuss discipline and described how parents, school staff, and students filed into the meeting room still "reeling from news of the carnage in a Colorado high school."

For those of you who have forgotten, April 20, 1999, was the day the school shootings occurred at Columbine High School. A somber, respectful tone beset the meeting. The shootings were of course mentioned by the participants, but all comments were very thoughtful and filled with concern rather than misplaced emotion. Later, this gathering was viewed by some as reactionary to the Columbine shootings even though it had been planned for weeks.

On May 3, a composite of the opinions and ideas collected that night was sent to our school board and district administration along with a letter informing them that this issue was on the agenda for their May 10 board meeting. They were asked to consider one of the anonymous written suggestions submitted that night. That suggestion was the idea of setting up a task force to fully explore all questions, comments, and recommendations that were expressed by the attendees of the town hall meeting.

On May 7, a letter came from the superintendent stating that, after thinking about the comments, they had moved forward administratively "to provide a forum and relief for the concerns expressed that night." They believed this structure would provide an "effective mechanism for dialogue and action surrounding the issues of school safety and discipline." In addition to the committees dictated by the existing disciplinary discrimination lawsuit, committees would also be set up in the elementary schools. The meetings would be monthly and were supposed to be designed to "meet the collective needs of our students and parents." Nice wording, and that was where we were told to go!

But written anonymous comments had been collected that night and compiled in a booklet and, as promised, they were presented to the school board on May 10. The idea of the school board sanctioning a task force was clearly indicated in the document. It was not a new idea. The same idea had actually been written up in our state's *Safe and Disciplined Schools Resource Handbook* published in 1996. This publication was very organized, easy to read, and reminiscent of livestock production handbooks, containing "proven" husbandry practices, developed by our agricultural cooperative extension system. This safety handbook contained "best practices," including an outline of who should be on a task force and what processes they should go through for evaluation of conditions, and it gave sample agendas and ideas for identifying research-based program elements useful in the effort to produce safe and disciplined schools.

As expressed to the school board and outlined for the community in an editorial, the "task" would be to sort through the recommendations and concerns that had been voiced on April 20 and to identify our school and community strengths, challenges, and limitations. The goal would be to come up with opportunities and *workable solutions* and to identify the people or institutions that could make those things happen.

Five separate times, our school board was asked to consider sanctioning a task force. At one meeting, it was presented with the differences between the existing committees and their functions, including how a task force would only serve the district for a short time period and in an advisory capacity with no real power. All five times, the school board said "no," while other communities in our state and our own state government moved ahead with similar ideas. The "mechanism for dialogue and action" was to be committees. So, with others that were equally willing to give of themselves, we sat on safe school committee after safe school committee. And, with persistence and patience, some progress was being made. Some issues were being addressed in a comprehensive district plan.

Time ran out on the discrimination lawsuit. Our middle school committee was excused. An invitation was extended to join the district Safe and Drug Free Schools committee that met quarterly; early in the morning, with an agenda so packed with presentations that little to no time remained for discussions before heading to work. I went, but it no longer met the "collective needs" for me.

On May 1, 2003, a letter was written asking the superintendent what suggestion he might have now on a direction to take to address the original issues of safe and disciplined schools that had been so clearly voiced that fateful April evening in 1999. No answer was provided. This is the point where one must turn to humor to remain sane. Do you know the definition of a committee? The answer: the unwilling, appointing the unknowing, to do the unnecessary. At the time, it was funny.

Four years on these committees and one has to wonder if the results justified the sacrifice of precious time. Improvements had been made at various levels and continued to be made by hardworking, caring individuals. Don't get me wrong. Things are better than they were, in many ways. As a district, we had gone from not wanting to give up an inch of our "site-based" decision-making powers, not wanting to even use the word "consistent," to having more consistent policies and common discipline language at all our elementary schools. We agreed that it was necessary because of the high level of mobility within the community. We even use the word "consistency" freely now and in a good way. And we had come up with a plan.

The experts on safe school issues long ago identified the importance of community involvement in planning and the implementation of plans. In this district, the tough issues of respect, fairness, and parental and community roles need readdressing. They were addressed in the original plans. They were good plans. But, honestly, being just a parent, and a working parent at that, one cannot keep pounding away at the administration to stick with the plan. The need for sustained parental oversight most certainly wears a person down.

When people's views get ignored, proven ideas get put down, well-constructed plans get forgotten enough times, people give up. I've often wondered if that very idea is some sort of technique or theory they teach in administrative school. It worked on me; a dead end on the issue of safety and discipline had been reached.

These stories may seem "tame" but think about it. When we allow adults to justify inaction and put children and other adults "in harm's way," we signal our own lack of respect for others. When we allow the institution of public education to set its boundaries of control to exclude its own communities in *the process of solving problems*, we accept selfishness, arrogance, and wrongdoing on the part of public servants. The incivility we see demonstrated by far too many children on school turf is nothing more than a symptom of our own loss of values. It is a reflection on how we are treating each other. Whether it is children against other children, or adults being repeatedly disrespectful to other adults, it is bullying. As Sara L. put it, "It's grown to be such a violent culture we live in and it's being accepted as the norm."

Now, the stories in my community come from parents or relatives of children who have been harassed at school to the point that they have to move to a different school or house, have to live with the thought that bullying was a contributing factor to suicide, have had their house shot up in drive-bys, or have a kid who quietly suffers waiting until the day they can get out of the daily "drama" of school. Victims are forced out, and the local terrorists, our gangs and bullies, move on to triumph over their next victims. The naked truth, as Peg C. can tell you, is that "bullying hurts."

Reflecting on the current stories (anecdotes) coming out of our schools, it is a statement from 1999 that is haunting. It was from a student attending the meeting on April 20 who said, "I think it's funny how people can come to meetings and complain, but do you actually see them stepping in and doing something about it?" Our youth know what we need to do. They know that building fences alone won't stop gangs and bullies from doing their damage to society. Will we ever listen to them?

Will we hear the call of others? Adults across our country continue to struggle to be taken seriously on the issues surrounding safe and disciplined schools. As Pedro Noguera put it in his book *City Schools and the American Dream: Reclaiming the Promise of Public Education*, "if we truly seek to create a different future, one that is more peaceful and nonviolent than the present, we must actively go about creating it" (2003, 141). Committees, meetings, discussions, and handbooks are not enough. We must cooperate, develop a vision for what we will accomplish, and set firm goals. Then, as Katherine C. says, we must "do rather than talk."

Without a shared vision, firm goals, and cooperation within our community, our safe schools plans vanished with the changing administration and the changing school board. Our district failed to follow through on its original plans. Other plans now exist, but I have yet to see this community have another meaningful open exchange of ideas, on a large scale, about discipline, bullying, and gangs in this dysfunctional school district.

# Chapter Two

# The Three R's, Plus the "R Rule"

Reading is our first and most basic educational process. From kindergarten through third grade, children learn to read. Thereafter they read to learn.
—The 90% Reading Goal

When schools struggle with discipline in their classrooms, some assume that it is just a reflection of the general decline of civility within our society. When classroom disruptions interfere with learning, the blame reflects back on our culture. With that in mind, the circumstances in our son's first grade class were taken as just such a situation, at first.

Five extremely disruptive boys were in this mix of twenty-eight students. Halfway through the year, it was decided to break them up by moving two of them out to other rooms. No doubt, continuous disruptions had been a setback for some and outright detrimental to the learning of the Three Rs for others. The fact that something else was to be learned from this experience eluded understanding at the time.

Things were being taught very differently than what my memory served. The general structuring of the class didn't feel right, but, being just a parent unfamiliar with the changes occurring in education, you go with the flow. And being a trusting classroom volunteer, teacher instructions about helping kids were followed unquestioningly. Instincts were saying differently, but the belief was that the "newest methods" were better. A blind element of trust existed, and no one had clarified what exactly a "pilot program" meant.

This was in 1992. It was obviously a period of experimentation in education in our state and the nation as a whole. This was a classroom being taught using the whole language technique for reading, inventive spelling without corrections for writing, and the touch point math technique for the basis of addition. Some would argue that phonics was being taught along with the whole language.

The obvious phonics instruction in this classroom was the use of headsets with a purchased program and worksheets that went along with that instruction. It used an instructional technique that is now commonly called "drill and kill," insinuating that a fact is "drilled" into a child's mind over and over again until it "kills" the desire to learn. Others associate this type of instruction with rote memorization, and the two ideas have been so closely related that they are considered one and the same by many, not all.

The idea behind inventive spelling with no corrections is to minimize any inhibitions to writing. It is to foster creativity and build self-esteem. As volunteers, we were instructed to have the students read their writing to us and praise them. We were to make no corrections.

Occasionally, uncomfortable moments would arise when kids couldn't remember what they wrote and wondered why you couldn't read what they wrote. They would flash you a look expressing their sentiments ("You dummy!"). That was acceptable and even amusing, but others, you could tell, felt differently. They were the ones that had disappointment written all over their faces. If it isn't readable, what's the point? Children are smart and should never be held down to a standard way of doing things, no matter which side of the teaching technique spectrum we adults have set our own beliefs.

As stated in *A Nation at Risk*, "Attention must be directed to both the nature of the content available and to the needs of particular learners. The most gifted students, for example, may need a curriculum enriched and accelerated beyond even the needs of other students of high ability. Similarly, educationally disadvantaged students may require special curriculum materials, smaller classes, or individual tutoring to help them master the material presented" (National Commission, 1983, 24). To promote only one way of doing things as "right" is wrong.

As Linda Darling-Hammond pointed out in *The Flat World and Education: How America's Commitment to Equity Will Determine Our Future*, teachers need to be able to use a "full array of instructional approaches" (2010, 296). And as many a person has stated, we must do things right the first time; let's call it the "R rule."

We must be wiser in choosing how we educate. We are obliged to consider the potential effect our decisions have on children before we put them into action in the classroom. And we have got to receive feedback and take it seriously. It's time to acknowledge that what we do in first grade sets the stage for the reading, writing, and math skills children need for the rest of their lives. Our actions need to speak to that fact. Mistakes can be devastating.

Why we thought taking a special education technique like touch point math and applying it to whole classrooms of able students was a good idea is beyond comprehension. It was not a smart decision. Consider your child very lucky if they weren't subjected to this arithmetic "pilot program."

This particular group of twenty-eight children got more than their share of pilot programs. In this case, the use of the word "pilot" means that these children served as a "trial unit for experimentation" (*Webster's*, 1976). In any experiment, you run the risk of failure. The big question becomes: How many were set up for future failures because of it?

Going from volunteering one day a week for the first grade class to two days a week the next year helped to foster a new realization. The instincts that brought about an uneasy feeling toward these new instructional techniques may have been correct; things didn't seem right.

But searching for answers wasn't the motivator to volunteer more days; the hope was that this would help free up time for the second grade teacher to provide more much needed individual attention to my own child. It had become obvious that learning differences were emerging.

Well into this second grade year and knowing this group of kids pretty well by then, it was fairly easy to identify who was falling significantly behind in class. Watching these children at work at their desks, some could easily be observed developing coping techniques. They were pretty good at being able to copy someone else's work, even upside-down.

At a glance, 20–30 percent of these kids were exhibiting various signs of having learning difficulties. That seemed like a lot of kids. In mentioning the observation to the teacher, her response provided insight into what the future might hold for these students. She looked at me sadly and said, "I think you are looking at our future dropouts."

Ours was one of them. That is one of those moments when motherly instincts slam smack into the face of reality. The need to concentrate on keeping my own from being part of that statistic became a goal. That class ended up with a state-reported 70 percent graduation rate. But, to put that into perspective, remember that real numbers are difficult to decipher, as are the facts. Maybe it doesn't matter to people. As Mark Twain said, "There are lies, damn lies, and statistics." Still, there were years that half the kids in our high school "disappeared" from the time they entered ninth grade until what would have been their graduation; they "moved away." Maybe Kathleen M. is right, "people don't want to hear the truth."

## READING: TRENDS, TECHNIQUES, AND RESULTS

As a parent, my grasp of the theory behind the whole language concept was that we all become sight readers. You aren't phonetically sounding out every word on this page. You quickly recognize the familiar words and move on. This is something you developed over time probably at your own pace as you became confident with your vocabulary.

The observed trend in the classrooms in the early 1990s was almost the opposite. They were teaching recognition of whole words first and large numbers of words at a time. Paper copies of reading books would be used at school, come home at night, and were used for testing. They seemed to be expecting the kids to memorize all the words. Looking back, was that "drilling and killing" the interest in reading? How should whole language be taught?

At that time, in the curriculum handbook for our district's teachers, their directive for the number one instruction on strategies to teach when a child didn't recognize a word was "to guess." An instruction to sound out a word was buried near the bottom of the list of reading strategies. And nowhere to be found was encouragement for students to seek to clarify words or explore their meanings if they weren't clear to them.

Sight reading and guessing alone may not sound too bad on the surface; with practice, children should eventually memorize most common words. It was when these groups of kids, taught by this method alone, began to progress to the next levels that it became apparent that no plan was in place as to how or when we expect them to "guess" correctly if they aren't doing so already. If they aren't given other doable approaches to reading a word, guessing is their only option and it is certainly the quickest and easiest thing to do.

Many children in whole language classrooms do pick up the ability to sound out words accurately. Those lucky kids may be "easy learners" who didn't need much instruction to get them reading accurately, they may have had more instruction at home or with a tutor, or they may have had a teacher who closed the door, ignored the district's directives for instruction and taught phonics. Somehow, some children got the tools they needed to progress.

Some people can't teach phonics. My mother clarified this phenomenon by sharing her observations on phonics in the public school system. She remembered watching phonics instruction come in and out of the classrooms repeatedly as my six brothers and I had gone through school. She said she could tell which of us had it and which didn't. I believe her.

Of course, that is considered anecdotal. It's just an opinion from another person who is just a parent without education credentials. Her statement might not mean much to the education elite but it certainly meant a lot to me. It explained my inability to teach our son the phonetic skills he seemed to be missing. Imagine how difficult it might be to learn to teach phonics if you were never taught it when you were younger. How should phonics be taught?

Good fortune presented the opportunity to observe a technique and structure of teaching reading that was totally different from what had been observed in our son's class four years earlier. In our daughter's first grade class, the phonics portion of the instruction process was remarkable. You can't begin to understand it until you hear and watch it being taught by someone that really knows what she is doing.

In this class, the phonics lessons were given with all kids gathered in a small circle at the teacher's feet facing her. This enabled the teacher to observe the shape of the kids' mouths and the position of their tongues as they mimicked the sound that she was making while their eyes were on the letter combinations (blends) that she was teaching.

It's hard to say if the object of these lessons was concentrated on specific blends or more on the idea that kids need to recognize that letters do not always "stand alone" in a word. This was not an intense effort to drill a particular combination into their heads. It wasn't even followed by a specific book focused on the lesson.

The class would break up into smaller informal groups or on their own to practice what they had learned. We volunteers had been asked to come at this time to be available to read with children that wanted us as part of their group. The teacher was then free to work with individuals that I suspect she was targeting as needing her expertise. We were on hand so the kids could practice with some guidance. If they happened to recognize a letter blend from their lessons, that became exciting for them.

It wasn't apparent from the structure of the instruction that any designation was made of which kids were the top readers and which were the bottom readers. Possibly if you watched the teacher closely enough you would be able to figure it out. That was in total contrast to previous observations, where children were almost immediately assigned to leveled reading groups with little hope of ever being in the top group if that wasn't where they started. Kids unfortunately figured that out very quickly. It is an observation noted by others.

In *Reaching Higher: The Power of Expectations in Schooling*, Rhona S. Weinstein, as a parent and educator, describes a study of three first grade classrooms. Her findings "revealed remarkably restricted mobility between groups: no member of a low reading group was able to gain entry into the highest reading group" (2002, 53). This is "leveling" or "tracking."

Weinstein also made this piercing statement: "That children know whether we think them smart or dull should give us pause" (289). Children observe, understand, and react in their own ways. And, as Darling-Hammond points out, "tracking persists in the face of growing evidence that it does not substantially benefit high achievers and tends to put low achievers at a serious disadvantage. . . . The disequalizing effects of early tracking continue throughout the remaining years of school" (2010, 60).

The awareness of their group "placement" in our son's classroom was at times obvious on the children's faces and reflected in their attitudes. While in our daughter's first grade classroom, when they broke up into groups or individually to read, they determined their own pace and the atmosphere of excitement about reading was obvious.

A difference also existed between these two classrooms in the reading material. Our daughter was exposed to stories that were about everyday life and the living things around us. It wasn't Dick, Jane, and Spot, but the themes resembled what you might think of as the modern-day equivalent to those old stories. The kids could relate them to their own lives.

On the other hand, our son had to struggle with nonsensical names and stories about faraway places that he couldn't relate to at all. Those stories may be excellent for established readers but certainly made guessing at words extremely difficult and the goal of reading to learn an iffy prospect.

## WRITING: PRACTICE OR REINFORCEMENT OF MISTAKES?

The theory that, above all else, we need to protect the self-esteem of students was never more evident than when it came to the teaching of writing during the early 1990s. Don't misunderstand—preserving a child's self-esteem and creativity is important. Children must come out of schools with their natural interest in learning intact. But it only seemed like common sense to make relevant corrections when they are younger rather than forcing them to face what amounts to failure as an adolescent or adult. That was obviously not the consensus in the teaching profession at the time.

Listening to children read back what they had written, giving them encouragement, and not making corrections are very reasonable approaches in the beginning. But just as with guessing at a word when reading, at what point do you start to teach accuracy with spelling and grammar? That was a question that should have been asked earlier rather than later, and would have been, had not that blinding trust also made us mute.

It would be many years down the road before it became clear that no consistent plan existed in this district for improving the writing skills of all students. A seventh grade English teacher clarified it by saying point-blank that no specific plan had been made for these kids that had not acquired the writing skills they should have to that point. She went on to say, "We don't know what to do with them."

In our curriculum, we had lists of frequently used words predetermined by grade that teachers were to have the kids spell. This was done in the traditional way of giving the kids a list of words weekly to memorize and then following up with a test on those same words. That is how many an American was taught spelling.

A similar approach was used for grammar lessons; the lessons were also done out of the context of a written piece. Class work took place on the board or a worksheet, where mistakes would be corrected. Many times it would be an isolated sentence or two written by some unknown about something that may or may not draw the interest of the students.

Writing assignments themselves were infrequent. Over the years, the most commonly observed writing practice was journal writing. Some would argue that a journal is too private an arena in which to do any correcting of spelling or grammar. Let's assume that is correct and then consider: couldn't a journal at least be used to get the students to clarify thoughts, to encourage some questioning by the students themselves, to demonstrate a deeper thought process, or as a place to encourage them to explore interests?

A quick glance at an old eleventh grade English journal was revealing. The check mark and good grade indicated that the apparent expectation for eleventh grade English was to be able to write three sentences in a form that looks like a paragraph but not necessarily make a point like a paragraph is supposed to do. No question marks existed where clarification was sorely needed. The absence of comments and marks, other than the check mark, indicated completion of an entry and no in-depth thought process was necessary to make the grade.

Not correcting anything was only reinforcing mistakes, not teaching good writing habits. Provided with an insufficient number of writing projects, students lacked the opportunities to learn to write adequately and with confidence. This seemed wrong especially when you consider that, when training an animal, repetition with reinforcement of good behavior is the basis for success. If you are forced to make corrections, it is best done when the mistake occurs or as soon as possible thereafter.

The importance of writing and spelling has eluded many. Being just a parent, who wasn't the best with grammar and writing in school and who has always been one of the worst at spelling, it was being part of the workforce that revealed their importance to me. You don't need to always be the best at everything, but mastery of the basics of communications and mathematics is essential.

# ARITHMETIC: MORE EXPERIMENTS GONE WRONG

How could we have gone so wrong with mathematics education? So many of us, in so many different ways, were wrong. In your district it may have been "New Math"; in mine it was "Touch Point Math" followed by some "New Math" techniques.

For those of you unfamiliar with touch point math, it is a proven effective method for teaching special education children who have been judged to be incapable of learning to add any other way. It is where the correct number of dots and circles are located on the number itself. For example, the number 8 has four dots which are surrounded by four circles. The child learns to touch and count the dots and circles and uses that method to add numbers.

What appears to have happened when this was used in non–special education classrooms was that a noticeable number of these children clung to this method as a crutch and, in the end, it slowed them down. Teachers began to notice the difference in test scores. If you watched a child in the classroom you could tell when they were counting incrementally to get an answer for simple addition. As the numbers that they were adding got bigger, the technique made the process of getting an answer painfully slow.

In all fairness to the technique, what may have also contributed to our district's failing math scores were the curriculum instructions to decrease attention to the rote memorization of math facts. So, if you hadn't learned what nine plus nine equals, you could start at nine and count nine dots and circles. What would you do if you had no confidence in your ability to recall an answer?

For whatever reason, the detrimental effects of failed math instruction techniques became obvious through classroom observations as the same group of kids advanced through the grade levels. It didn't matter what test we were using to track them; the scores were falling and later failing to make the grade.

In the upper grades, teachers didn't seem to know how to go about reversing this downward trend, while some teachers in the lower grades acted as if it really wasn't a big deal. If those teachers weren't communicating with any upper-level math teachers then they weren't hearing what the upper-level teachers had to say about the poor performance of the students they were receiving. The elementary teacher would only know that the children seemed to be able to add and subtract at a first, second, or third grade level.

When our district finally dropped the touch point pilot program, the need for our school board to address the issue was long overdue. They deserved to be applauded for dropping that particular pilot program, but they needed to address plans to correct the problems that this technique had created for certain students. What do you do when an experiment goes wrong?

Scattered throughout this community were parents who were thinking that their child wasn't good at math. The parents had no way of knowing that their child may potentially have succumbed to a mistake in the teaching technique. After approaching our school board to answer the question of what to do next, their response came in a "thank you for your time and concern" letter. No action was taken to try to correct the problem the schools had created with this pilot program.

These unfortunate kids may forever have numbers in their brains that have dots and circles on them and they may continue to use them. If they had been cars, a recall would have been forthcoming. In medicine, if you make a mistake, you attempt to correct it as soon as possible because you know it will snowball on itself. They didn't do that in our local education system; they just passed on their failures. And we moved on.

In mathematics instruction, we moved on to the next fad. This one seems to have been more widespread in the United States. The theory is to introduce multiple concepts and come back to revisit and reteach them on a regular basis. At this point, the trust was gone and skepticism was the new order of the day. Every aspect of every change deserved to be looked at with a critical eye.

The work papers and tests with this new program did not physically have enough room for a student with crude fine motor skills to show their work. Teachers allowed students to just put an answer without showing their work, thus making it difficult for upper-level algebra teachers to later break that bad habit. Nowhere did it appear that we were teaching kids to check their work, every time. And where this teaching "program" really appeared to fail kids was in the fact that they didn't seem to do enough of any one type of problem to master it and cement it concretely in their minds.

This time, the intuition of this parent was confirmed in a scientific study known as the Third International Mathematics and Science Study or TIMSS report. Since that time, the word "Third" has been replaced with the words "Trends in" to maintain the acronym TIMSS. One conclusion of its chief investigators was that when we, in the United States, think about the basics we think of repeating concepts over and over.

In other countries outperforming us in math and science, they consider that "the basics are so important that when they are introduced, the curriculum focuses on them. They are given concentrated attention so that they can be *mastered*, and children can be prepared to learn a new set of different basics in following grades" (Valverde & Schmidt, 1997–1998, 63).

With the three R's, it appears that other countries, and in many areas of our own country, an expectation of mastery is set and met. It appears that there are ways to do things right the first time. Now, what about science?

## Chapter Three

# Where's the Science?
# Using What We Know

> Students should develop a conceptual understanding of the natural world, criti-
> cal-thinking skills, and scientific habits of mind, including curiosity, respect
> for evidence, flexibility of perspective, and an appreciation for living things.
> —South Carolina LASER Institute (2002)

Consider yourself among the fortunate if your children experienced an adequate amount of hands-on science in their elementary school. And your
children are extremely fortunate if that practice continued throughout their
middle school and high school careers. This is not the case consistently
across the United States. That fact became painfully clear through experiences within my local education system.

After several years of volunteering in classrooms, it started to become
apparent that little to no science was being taught in many of the elementary
classes. Conversations about the topic would include such remarks from
teachers as: "We don't have time in the day" or "We don't have the equipment to do it." From the parents you would hear, "The teachers don't like to
teach science" or "They don't feel comfortable teaching science."

A trip to the district office was in order. The question to the then–acting
superintendent was "Do we have a science curriculum?" His answer: "Our
kids are good in science." Really?

At this point in time, our district was using the Iowa Test of Basic Skills
(ITBS) and the first time it was given to children was in the their third grade
year. On our son's first test, the area he scored highest in was science. It
appeared the acting superintendent was right. In some unknown way, our
school must have been doing a good job teaching science without being
obvious.

Years went by, and the now yearly ITBS scores were recorded, put in the student's file, and a copy sent home to the parents. As a parent, on a standardized national test like these, you at least wanted to see your child hold his ranking. Our son's percentile ranking in the United States had actually been steadily rising in language and reading, dramatically rising in math (after some unteaching and reteaching), but steadily dropping in science. The ITBS was last given in his seventh grade year, with his score in science being twenty percentile points below where he had started in the ranking in third grade.

How much emphasis a person should put on test results is questionable, but this looked like a red flag waving. It was time to carefully watch what was going on in the science classes. For the next three years, as a junior high and high school parent, "watching" became difficult. Parents were no longer wanted as volunteers and "hovering" is not a good idea. So, seeing the whole picture was never possible. The problems that were obvious were both unbelievable and unforgivable.

It's doubtful that any single situation was unique to this school and this moment in time, but the hope would be that such a combination of things happening to one kid was just bad luck. Keep in mind, every situation our son encountered was what approximately 150 of his classmates also experienced.

Eighth grade brought an episode with a first-time teacher attempting to teach physical science without even a model of an atom in the room. She honestly was trying to do the best she could with very little in the way of materials to do her job. She basically ended up using the "drill and kill" instructional method. She sent home the science vocabulary words, had the children memorize them even if the words made no sense, and then expected them to regurgitate them on a test. At home, the best that could be done was to try to lend some understanding and relevancy to the words. Perhaps a complaint should have been made to the principal or higher-ups, but experience thus far had taught that you more than likely would not see the problem resolved. And besides, this situation wasn't this teacher's fault, and potentially she could have been blamed. She didn't return to our district the next year.

That next year brought a new subject, with an experienced teacher, but the same "drill and kill" technique. To add relevancy to earth science is tricky when a person has no expertise in the subject or any previous interest in it. To be accurate and helpful, a book at home was necessary. When the teacher was asked about a book coming home, the answer was "There aren't enough books for kids to take them home." The arrangement was that kids were to come to the classroom after school, check out a book, and make sure it was back before school the next morning. But the teacher was also a coach and wasn't always available after school to check the books out. After jostling with that situation in the fall, a book was finally assigned to us.

When it was time to study for the cumulative final in this class, it seemed to be the perfect opportunity to demonstrate how a person can make use of previous tests to pinpoint areas of study where they should focus their attention. Since the answer sheets but never the tests themselves came home with the student, we went in after school one day and asked the teacher if we could go over the previous tests. He said he had already gotten rid of them; he was moving to a new room the next year. Frustration and disappointment had a battle to see who reigned supreme. The moment to teach a useful study skill, a teaching moment, was lost. But that year still didn't compare in frustration level to the next.

The biology class was being taught by a coach in his last year of teaching. No syllabus was used to inform us or the student about the subjects to be covered and when. Few class notes existed, and again there was no book that could come home. The tests were all essay without a guide as to what they were graded on and, again, they never came home. Our son was getting a good grade. But of more importance was the answer to the question "Was he getting a good biology education?" Although in later years temptation would rise up, this was the one and only time we ever pulled either of our kids from a class. All that could be said was "Enough!"

## THE THEORY OF ACTION

What may have added to the unbearable intolerance of this situation was a revelation during the previous summer. An administrator had given my name to a high school science teacher working on a grant to attend a K–8 Science Education Strategic Planning Institute in South Carolina. Along with a team of teachers and the superintendent, the job of the designated community scientist was to bring back information to the community and stimulate interest in science education. In June 2002, this institute made clear to us the ideals (philosophies and principles) underlying quality science instruction.

The title of the institute was Leadership and Assistance for Science Education Reform (LASER). The institute's emphasis was based on the National Science Resources Center (NSRC) model of systemic science education reform. The teaching philosophy promoted was that children learn science best in an inquiry-centered environment. For those of us without education credentials, this translates to giving a child something to work on or with and allowing their natural curiosity and interest to guide them in asking and answering questions. In other words, we parents might call it "hands-on" learning and those that are lucky enough to have schools following the philosophy behind this type of learning may know it as "experiential" education.

Using a variety of lectures and activities, the institute presented the important concepts behind understanding and establishing quality science instruction. Topics stretched from brain development to the essential factors in changing a local education system. One very fun and insightful activity was The Change Game. It provided descriptions of people and circumstances and required that we "players" make decisions regarding which people we would reach out to for help first and how we would approach "the change process" strategically. It served to make the point that change must occur first in the minds of people, before they will act on that change.

Another essential piece of this institutes education process was for us to understand the National Science Resource Centers' Theory of Action (see Fig. 3.1). This theory is presented in the shape of a pyramid. What makes a pyramid strong is the wide base on which the rest of the structure is built. The theory demonstrates that in order for us to support and guide our student's academic progress in science education, we must base our actions on sound knowledge of research and best practices. Science was their topic of focus, but the theory can be applied to any and all topics related to educational progress.

Once a wide base of information is established then collaboration must occur with those who will be involved in the changes and, collectively, they must develop a shared vision for moving forward. If this process is used for a particular subject being taught, then, based on the vision, curriculum is developed, relevant and appropriate assessments of learning are created, and education of teachers is provided along with the necessary materials. Good programs and plans of action are most successful and sustainable when they are encouraged and supported by both the school establishment and the community.

Another objective of the LASER institute was to teach us how we can help students become problem solvers using critical thinking skills while teaching them relevant science facts. The goal of the institute was to have the districts in attendance come away with a plan to improve the teaching of science in their district.

We met the goal of the institute. We did come away with a plan and it was a good plan. Unfortunately for the kids in our district, economics and politics would prevent this team from implementing the plan. Our daughter, even though she trailed her brother by years, would not see any benefit from the knowledge gained or the efforts of this team to improve science education instruction in our district. However, years later an opportunity would present itself to use a small portion of what had been learned at that institute.

Figure 3.1. Reproduction here is with the permission of the National Science Resource Center. This diagram cannot be reproduced in any form without the expressed written permission of the NSRC.

FAILING TO USE WHAT WE LEARNED

In the fall of 2006, inquiry led to information about a federal grant administered through our state's Department of Education. It was a Math and Science Partnership Program grant aimed at professional development, which is another term for continuing education for teachers. At the time, this appeared to be an opportunity to practice partnership building skills and use the previously gained knowledge of science education at the same time.

The situation in our district at this time was that the administration was severely limiting the amount of time teachers could spend on anything other than reading, language arts, and math because of our poor performance on our state's tests. We hadn't started testing for science yet. Our school district is surrounded by districts that were teaching science starting in the elementary grades using the best practices of hands-on techniques. These surrounding districts were performing better on the standardized tests in reading and math.

Curiosity and an inquiring nature leads one to ask: Were they performing better and as a result had the luxury of teaching science, or were they performing better because they had been teaching science in a way that stimulated the naturally curious young brain, making learning in reading and math more relevant, interesting, and therefore more productive? In the end, the hope was that the readers of our grant would be thinking along the same lines.

To even begin this grant process, a partnership needed to be developed between an institute of higher learning and a school or school district labeled as "failed" by the federal law, No Child Left Behind, rules. Then, according to what had been learned about the change process at the LASER institute and based on the NSRC Theory of Action, we needed to establish a common knowledge of research and best practices among the key leaders in this project. Together, we needed to develop a common vision for moving forward with science education at the elementary level in the district.

Three months later, we had completed the grant writing project and had built an excellent team that would be ready to work should we be awarded the grant. The main writers consisted of the knowledgeable principal of our "failed" downtown school, a very brave education professor from our local private college, and myself. As part of the larger team, we had several elementary teachers, both middle schools represented by science teachers, and a district administrator that was becoming very open to the idea. That, in itself, was a huge accomplishment.

We began this endeavor knowing it was a competitive process. In our state, they would be awarding three to four grants. The grant proposals were being sent to evaluators outside the state to ensure fairness in judging them with the final decision being made at the state level. Idaho is one of very few states that elect their chief education leader referred to as a superintendent in this state. We were reassured, as postelection State Department of Education personnel changed, that the evaluators had been hired ahead of the changeover of administration and all was a "go" for the process to proceed as previously indicated and in a timely fashion.

Our grant proposal, *Bringing Science into the Elementary Classroom*, was ranked second overall in the state by the independent evaluators. In defense of that ranking not being first place, we would have scored higher had the out-of-state evaluators connected with the fact that we had no baseline state statistics in science because we had yet to develop those tests. We were not awarded the grant. The number of awards to be given had supposedly been cut.

The reality for us was that new personnel in the State Department of Education had worked with a math partnership in our district previously and math trumped science, no matter how good the proposal. As with many situations that are tied to politics, somebody knew somebody. Our partnership got the proverbial political shaft. It felt like time wasted. Now, there is some comfort in being told by Betsy A. that "There are no mistakes; they are learning experiences." But one does need to face the facts.

The grant proposal had failed to demonstrate to our state administration the importance of inquiry-based science education and its direct correlation to the improvement of math and reading scores. So, in no way did they even come close to comprehending the importance of inquiry-based science education in the development of young minds and their future ability to think critically and apply their education in the sciences for the betterment of our social and economic needs.

Medicine, energy usage, and environmental issues are all perfect examples of the relationship between social and economic needs and quality science education. Talk abounds about improving the health care system in the United States, but not nearly enough of it is about real preventive health care. In veterinary medicine, especially in the food production fields, the debate no longer exists that responsible preventive medicine costs less than treatment of illnesses and the loss in productivity that sick animals experience.

The key to effective preventive medicine is education. When you apply that idea of educating people to the economics of wise use of resources, consider how much better off we would be if people were better educated about energy consumption. Conservative practices make sense.

We must consider education's potential as a powerful tool in helping to alter the problems we have created with the pollution of our air and water. If all people understood and applied just the basics of wise use and conservation of natural resources, the situation would dramatically improve. Clearly, we must address science education issues to address the social issues of health care, energy usage, and our world environment.

Seeing that children in my community would continue to be deprived of quality science education was tough to swallow. The humor of the situation can be found in sad irony. The tunnel vision produced by standards and testing for reading and math had limited or excluded the use of quality science education as a potential tributary to the lifelong successes of our students. It seemed we were forced to teach to the test. In the 20/20 hindsight we all have, seeing "No Child Left Behind" on the title page of that grant application, we should have known better than to have gotten involved. Participation in what you know is wrongful won't make it right. Never sell your soul.

# Chapter Four

# Along Came "No Child Left Behind": With Unintended or Foreseeable Consequences?

> A school cannot be studied satisfactorily, nor judged fairly, except in terms of its own philosophy of education, its individually expressed purposes and objectives, the nature of the pupils with which it has to deal, and the needs of the community which it serves.
>
> —Cooperative Study of Secondary School Standards

Before the No Child Left Behind law came into existence, our state and our local school district were attempting to straighten out the mess created during the most recent downturn in a variety of test scores. It appeared we may have let the teaching pendulum swing too far in the direction of experimentation with techniques that had gone wrong. Those tracking the data concluded that statistical trends were of concern; issues needed attention.

The state and local education agencies were starting to make what looked to be real improvements as they were coming to an understanding of where they had gone wrong and attempting to adjust accordingly. The process was proceeding at a snail's pace but it was slowly floating forward. Then along came the "outcome-based" theory of reform. Suddenly, we were to hold students accountable by denying them a high school diploma if they failed the "exit standards test."

# STATES LEAD THE WAY ON STANDARDS AND TESTING

The theory behind "exit testing" *sounds* reasonable. The idea is that we develop a set of standards that we can basically agree on as to what we would like all graduates to know and be able to do before receiving a diploma. This move was supposed to ensure that a high school diploma really meant something more than the fact that students attended school—what some refer to as "seat time." It was to ensure that a basic set of skills had been *mastered* by each student, and the high school diploma would serve as a testament to that fact.

In my state these skills had been defined many years before in Idaho Code 33-1612 mentioned previously as defining a *Thorough System of Public Schools*. Those skills were identified and stated as "the skills necessary to communicate effectively; the skills necessary for students to enter the work force; the skills to enable them to be responsible citizens of their homes, schools and communities." In addition, the law states that "schools will provide a basic curriculum necessary to enable students to enter academic or professional-technical postsecondary educational programs" and that they will be "introduced to current technology."

The writers of this law did an excellent job of defining what the people (the business community, parents, and community in general) want from their public school system. The question becomes whether or not anyone at the State Board or Department of Education or our local school board read and understood these words. They obviously did not keep the ideals represented in the law in the forefront when planning their next move.

Considering the fact that my state was many years behind other states in this "exit standards" process, brought on by the "standards, assessments, and accountability" movement, it would have been easy to learn from other states about their mistakes as well as their successes. Instead, we proceeded by first writing our own set of standards for language arts, math, science, health, and social studies. This was done through committees of chosen people, along with taking comments at some not-so-well publicized public meetings.

The developed standards were taken to the state legislature in 2000 for its approval, and the first class to be held accountable to pass this new testing was slated to be the class of 2005, our first child's graduating class. Being one of the few parents knowing intimately what that class's learning experiences had consisted of in my district sealed the obligation to testify at the State Joint Legislative Education Committee Hearings.

Careful preparation was called for, given the fact that they might only allow about three minutes for a person to voice their view. Thoughts on the experiences of the past nine years needed to be condensed. The message needed to open their eyes to the existence of poor learning environments, poor teaching techniques, or lack of instruction in some subject areas, and the lack of proven effective remedies for problems that the aforementioned had created. The intention was to try to put the legislators in the shoes of a "failing" child of the class of 2005.

At this point, in 2000, these students had been in the school system for eight years. In the next five years, according to the State Board's proposal, we would be able to identify the problems of each individual and address those problems with "research proven effective remediation." Remediation means "to find a remedy." We were only at the point where we could admit in our own minds that mistakes had been made. We had yet to say out loud that some experiments went wrong. How do you find a remedy when you won't discuss all the causes?

We were actually being asked to put our faith in the system's ability to identify and fix problems it had partially created itself. Numerous teachers in the upper grades had no idea why their students were coming to them unprepared. Certainly, parents and the public weren't informed. As a parent, I never got a "recall for faulty instruction" notice. How could a student be held accountable by denying them a diploma when nobody had openly admitted that mistakes had been made, let alone worked cooperatively to correct them?

Just before the testimony started, the chairman announced that they would not take comments on implementation of the standards, only on the standards themselves. Putting aside the much-rehearsed outline that mainly addressed implementation, finding a copy of the standards, and going through it like a mad woman with a marker, a new approach to deliver the message was devised. Improvise.

First, the message was politely delivered that some of us had come prepared to talk about implementation of the standards and testing and would be looking forward to addressing those subjects at a different time in the future. A nod came from the chairman indicating that input on implementation would occur at another time but it was apparently not a promise. That opportunity never came; implementation of standards never received its public hearing with the legislature—these policymakers would never hear directly from those of us in the trenches.

After testimony had been given that morning, the room emptied into the hallway, where the chairperson's secretary seemed to go out of her way to deliver the following observation: "If they were listening, they got your message." For what had been expressed to the legislature was a comparison: a compliment on a specific, well-intentioned, relevant standard followed by a statistic or observation to point out where the average students really were at this point in time in relation to that particular standard.

The hope was that a light would go on and it would dawn on them how unrealistic it would be to get these students to the desired level in such a short time *without extensive support*. The object was not to say that standards aren't a good thing. The point was that if "exit standards testing" was the direction that they were bent on going, the students needed the standards and curriculum in place eight years ago! Plus, these students needed every ingredient that goes into creating and supporting highly performing schools— *effective* leadership and instruction, a safe and nurturing *learning climate*, and family and community *engagement* in the learning processes.

The legislature was apparently not listening to the few of us that were in attendance without a political or monetary agenda. Our state then proceeded to hire a testing company that was inexperienced in exit testing. The testing company, along with the State Board, held some, again, not-so-well-publicized public meetings. The principal of the middle school, where our local class of 2005 attended, was asked if a notification could be distributed through his school to the parents informing them of this meeting. His response was "It is not my responsibility to inform parents about educational issues."

So it goes. The testing floodgates were opened with a resultant current too strong to swim against alone. No good way to reach others who might have cared to help could be found. I attended that meeting as the lone self-appointed representative of our students. An employee of the testing company came up afterward to tell me to "fight the good fight," for even many of them did not believe in "exit testing."

At the time, it appeared that this test company employee was "just" one person expressing a personal opinion. Looking into it further, ethical testing industry professionals follow a code that provides guidelines for what is considered "fair" including "the recommended uses" and the necessity for understanding "the strengths and limitations of the test" (Code of Fair Testing Practices in Education, 2004). There are ethical and unethical uses of testing and the data they produce. Many could foresee the abusive uses of standardized testing that were to come.

With disappointment imminent, without very large numbers of parents knowing and understanding what was happening, it was too hard to prevail; it was impossible to fight. The people promoting this project were so sure of themselves; they didn't need to listen to the voices of the scores of dissenters from all over the area and across the education spectrum that had voiced similar concerns.

Keep in mind that in 2000 the process of using standardized tests as the basis for "accountability" was referred to as "high stakes testing." A diploma was what was at stake. If you don't consider that a high stake, look at the difference in the earning potential of those with and without a high school diploma. In many states, this process associated with "exit testing" had caused a public backlash.

Before No Child Left Behind (NCLB) came fully on the scene, the spin-meisters worked their magic on the name of the testing. It became "standards achievement testing." Everybody wants achievement to occur. Everyone wants standards set to achieve. Significant resistance had been averted with a change in wording. It was excellent execution of propaganda.

We skeptics tread water and waited to see what decisions would be made for us next; anxiety about the future was welling up while we wondered if they would really deny diplomas—if they would really allow the torrent that had been unleashed to wipe out the undeserving students. The wait wasn't long. It was truly amazing to see how quickly the system could change when the right people said "go."

By the summer of 2001, our Assessment and Accountability Commission proposed the rules for our standards achievement test. Their recommendations stated that students who failed the test could still be eligible to graduate if local districts decide to issue them diplomas based on alternate routes to graduation. That left the debate about the true worth of a high school diploma up to the local district. In the name of "flexibility," it was accepted that diplomas could be awarded without proving or improving achievement as designated by law.

So, in the end, the objective of the development of standards achievement testing went from giving value to a diploma to identifying the child's needs and addressing it in their instruction, right? That sounds good. That sounds like what should go on in every classroom every day. But, now being a skeptic, doubts were overflowing. How this was going to work would all be in how it was implemented, and that hadn't been openly discussed.

At that point in 2001, as a taxpayer, the big question at the local school board budget hearings was: "How much money would be set aside for remedial instruction for those failing to pass our new state tests?" At that time, blank stares and shrugs exchanged between the school board members and the superintendent answered the question. There was no money set aside. The money for the purpose of addressing individual students' needs as identified on the new tests wouldn't be designated until this district's 2007 budget; a six-year lag!

As a parent, I went from closely following my oldest child's standardized test scores through the fall of 2001 to being totally in the dark while they piloted the new tests. I watched him and his classmates once more become guinea pigs for the system. I anguished as they spent precious instructional time testing those students two and three times a year.

In the fall of 2003, the targeted class of 2005 emerged from the darkness with their ACT scores. It indicated, as did the state tests, that our son could use some additional help. However, the district could not provide any instruction specific to our son's needs. He wasn't bad enough compared to the others in his class. Sound like a child left behind?

At that time, since they had no intention of doing anything beneficial with his test results, a request was made that they not waste his time any further with testing. But, due to poor communications within the school, he was tested again, prompting a letter to our State Board of Education. That letter stated: "You were *responsible* for setting in motion the testing of the children in the class of 2005. You took away a portion of their instructional time and gave them nothing in return. Once again, the education *system used children* for experimentation without benefit to them. These children have been cheated. You're just lucky most parents don't know enough to realize it." To the then-governor of our state went a letter saying, "Please tell me where *the accountability for the administration* fits into achievement testing." That request still hangs in the air.

Apparently, the public education resources to help a child being left behind were in reality nonexistent or had been exhausted (like myself). Where does one turn for help within the public education system?

## HOW "NO CHILD LEFT BEHIND" WORKS (OR DOESN'T)

In the fall of 2004, the machinery behind No Child Left Behind was in full gear. If you were a parent with a child in a school labeled as "needs improvement," you received a letter required as part of the NCLB "sanctions." This was part of the penalty for not scoring well on the new standardized tests. Our letter read: "Under federal and state laws and rules, students in schools identified for improvement are eligible to apply for transfer to another school within the district that has met state academic goals. However, our district has no transfer options available at this time because we have only one high school in our district."

Within this public school system, this letter just confirmed that we were sending our child to a school that needed some improvements; it confirmed our need for *help* and it only took three years to do it. It changed nothing for the students; the damage had been done. In the future, similar letters would be delivered again and again.

It never made sense. Each state, independently, for the most part, spent time and money developing standards, developing tests, and in some cases redeveloping tests, used students' instructional time to validate the tests, and used the results to put in place (in this case) meaningless sanctions such as letters to parents from schools that "failed" repeatedly. Now, what exactly is No Child Left Behind (NCLB)?

In *Why the No Child Left Behind Act Needs to Be Restructured to Accomplish Its Goals and How to Do It*, lawyer Gary Ratner states, "NCLB is a massive and complex law regulating scores of federal education grant programs. . . . [It was] heavily modeled on the states, then decade-old "standards, assessments and accountability" movement. (In fact, NCLB may be thought of as the federalization of that movement)" (2007, 8).

From the perspective of a parent who has suffered through trying to figure out what this law does without actually reading the law, it can be said with certainty that it is a federal law over nine hundred pages long that was passed in 2001. One should at this point question whether most lawmakers read and/or understood it. The reason we should wonder is not its length alone, but also the fact that it sets as its goal that all students, 100 percent, will be proficient in all tested subject areas by 2014.

The thought behind that is certainly an appealing one. Who wouldn't like to see us shooting for 100 percent proficient students? "Proficient" means "highly competent, skilled or adept" (*Webster's*, 1976). That definitely sounds like what people want in our students, 100 percent; no doubt. We can give 100 percent of our students an *effective* education *relevant to their needs*. However, consider whether, when dealing with people in the arena of statistics, how frequently do we get 100 percent on anything? What were our representatives thinking?

With the current standards tests we were supposed to use the results to tailor the instruction to the students' needs. In our dysfunctional district, we saw how that was "working" by 2004—it wasn't. And testing itself was never going to work to advance the *quality* of student learning in the schools that so desperately needed it, because a score can't distinguish between a test preparation curriculum and quality education.

As Douglas B. Reeves, in *101 Questions & Answers about Standards, Assessment, and Accountability*, stated in discussing standardized tests, "What these tests can never do is measure a broad concept such as 'educational quality' of schools and teachers, and the tests certainly do not measure the general knowledge of students" (2001, 27). He explains how they provide a "brief and limited" picture and in the best accountability systems are only *one of many "indicators"* that could be or should be used. We knew this before 2001!

And even earlier, the Cooperative Study of Secondary School Standards clearly stated its objection to testing as "a sole method of accreditation or for similar widespread comparison" because testing tends to make "instruction point definitely to success in examinations," cultivates "a uniformity that is deadening to instruction," can "thwart the initiative of instructors," and can "destroy the *flexibility* and individuality of an institution" (1939, 163). In addition to bringing about a rigid curriculum, the study concluded, this type of testing had little validity for identifying superior and inferior schools and *a better method was available.* In 1939!

But we moved "forward" with the goal of NCLB to "close the achievement gap" through "accountability, flexibility, and choice" basing our evaluation of "the gap," "accountability," and the need for "choice" on only one indicator of achievement: standardized test scores. As Diane Ravitch acknowledges in *The Death and Life of the Great American School System: How Testing and Choice Are Undermining Education,* "Scores matter, but they are an indicator, not the definition of a good education" (2010, 90). "Good education" was what we all wanted, right?

No, the call for school "accountability" was the big driver of this law. So, based on what a school's original proficiency level was when first tested and finding the difference from 100 percent (its goal), a school's yearly target is then calculated by dividing that difference by the number of years to the target year 2014. That is one way an annual yearly progress (AYP) goal can be determined, but it may be set differently depending on where you live. Your state may also decide that it won't increase the goal yearly. And most currently, we face the idea that after a decade we might just waive away this whole idea without really discussing what is at the root of our "experiences."

Your school's test results are further broken down into twelve subgroups of student demographics to ensure that no particular group of children gets left behind, thus clarifying the real meaning of the name No Child Left Behind. A school needs to make progress toward its yearly goal in all categories. When schools don't meet those goals, they have "failed" to pass their AYP and are labeled as "needs improvement."

As NCLB proceeds, the public is beginning to hear and will hear more about how all schools will become "failed" schools; more and more schools are being labeled as "needs improvement," insinuating failure. The public will hear that being labeled as "failed" doesn't mean what it implies. That is true. That is what happens in cases like this when you set a statistical measurement of 100 percent as a goal.

Eventually, almost all schools miss the mark. You will hear that you can easily get the "failed" label by missing the goal in one subgroup or by a few students. That is true. But what about a school that failed to serve large numbers of students from the beginning in multiple categories and is given chance after chance after chance? That is a school truly in trouble and in need of help. And when it is a high school where a diploma is given by an alternate route after failing the standards tests, that school graduates students that are children left behind.

The NCLB law allows schools to fail to pass their AYP for two years in a row before being labeled "needs improvement." NCLB began to count the test scores in 2002. Our district's only high school failed to meet its goals in 2002 and 2003, so we got our first parent letters in the fall of 2004. That same year, ninth graders were brought into what was originally built to be a three-year high school. When you fail to succeed with some students, making a school bigger by adding more to the mix is allowable, I guess.

The logic is baffling, but under NCLB law it was considered a reconfiguration and gave the school an additional year to fail and not face additional consequences. So, in 2007, we received the notification required of schools that have failed for three years in a row, when in actuality it had been five years. How many ways can you think of to use statistics to hide the truth? But we did get our letter that proves "transparency."

This letter stated that "The district must make available additional help for eligible students upon parent request." This help is referred to as supplemental services. Three months into the 2007 school year, the district hadn't had a single request for services. The letter went on to indicate that the services would be allotted based on income level and how far the allotted money would spread.

With each letter came more unanswered questions. Honestly, it doesn't seem right to bother school board representatives with numerous questions about the law when they are acting as unpaid volunteers, such as they are in my district. Logically, a call to the paid state educational agency employees would be in order.

First, they were asked to confirm that the statistics were correct in that our high school had never passed its annual yearly progress goals. Finding the person to confirm that was not easy. The fact that it took a lot of time with each person in the chain of command to verify the truth revealed that not enough people were paying attention to the reality of who had failed from the beginning and repeatedly.

So, what about accountability? NCLB is a federal law implemented by the states. Who is supposed to be watching at the state level? The first year of "needs improvement" status requires that a two-year improvement plan be developed. Our state department of education wasn't really sure who was responsible for reading those plans and they referred the inquiry to the State Board of Education, which tried to refer it back to the state department. Since no one could be found that had actually read the improvement plan at that time, it was time to get a copy.

After reading it, it was apparent that nobody had read it very well, if at all, since goals had failed to even be set. They really had forgotten or omitted goals in most subject areas; blanks were obvious where goals should have been found. Really! When asked again who was accountable, state officials either explained that it was up to the local school board or they quit returning phone calls. After all, when you are just a parent, you don't carry much weight, even though they tell you "you are important." So, with nowhere to go but up, the U.S. Department of Education was next on the list.

On the first call to them in the fall of 2007, upon inquiring about the complaint process, the response was that no complaint process for No Child Left Behind existed. The second time, upon request, the comments were supposedly noted and passed on to the Secretary of Education. The helpful person answering the phone did confirm the fact that my local school board is ultimately responsible. The conversation also established that, indeed, my state was supposed to identify its "failing" schools.

So, when you put all these conversations together, it really becomes clear that we have armies of well-paid bureaucrats set up to administer the No Child Left Behind law but, when it comes down to accountability for implementation of the plan, it's a local control issue. It is the implementation of a huge plan that we at the local level were never given a chance to critique. The effectiveness of NCLB depends on, in our case, unpaid local school board members. And the time has come where we must see that we have come full circle, again.

These experiences in my dysfunctional district are not unique. From coast to coast, the failures of this law, and the flawed theories it was based on, have been coming to the surface.

So, this becomes the moment in time when we need to better understand what this law was originally intended to do. We must look back to President Lyndon Johnson's "War on Poverty." The Elementary and Secondary Education Act (ESEA) of 1965 was passed as part of that war because of the sentiment that the needs of children living in poverty were *not being met by state and local officials*. This law requires review and reauthorization by Congress every five to six years. This law was intended to target a very specific group of children, those from poverty-stricken families whose schools were failing to meet their educational needs.

The majority of public schools are meeting children's needs. Highly functional states and functional districts have highly performing schools. We should now honor the intentions of the original law while following the business model rules that so many believe we should. As James Lewis Jr. points out in *Achieving Excellence in Our Schools . . . by Taking Lessons from America's Best-Run Companies*, "We must learn not to tamper with success" (1986, 183); not in practice and not in policy. No Child Left Behind is the 2001 reauthorization of the 1965 ESEA.

This education law has become too complex and confusing to be *implemented effectively* at *the local level* particularly by *dysfunctional districts* whose schools contain the very students the law set out to help. The law is confusing because it makes no sense. We need "failing schools" to take the necessary actions to improve themselves. But they aren't capable, that's why they struggle. But instead of using what we know to guide students' academic progress, Congress strapped us with a top-down, across-the-board, one-size-fits-all mandate for better test scores, the falsely assumed judge of "achievement." It put the proverbial cart before the horse, results ahead of responsible action. It flipped the Theory of Action on its top. An upside-down pyramid is destined to crash.

As Ratner realistically assessed the situation, "By treating increasing test scores as the end in itself, the Act pressures schools to drill and kill students with test preparation, narrow the curriculum, and take other steps to artificially raise test scores" (2007, 3). And not only did this law produce these consequences; it further deprived students of opportunities and fueled the tumult of "education reform" efforts as explained by Kathy Emery and Susan Ohanian in *Why Is Corporate America Bashing Our Public Schools?*: "Schools labeled as 'low-performing' have their arts and physical education programs cut and replaced with hours of reading and math drills. Schools labeled as 'high-performing' are besieged by parents fighting to get their children into these schools, turning districts into battlegrounds of parent fury and futility" (2004, 202).

What else should we know about NCLB?

Under the "accountability" mechanism of NCLB, if your school fails a fourth year in a row to meet its AYP, in addition to the sometimes nonexistent school choice and the supplemental services for those comprehending and acting on their right to make that request, the school may be required to replace "certain staff " or "fully implement a new curriculum."

If your school moves on to a fifth year in a row, which technically in our district we had long ago surpassed, it is supposedly required to "restructure." What restructuring may mean is that the school may be closed and may be reopened as a charter school; it may be required to replace all or most of the school staff or turn over school operations either to the state or to a *private company* with a "demonstrated record of effectiveness"—based on test scores?

You may be thinking, after all the bungling that has occurred in some schools that it is about time someone else took charge. Think again and real hard about how scary that last step really sounds. Will privatization build and maintain the public trust better than what our long history of quality public education has demonstrated?

There can no longer be any doubt that the public schools and their teachers are being bashed by the media and bad-mouthed by various groups with their own agendas. As Emery and Ohanian point out,

> The truth is that there is a long-standing problem of children in these [NCLB demographic] subgroups failing to thrive in school, but business interests, instead of working to solve the problem, redefine it to their own ends. The

business plan is to declare schools failures, vacating the principals and teachers. Pit teacher against teacher, school against school. Get conservatives fighting against liberals over vouchers and charters so they don't join together
against their common enemy. (2004, 78)

Have the consequences of this law been unintended, unforeseeable by those
in power who were unwilling to listen—or intended? All I know for sure is
what I saw with my own eyes and what I hear from others including teacher
Sarah P: "we have done what was asked without results."

Whether or not you are a big believer in conspiracy theories, you have to
think twice. Years ago in a conversation with one of my brothers, the talk
drifted to something along the lines of "either these people in power toying
with education are really stupid or just evil and greedy." We decided it was
probably a combination of both.

With that dialogue echoing in my mind and someone else's words about
the "dismantling of the public education system" resonating loudly as I read
about the fifth year's sanctions, I have to wonder where we are headed next
with No Child Left Behind, the former Elementary and Secondary Education
Act, and our public education system in general.

One thing is certain, as Monty Neill declared in *Many Children Left
Behind: How the No Child Left Behind Act is Damaging Our Children and
Our Schools*, "Real change will happen far faster if the nation decides it
really means to leave no children behind and takes appropriate measures, in
education and elsewhere" (Meier, Neill, et al., 2004, 116). Education happens both in and outside classrooms. It is an adventure, a journey of lifelong
learning. We are all educators.

*Chapter Five*

# What Is the Problem? Why Children Get Left Behind

> When we leave the natural method, and adopt a fixed program, and insist upon uniform required subjects, and draw in large numbers of students, then we are tempted to introduce rules, organization, discipline and bribes. Then, education becomes a ritual, not an adventure.
>
> —Ralph Waldo Emerson

A whole system has developed around educating children. We call it a system, anyway, and most will continue to do so out of habit. A better descriptor would be "bureaucracy," which *Webster's* defines as "the administration of government through departments and subdivisions managed by sets of appointed officials following an inflexible routine." A "system" would imply that it is working in "a unified way in an orderly form so as to show a logical plan linking the various parts" (*Webster's*, 1976). The word "system" better describes our ideals in public education rather than the current reality for many of us.

This educational bureaucracy we have created includes the president of the United States, both houses of Congress, the Supreme Court and lower courts, the secretary of education, the U.S. Department of Education, each state's department of education and board of education, the school district administration, and ultimately the local school district board, administrators, teachers, and staff. In functional states, districts, and schools, some education experts and everyday people are allowed to be a part of the decision-making process.

The total cost to keep our education system flowing, from top to bottom, probably wouldn't matter if we were all happy with the end results; but that is not the case. It is a fair assessment to say that the distribution of educational opportunity in this country is through a bureaucracy that is huge and complicated and supposed to be largely based on state control and the idea of local control; the distribution of quality education is unequal.

Local control is a grand idea. The theory is that the people at the local level know what they need and are best able to exert control, direction, and change at that level. They, the people, become the built-in accountability factor. That accountability factor, local people, is a virtue in the concept of localism.

The flaw in the local control concept is that it is based on the vigilance of the people. It requires that people be watchful, informed, involved, and vocal. Therein lies the problem, in various ways.

Local control can go wrong. Community members can organize around their own agenda and be successful. Take sports, for example. A group of well-meaning parents can push for administration and board members to be selected based on favorable attitudes toward sports. If those selected to carry out the sports agenda do not have satisfactory attitudes toward and knowledge about academics, academics suffer. For that very reason, some education experts don't trust communities with being able to establish effective schools on their own. Without constant vigilance by the community, you can see the justification in their thinking.

Vigilance means more than just looking out for your own child. It takes looking out for the children of your neighbors, friends, and relatives. It takes people that care about the next generation—that is, really care, not just giving lip service to the idea of caring, using it as a sound bite, or tossing around the now-standard rhetoric like "no child left behind."

The public education system is great where the local control concept is functioning well. When all the factors necessary for the local control system to function are in place, it works. If even some of the ingredients of success are present, there is hope. But, when all factors falter, we find "failed" schools. We find kids going under, going down with no life preserver in sight. When local control of education fails, children have been, are now, and will continue to be left behind.

Early in my battle over safe and disciplined school issues, I came to believe that three major factors led to the declining state of our local schools. Those factors are: (1) lack of accountability of administration, (2) no "checks and balances" provided by the school board, and (3) apathy and the "me and mine" attitude of the public.

## LACK OF ACCOUNTABILITY OF ADMINISTRATION

Accountability means you are "obligated to be *responsible* for or able to explain your actions" (*Webster's*, 1976). Administrators are people whose job it is to manage or direct the affairs of an institution. Laws governing the schools, and now standards, are set by the government. And policies and curriculum are approved by the local school boards. School administrators manage the people carrying out the rules. They are managers. They should be accountable to all those above and below them in the hierarchy of the school system. Their actions must be based on the rules they are responsible for carrying out. They shouldn't make their own rules.

Observations, during the dealings with the safe and disciplined schools issues in 1999, led to the conclusion that many times the administrators didn't know or understand policies or laws. It is their job to know the rules under which they must function. In questioning the administration for clarification of the rules, you run the risk of setting up barriers between yourself and them. Ever feel like walls are going up between you and the person from whom you expect answers?

Others can see these "walls" in a different light. Marilyn Price-Mitchell explains in "Boundary Dynamics: Implications for Building Parent-School Partnerships" that "many of the boundaries between parents and schools are perceived as walls rather than places to interact and learn" (2009, 17). She acknowledges that "mandates may be needed to overcome natural organizational resistance to change, yet mandates alone will not create new *conditions* where *partnership* can thrive" (13–14).

If administrators do not feel obligated to give explanations to those below them, as we parents are seen to be, you are forced to give up or go around or go above them for your answers. If you choose to persist in seeking the facts, you may encounter the walls building ever higher and the wagons may circle. You may be made to feel like the enemy for asking questions.

Human nature explains this behavior to some extent, in that many times a person views comments as criticism and may take it personally as a direct reflection on them. The scope of this phenomenon and its potential detrimental effects to the education system were not apparent until after reading *Parental Involvement and the Political Principle* by Seymour Sarason.

Dr. Sarason explains that the political principle justifying parental involvement is the belief that, when decisions are made affecting you or your possessions, you should have a role, *a voice in the process* of that decision making. He describes the "rigid boundaries professionals erect to insure that 'outsiders' remain outsiders." He refers to this behavior as the "cult of professionalism" and uses the example of medical doctors, where you are "the 'outsider' trying to get an 'insider professional' to take your ideas, feelings, and recommended actions seriously" (1995, 26).

Accountability won't happen when the person asking for it is seen as someone whose experiences or desires are not relevant to the decision-making process. When explanations aren't to be found and no one hears or listens to your views supporting your concerns, you have hit a brick wall. Breaking down that barrier created by the cult of professionalism is too tall an order for just one parent. In the hierarchy of school systems, your local school board should be able to help.

## THE "CHECKS AND BALANCES" OF THE SCHOOL BOARD

If you recall, our local school board was asked five separate times to be part of spearheading a community group to explore safety and discipline issues and solutions. They said "no" for reasons that to this day are not fully clear. They threw up a barrier to letting others be a part of the decision-making process. The cult of professionalism includes more people than what fits the technical definition of professionals. The cult appears to have been in play at this level, with this school board. However, this particular school board was actually very effective in many ways compared to what followed.

The next group of school board members did not stick with the job for more than two terms and several did not even finish one term. This turnover seriously affected the functioning of our board, given the large amount of information they should absorb and understand. The learning curve is steep, especially in the beginning and with the changes in our laws. Thinking back over the reasons for the comings and goings of our local school board members could make for a book in itself.

We had a member unseated by a challenger whose child, along with friends, got caught drinking beer at an away game. That same new member saw through the demise of the administrator that enforced the admittedly wrongful alcohol policy. Another member sought a seat on the board to get rid of a softball coach, while yet another used his power to promote sports in general, and a friend in particular, to high places.

In dysfunctional districts, the shenanigans that go on behind the scenes are generally not noticed by the public. Occasionally an incident surfaces and the community acts as if this is the first time a board member "used" their position for less than stellar intentions. The peoples' attention is short-lived, and long-term problems continue. Board members are one part of "officialdom" who Sarason explains are probably for the most part pure in their intentions but lack "experienced knowledge of education reform" (1993, 9). Regardless, they have power.

It appeared that our board members understood their power, all right. That position gives them the authority to control others. We would hope, *we trust*, that they would use that power to make decisions based on knowledge gained and analysis of the issues at hand for the betterment of education for all. For them to make excellent decisions, it would seem logical to seek more than one source of information or perhaps even listen to more than one point of view. They, like many elected people in positions of power, may not have heard the Thomas Jefferson quotation, "Difference of opinion leads to enquiry, and enquiry to truth."

To follow Jefferson's line of reasoning would require that the board members actually take the time to listen to differing views, possibly even seek out different opinions and ask questions to seek to find the truth. To find direction as a board, discussion would be necessary, as a board. If the board bases its decisions only on the information provided to it by administration and no questions are asked and no discussion ensues, then administrative decisions are "rubber stamped"; no "check and balance" exists.

To do justice to schools that need improving, school boards need to have some working knowledge of the best ways to guide student's progress. They need to understand and be able to foster responsible action. They need to comprehend the Theory of Action. But first, they need to hear the reality. As Jason C. has stressed, "we need data transparency."

The school board is supposed to act as the go-between for the school district and the community. The school district administrators and staff must provide the school board with the facts. And it will save a lot of time and prevent some confusion if the public is informed because, ultimately, the community needs to be able to voice their concerns, address problems, and voice their desires to the board. It is up to the board to then drive policies and instruction by sorting out the details and giving direction to the district based on their combined educational philosophies. They need to assist in fostering a vision upon which to act. The three elements of the local education system—administration, the school board, and the people—are interconnected, and barriers among the three in any form lead to dissatisfaction or dysfunction.

Recently, in a frustrated conversation with me over science education, one of my board members put it this way: "I'm an unpaid volunteer who doesn't understand the budget, has no expertise in the field of education; I don't have the answers to your questions and don't have the energy to chase them." This is an elected official who ran unopposed to represent the public. Does the public not know or not care or both?

## APATHY AND THE "ME AND MINE" ATTITUDE OF THE PUBLIC

Apathy is a little difficult to discuss because of the potential for the misconception that understanding a concept equates to agreement, forgiveness, or tolerance of the situation. As this word applies to support for public schools, I view apathy as unacceptable for any reason. Apathy means "a lack of interest or indifference" (*Webster's*, 1976). It is certainly important for all of us to understand why and how so many people in our society display so much apathy but it does not excuse it.

Apathy is not directed just toward the school system. Look at our political system and this country's previous voting record compared to other democracies. We the people are supposed to serve as the ultimate check and balance through our power of the vote. But instead of being enthused about the democratic process or even being interested in the local control of schools, we find a very large number of people disconnected.

To understand this disconnect as it relates to schools, we have to think first about the people with the potential to be involved in the education system. We have those that care about all children, those that care only about their own children, and those that don't know enough to care. Some would argue that another very large group of people just don't and won't care. In my mind, that group is lumped in with the group that doesn't know enough to care until proven otherwise.

It's easy to understand how a person who cares about all children can get caught up in the workings of a defective education system and become apathetic. If obvious mistakes are being made and you confront authority with facts, you risk being called "confrontational." If you critically evaluate a situation and let those findings be known, you are "nothing but critical." If the powers that be use the theory that they want their enemies close and place you on committee after committee, you run the risk of letting them "committee you to death."

When a person who gives of themselves for the betterment of all children sees things change for "the better" only to later see them change back to "the easier," you have to think about how much easier indifference would be. When you work hard and long to change things only to realize that change doesn't last, that might make you give in to the easier path of apathy.

Developing apathy may be the sanest thing to do. If you are a parent who cares about the children around you and knows that you have your own child in a dysfunctional school environment, you have to turn your concern toward your own child.

Caring about your own children and staying focused on and fighting for them is really what you are obligated to do as a good parent. Those parents that are out to "give their child every advantage" are another case entirely. If your attitude comes not from self-promotion but from the true need to survive a bad situation, no guilt should be felt about the focus of your efforts being on your child. But the "me and mine" attitude of the public makes it easy for administration and school boards to bulldoze over any single issue.

When parents or patrons see or hear of something that seems fundamentally wrong, as long as it doesn't affect them or their child, many of them aren't inclined to do too much about it just to defend a principle. This leaves individual parents with individual issues for any one administrator to handle. Administrators usually can easily defuse any single situation and go on their way to the next thing without "fixing" the root of any given problem. Do we really wonder why we continue to have problems?

The other aspect to consider when discussing apathy and the "me and mine" attitude of the public is the number of people that are ignorant about the inequality of our education system and the glaring problems occurring in many schools in the United States. They appear to be indifferent. They appear apathetic when, in fact, they may not know enough to care. Edwin E. Slosson in his book *The American Spirit in Education* stated this: "The very districts that needed good schools most were from their ignorance least conscious of the need" (1921, 107).

Ignorance can be overcome through transparency and diffusion of knowledge. You can't expect people to be involved in their schools when they perceive that nothing needs to be done. No doubt, *effective local control* depends on an *informed public*. That is a problem, especially when we aren't even sure whose job it is to keep us informed about educational issues.

The easy part of communications is laying out the information for someone else to deliver. We have an abundance of good information. What we need is systemic assurance that it will get out to the communities and people that need it most. And the country in general, good district or bad, must be better informed about major education policy.

The movement to standards, testing, and the resultant No Child Left Behind law is a perfect example of what can happen when government moves ahead without the people understanding the intent and potential consequences of the law. That is how many government programs get put into place without the true informed consent of the people. If the people of the United States had understood the NCLB law before it was put in motion, they never would have approved; we wouldn't have spent so much money on testing and we wouldn't be looking at yet another change in the law. If we can't read it, understand it, and think it through before acting, maybe we shouldn't do it.

Historically, newspapers were seen as an essential vehicle for informing the public, for the public's voicing of opinions, and for opposing views. Today, they seem to instead interfere with the democratic process. We no longer can trust that we are getting a fair representation of the "sides" of any issue. And public relations stories do not equal information; fluff does not equal facts. Propaganda has an objective.

From our local communities that look blindly at dysfunctional schools to our nation of citizens who see no urgency to act on anything not directly affecting them, it's time for all of us to consider the risk to our country when we remain ignorant of the fact that when schools are left to decay, literally or figuratively, that decay will rot communities and cost our country greatly. Some believe, as Dr. Noguera expressed, that "Ultimately, the lack of a concerted and sustained effort to respond to failing urban schools can be explained only by understanding that America simply does not care that large numbers of children from inner-city schools and neighborhoods are not properly educated" (2003, 14).

As the years have passed, I continue to believe that school administration, school boards, and the public are the three problems at the heart of our education system's failures. We have a people problem. When we begin to think of solutions, keep that fact in mind. But certainly, in the perpetual flow of the system, major tributaries have contributed to the turbulence that has muddied the waters of education "reform."


## CURRICULUM AND TESTING


"Curriculum" is technically defined as "a fixed series of studies" (*Webster's*, 1976). Traditionally, the need to speak, write, read, and persuade drove the universal language curriculum elements. Our American predecessors also considered the concepts of mathematics and the ideas that belong to ethics and politics as essential. And nature study or the sciences were given importance in the schools of the past.

This all sounds easy; we should be able to set a fixed series of study down on paper. The problem is that what should be studied is not necessarily fixed. It varies based on the time, place, and needs of the local region, and let us not forget the needs and interests of the individual child.

Possibly, if we had focused our efforts longer and harder on our goals in education and the ideals of a balanced curriculum that should have followed, we could have solved the age-old problem of what we, as a society in the United States of America, want our children to learn and how we want them taught. Or, we could have looked back at *The Story of the Eight-Year Study* and considered one of the major guiding principles the study asked us to consider: "that the general life of the school and methods of teaching should conform to what is now known about ways in which human beings learn and grow" (Aikin, 1942, 17). And what the study concluded about secondary schools' curriculum content was that it should be determined by "two criteria; the demands of adult society and the concerns of adolescents" (74). Instead, we limited input from the public and dove into the testing aspect of education. And the dollars flowed in that direction.

What is the purpose of testing? The long-standing belief is that you use testing to find out what you know and don't know. It measures your knowledge. When testing takes place in a classroom situation, the test can be used by the student, with the help of the teacher, to pinpoint what the student may have misunderstood or failed to learn. The students can then go back and learn that information if they are so inclined.

The baffling thing is that somewhere along the way we have lost sight of that ideal. We aren't necessarily using tests that way; sometimes not even regular tests in the classroom. As previously mentioned, from about seventh grade on, not a single science test ever came home. Answer sheets with check marks and a grade arrived but without any indication what specific concept needed clarification.

It appears that the standard practice is for teachers to go through the test one time in class. That is probably fine for kids that don't miss many questions. But, if you have children who make many mistakes or have learning difficulties, asking them to grasp and remember all their mistakes during one review may be asking too much. Apparently the value in time spent contemplating and learning from mistakes has eluded many. Testing can become a barrier to learning rather than a tool for improvement.

The standards achievement tests deserve consideration as to whether they are of benefit or a barrier. Their purpose and use need to be scrutinized. When these tests first came out, no one seemed to know who was responsible for tracking a given child. A note might say that, based on test results, a child needed extra help, while the teacher handing it out might downplay that advice. That confuses parents.

In our district with its "failing" record, three months into the 2007 school year no one had asked for the supplemental services that were being offered as part of No Child Left Behind. Questions should be asked. The situation should have been a red flag as to inadequacies in public understanding of test results, how they should be related to learning, and what the NCLB law was put in place to do for children. In multiple ways, testing is not working as it was intended.

And we certainly don't have a single test that shows us how well our education system has prepared our children for life.

When the National Commission on Excellence in Education made the call that we were *A Nation at Risk*, they used eleven "indicators" (1983, 8–9).

1. International comparisons of student achievement,
2. Number of adults deemed functionally illiterate,

3. Percent of 17-year-olds considered functionally illiterate,
4. Average achievement of high school students on standardized tests,
5. The population of gifted students whose school achievement does not meet their tested abilities,
6. The trends in College Board's Scholastic Aptitude Tests (SAT) scores,
7. Percent of 17-year-olds demonstrating "higher order" intellectual skills by

   (a) Drawing inferences from written materials,
   (b) Writing a persuasive essay,
   (c) Solving a mathematics problem involving several steps,

8. Trends in national science achievement scores of 17-year-olds,
9. Percent of remedial mathematics courses in public 4-year colleges,
10. Tested achievement of college graduates,
11. Dollars spent by businesses and the military on remedial education and training programs.

And this report spoke to the nation: "We are confident that America can address this risk. . . . This would also reverse the current declining trend—a trend that stems more from weakness of purpose, confusion of vision, under-use of talent, and lack of leadership, than from *conditions* beyond our control" (15). They did use standardized test score "trends" but their curriculum recommendations were based on much more than test scores.

How well we live life is the ultimate test. The economy and our standing in the world on environmental, health, and other social issues including education are a few indicators among those to watch. The biggest question right now may very well be whether we are winning "the hearts and minds" war. You may think this is drifting off the subject of testing and the curriculum in alluding to the Iraq war and our wider "war on terror," but our global problems were actually predictable in some individuals' eyes.

In the 1956 book *A History of American Education*, author H. G. Good states: "There are some danger signs. One is the decline in the study of languages, mathematics, and the sciences. For economic development, for defense, for cooperation with our allies and the winning of new friends, these are important studies" (17). We are headed down a dangerous road when we narrow our curriculum to fit the test. Politics has taken us there.

## POLITICS AND MONEY

Which is worse: local politics or national politics? Or is politics just politics? Certainly the word itself leaves a bad taste in the mouths of many. The root of the word is "politic," which confusingly has two very different meanings. One is "having practical wisdom," while another is "unscrupulous" (*Webster's*, 1976) or unprincipled. Perhaps we should point the finger of blame at confusion.

Ideally, in our country, the public decides what it wants its young people to know and passes that information on to the school board, which sets the direction for the schools to be carried out by administration. Some of the questionable activities of our local school board, as previously described, illustrate one aspect of the downside of small town politics. A person's reason for seeking a board position and their reasoning behind the decisions they make should be questioned.

We voters don't always get many facts on which to base our decisions, forcing us to vote for or against whom we know or consider not voting at all. Rather than basing our vote on the beliefs of the candidate, many times personal rather than philosophical issues enter into the election of a local school board member. Or, in the case of an extremely apathetic public, one just needs to put their name in the hat to fill a vacated seat.

Our local board has five members and there has been a time when only one was seated in a regular election with an opponent. When something like this happens, no open discussion occurs concerning the desires and direction the board members wish to take. If no real candidates emerge, the philosophical direction your education board takes may never be revealed to the public. That is politics at its very worst, locally. On the state and national levels, education hasn't fared so well either.

The functions of state boards of education vary from state to state depending on state politics and policies and differing structures and functions of state administration. Our district is located in one of the most Republican states in the union. Our state legislature is dominated by Republicans with a Republican governor and a Republican state superintendent of schools, who is an elected official (a rarity in the country).

The direction of national education policy in the early 2000s was dictated by a Republican president who passed major education legislation with a then-Republican Congress. If the No Child Left Behind law was going to work well, wouldn't you think it would be apparent here? It's their party.

That chiding of the Republican Party is just for amusement; the reality is that throughout history it really hasn't mattered which party set the direction of the education plan. It is the surest bet that a plan will fail to fulfill its goal. In part this is due to the fact that the plan changes every four to eight years with the election of a new president.

President Johnson's 1965 education law was aimed at "educationally deprived children" with funding appropriations that were never fulfilled. The first President Bush set goals for the "America 2000" program; President Clinton gave us "Principles of Effectiveness" under "Goals 2000," while the second President Bush gave us "No Child Left Behind." You would think that the U.S. Congress would try to hold things steady. Many of them have been holding a seat for twenty or more years.

It really should not surprise us that these long-standing representatives have failed to adequately represent our children. They are so far removed personally from the education system; they may not realize what is going on. They just govern it! Do you think we might be at the point yet where we consider that it is time to quit allowing the children of the United States to be used as pawns in the political games being played out from our local districts to our state houses to Washington, D.C.?

And the political pendulum of control swings once again as Ravitch reminds us: "The school reformers of the 1890s demanded centralization as an antidote to low-performing schools and advocated control by professionals as the cure for the incompetence and corruption of local school boards" (2010, 5). Does the pendulum of power have to be at one end or the other? Can we make it stop?

I agree with Dr. Noguera that "education is a political issue"; and he asks, "which side are you on?" (2003, 156). Fair enough, let's define the sides. Give all of America's children equal opportunity, or not?

Technically, education is a responsibility of each state, but realistically we should be facing the facts. By definition, chronically low-performing schools are evidence that state and local officials have not met their responsibilities. Economics is tied to education. What happens economically in one state of our United States affects the country. As President Reagan pointed out, "This country was built on American respect for education" (National Commission, 1983, 16).

Instead of working cooperatively with the people most directly affected by education policy, the federal government and, in some states, oppressive state governments are restricting and directing our decisions. They don't seem to understand that success has more to do with the implementation of a plan than the plan itself. Or they don't care. The costly flaw in the lawmaking process is the failure to listen to the people in the trenches—parents, teachers, and students. It is a repeating pattern.

Being at the mercy of political whims, it should be no surprise that we are looking at the same problems in education that we have been trying to solve throughout the history of education in the United States. Except now the money connection is stronger than ever.

Education is big business. Among the common people, it is a widely accepted view that our political system is directed more by money than the desires of the people. The result of that is that we are letting politics and money set our educational philosophy. As Ravitch put it, "Untethered to any genuine philosophy of education, our current reforms will disappoint us, as others have in the past" (2010, 225). No Child Left Behind, once again, can be used as a sad example.

NCLB forced us to collectively and separately spend billions on development and testing of tests. Individuals then spend countless dollars on what can be called the "cottage industries" of education. These are all the businesses that have sprung up to help children pass the tests and also to fill our system's educational gaps. If parents become concerned about their child's education or test scores and they find they aren't getting help or cooperation from the public education system, they can turn to tutoring or publications for help—if it is something they can afford.

The very nature of the funding for NCLB leaves children behind. In particular, it is leaving behind those that are getting their last chance to make their diploma mean something, our high school students. They are worth mentioning again, as is the money trail.

Funding is based on formulas and grants, and, in districts such as mine, we reached the maximum allotted formula funding for Title 1 schools, meaning low-income schools, and are forced to decide where to best use those funds. It has become common, recommended practice to use fewer of these dollars at the high school level because the students' test scores only count once for NCLB in grades 9–12.

In other words, the children at our high school were eligible for funds because of the high poverty rate, but the government emphasis has directed schools to put their money into the earlier grades, resulting in what amounts to turning their backs on the failing high school students, giving them their diplomas and sending them into the world.

Look at the money trail of No Child Left Behind. Look into the eyes of the failing high school students that are left with the crumbs of a remedial program because the money was directed to the lower grades and tell them they aren't being left behind. Look them in the eyes and explain how the money is better spent in the early years. Tell them what the research shows. And tell them that No Child Left Behind isn't just a slogan.

But the money trail and its political connections don't stop at this point. When your schools fail to make adequate yearly progress (AYP), the law tells you that you may have to fully implement a new curriculum. Your district may be led to believe that it has to buy into a research-based "program" to fix its problem. Companies that have gotten their programs on the right list have done well.

NCLB directives have pushed districts toward investing in programs rather than developing their own teaching philosophies, curriculum, and instruction to fit their needs. And there is more to the money trail with NCLB. When this overstepping federal law talks about turning schools over to private companies with "a demonstrated record of effectiveness," we need to really be looking hard at educational research.

## RESEARCH AND REALITY

Educational research has fascinated and baffled me. A scientist thinking about research thinks about holding all variables constant in an experiment except the one being tested; that is impossible in the education system. Educational research deals with individual little people and their attached individual families. Variables are plentiful. That was the baffling part for me.

The fascinating part was coming to the realization that "research" can also be defined as "careful study and investigation to discover or establish facts or principles" (*Webster's*, 1976). Put in that context, research in education is much more open to interpretation so it's much less absolute than pure scientific research, if such a thing as absolute or pure exists. Yet, time and again, administrators and others defend their position on an issue based totally on what the research shows. Educational research has to be taken with a grain of salt, given its very nature. It's not the same as scientific research in other fields. In education more often it's about correlations rather than establishing a cause and effect relationship.

The flaw in relying strictly on research, and therefore our often misdirected efforts, can best be explained by again making a comparison to the practice of medicine. Practicing medicine is not a pure science. Scientific facts are used as guides, but, when dealing with a living thing, variables are going to change your expected outcome. These are things we have no control over.

Many continue to point the finger of blame for our "failing" schools at poverty. OK, how are you going to solve that issue today? My children were schooled in a poverty-ridden district and I'm here to tell you that there is a multitude of things we can do, today, because the problems I encountered were not directly due to poverty but due to a "dysfunctionality" created and permitted by people. We can change that reality.

Each living being is unique. That's the reality. That is why the "practice" of medicine is referred to as "an art and a science." In the practice of good quality medicine, prevention of medical problems and response to any necessary treatment should always be gauged on an individual basis. The practitioner must make decisions based on both test results and the circumstances in front of them. At times they are in conflict. In the education setting, the people that are best able to judge the needs of a student are the ones the children see daily—their teachers and parents.

Deborah Meier summed it up nicely: "There are times when expertise overrules popular opinion, and vice versa. But we cannot and will not do a better job of resolving these conflicts by getting rid of the crucial local voice of the people" (2004, 78).

## LIBERTY AND LISTENING

Teachers and parents are the groups you would hope to be hearing the most from when discussing improvements in education. They are the ones most intimately connected to the education system through children on a day-to-day basis. You would think their input and feedback would not only be welcomed but recognized as essential to a quick response when a problem is sensed.

Unfortunately, these two groups are the ones most afraid of the repercussions of expressing dissatisfaction, concerns, or reservations over a whole host of issues at multiple levels. Some parents fear that what they say may lead to more difficult times for their children. It happens. They don't want to risk it. Some teachers fear reprimands or fear for their jobs. That happens, too. Overridden by fear, these groups are keeping their opinions to themselves. They are giving up their voice in the decision-making process. The very people that the system should be responding to in order for continued improvement to occur are the ones feeling least at liberty to speak.

Teachers are being arbitrarily controlled by inflexible or overbearing administrators and now changes in law. They are being controlled by the government through testing results. Parents are being controlled from multiple directions including by administrators, teachers, and coaches. This suggests that we have decided to give up a piece of our liberty. Liberty means "freedom from any form of arbitrary control" (*Webster's*, 1976). Here in the United States, we are supposed to be at liberty to use our freedom of speech. It's not working well in the bureaucracy we call the *public* education system.

Fortunately, some teachers and parents exist as exceptions. They are the individuals that "buck the system" or, in some people's analysis, are just plain critical and cause problems. Thank goodness for them, because they are the ones that keep poorly performing schools from totally falling apart. These are the people that some would laughingly refer to as "watch dogs." These brave individuals make noise, but is anyone really listening?

Listening skills appear to be something that fewer and fewer people possess. Not too long ago a magazine wrote about things that other countries do better than we do in the United States. One of those things was the art of conversation. That should be no surprise.

To converse, you have to patiently listen before responding. In our hurry-up world, we are modeling ineffective communication skills to the next generation. We also have people that know how to listen but make the choice not to listen. So, in the bigger picture on the subjects of liberty and listening, think about how it doesn't take decisions being made behind closed doors to kill a democracy; for those in power to destroy this republic, all they need to do is quit listening.

As Bill C. wrote, "Lots of decisions are made based on perceived definitions. The labels might not be true, but once the label goes on, the questions go off and thus we are often stuck with politicos and policies that are not what we wanted. Communication becomes non-existent; there may be hearing, but little listening." And the "ideology wars" are sorting and labeling us all. Plus, those fighting and listening to the "war of words" aren't asking for clarification.

If you have been listening to discussions about education, it has become fairly common to hear folks voicing the opinion that the blame rests on the shoulders of the teachers, parents, and kids. Many would argue that teachers, parents, and students are the whole problem. These people must consider and understand that the system has failed time and again to train and retrain educators properly, it has failed to inform parents of their role in the task of educating, and it is mismanaging too many students to hold them accountable.

## WHAT WE HAVE IS A SYSTEMIC FAILURE

The system has failed to thoroughly educate the public about educational issues. Our inaction on this long-ago identified problem has led us to accept the unacceptable. As Yong Zhao observed in his book *Catching Up or Leading the Way: American Education in the Age of Globalization*, "The American public, short of other easy-to-understand measures, seems to have accepted the notion that test scores are an accurate measure of the quality of their schools" (2009, 33). It is not right.

The takeover of our education policy and practices at the exclusion of "us" in the process has not been a result of the "business-model"; it has been a result of a greed-driven, self-serving society. It has brought more education wars: competition in opposition to cooperation, choice against commonality, rigor versus flexibility. Stop. The collateral damage has been too great.

The system has failed to show understanding of the learning *environment* that needs to be created in classrooms and in communities to provide what children need to be educated to their fullest potential. We have unknowingly created another "gap"—the wisdom gap. It is reminiscent of the story of the old man picking up starfish on the beach and throwing them back. A young boy thinking it foolish tells the old man that "it doesn't matter; they'll wash up again tomorrow." The old man flings one far into the sea and says, "It mattered to this one." That story didn't just demonstrate we can save one at a time; it also expressed the vision of the elder passing on wisdom to our youth.

Wisdom comes from knowledge, experience, and understanding. It comes with time. And as John Taylor Gatto expressed in *Dumbing Us Down: The Hidden Curriculum of Compulsory Schooling*, "without children and old people mixing in daily life, a community has no future and no past, only a continuous present" (2005, 21). Gatto originally wrote that book in 1992 and used the term "pseudo-community." In far too many places today, our "present" is no different from our past. Our nation is at risk.

But remember, not all schools are a problem. Schools that fail to properly educate children have a common underlying issue, as expressed by Ratner, "the absence of the key human resources" necessary to be *effective* (2007, 22). And if "academic proficiency" is our educational goal, current policies incorrectly assume "that schools and districts already know what to do to accomplish this goal and have the *capacity* to do so. . . . And it incorrectly assumes that if districts cannot turn failing schools around, the state departments of education have the *capacity* to assist them to do so, or, if necessary, to do it themselves" (49).

Capacity means possessing the knowledge, skills, abilities, motivation, and desire to accomplish a goal. In the case of *school improvement*, it means being able to take the handbook off the shelf and make things happen. First, we have to stop blaming each other. And then as Philip K. will tell you, "We must put aside our differences."

We've all heard teachers who complained about how "the families of their students simply did not value education" (Noguera, 2003, 47). Yet it turns out that this statement, as Noguera points out in his story, was made by people who in reality didn't know this to be true. It was and continues to be an assumption. If lawmakers and educators are out there "blaming uncaring parents, lazy students, or a society that does not provide adequately for the needs of poor children" (49), they need to stop playing the no-win blame game so we can get on with meeting *our shared responsibility* to serve the educational and developmental needs of all children.

When we have underperforming schools anywhere in our country, we have a systemic problem. If you believe there is no way to "reform" the public school system, then it is understandable that you would want to throw in the towel and privatize the whole business. But there is another *choice*.

We now understand better than ever what needs to happen and where that change needs to occur first—in the boundary waters where teachers, parents, and kids are found floating around searching for solutions to grab onto.

*Chapter Six*

# We Have the Answers

Ask Counsel of both Times: of the Ancient Time, what of it is worth keeping, and of the Latter Time, what is fittest for the new day; but seek as well to create Good Precedents as to follow them.

—Francis Bacon

At one frustrating moment in time, the thought occurred to me that providing equal opportunity to a good quality education was too complicated a proposition to ever achieve. Now, through observation, inquiry, and research, the facts are very clear that the "fixes" are laid out before us; they have been for a long time. They have surfaced and are within our grasps. The question is: Will we pull them from the stream or watch them once more float away, go under, only to resurface again in the future, too late for us?

H. G. Good made the observation: "American education has been brought down from the clouds to deal with the needs of the office, farm, mart, shop, and home, where people work and live. This is good precedent. But the problems of philosophy, government, and pure science are not therefore to be less studied" (1956, v).

This statement implies that, in looking at providing a quality education to all children, we must be looking at our needs while keeping the idea of *balance* in mind. To achieve balance, you wouldn't jump from one side to another. You wouldn't pull one thing off or shove on another. You wouldn't make any sudden or radical moves. You would sense your imbalance, adjust accordingly, and attempt to inch your way to success.

# SAFE AND DISCIPLINED SCHOOLS: CREATING COMMUNITY CIVILITY

The teacher should find the cause of misconduct and should treat that rather than the symptoms.

—Christopher Dock

Christopher Dock's statement should not be misconstrued to mean that the teacher is solely responsible for the cure of students' misconduct. It should be looked at from the perspective that when children intentionally misbehave, they may very well be indicating that something is amiss in their lives or in the immediate learning environment. The "bad" behavior is a symptom, not a diagnosis of "a bad child." Discipline problems in our classrooms and communities will always be in need of being "solved" so that we can ensure instruction without interruption and maintain a civil society. The solution to the tough issue of creating disciplined classrooms lies in the ideals of creating safe school *environments*. It starts with understanding the causes behind the symptoms.

Having spent years listening to discussions about the issues surrounding safe schools, the fact is that collectively we have a good understanding of most of the causes of misconduct and the prevention and interventions that are effective. In *Hope Fulfilled for At-Risk and Violent Youth: K–12 Programs That Work*, Robert Barr and William Parrett claim: "We now know beyond a shadow of doubt that all children can learn, that effective schools can overcome the debilitating effects of poverty and dysfunctional families, and we know exactly what schools must do to accomplish this reality. What remains is the collective will to act" (2001, xii). The *school climate* and *classroom conditions* that are conducive to learning are the same climates and conditions that prevent bullying and other disruptive behaviors.

Another author, Peter Sacks, opens his book *Standardized Minds: The High Price of America's Testing Culture and What We Can Do to Change It* by stating, "In my research for this book, I was struck by a profound disconnection between knowledge and practice" (1999, xi). Sacks, Barr, and Parrett are experts in their chosen areas who live in my state. They are homegrown experts, so to speak, but they, their work, and their findings are unknown to my community. Their voices have been missing.

So many authors have written down "pearls of wisdom" waiting to be found. In notes I uncovered recently was this outline of ideas offered by Carl Bosch in *Schools Under Siege: Guns, Gangs, and Hidden Dangers*:

1. Hold high expectations—clearly defined expectations of respect, dignity, and responsibility,
2. Have a clear and defined set of rules,

3. Parental involvement is essential,
4. The teachers role is key—being an "open ear" and caring,
5. Administrators must have a strong presence, open rapport, be fair and decisive when needed,
6. Stay one step ahead,
7. Promote positive school activities,
8. Respect community influences.

My notes indicated Bosch stressed that primary prevention of discipline issues resided in uncovering the reasons behind inappropriate behavior, the proper training and teaching of the skills children need, and that *consistency* and *fairness* were important qualities for children to learn that adults should model (1997).

Teachers, administrators, parents, and the greater community need to make better use of the existing body of expertise and their available community resources; putting knowledge into practice. It needs to start with a common understanding of the language we use. As Dr. Price-Mitchell notes, "In recent years, the language has changed, from parental involvement and participation to *parent-school partnerships*, which implies the shared and equally valued roles in education. . . . Another term gaining wide usage is parent engagement, emphasizing the importance of parent's active *power-sharing* role as citizens of the education community rather than people who participate only when invited" (2009, 13). We need to establish common terminology and mean what we say.

The solution to schools that struggle with disruptive behaviors could quickly begin to take form by using existing human resources and other supports already in place to help our youth. Through a community position designed to coordinate the multiple government bureaucracies, private youth foundations, and other public institutions, we can bring knowledge into the hands of those that can use it and resources to the feet of the children that so desperately need it. We can call this position a "community education organizer," keeping in mind that it should be a community position not another school district job.

Existing in our current education system are federal, state, and school coordinator positions referred to as safe and drug-free schools coordinators. "Drug-free" has been lumped together with "safe schools" in that title and job description. We need drug education. It is an assumption that it is part of school curricula. But we need to remove the "drug-free" wording and emphasis from these positions, not because we should remove drug education, but because we need to fight our human nature to do the easier thing. It is easier to focus on the drug education piece when you are a safe and drug-free schools coordinator than to tackle safe and disciplined school issues. If these current positions only focused on safe schools issues, these school coordinators would quickly come to the same conclusion many did years ago.

Safety and discipline are community issues. These are issues of establishing civility on our streets and in our classrooms. This is about establishing socially accepted behavior. Communities need to set their expectations, make those expectations known, work together to meet them, and constantly remind each other that we are to model them in all aspects of our public lives. Adults need to support each other in this endeavor. Teachers and parents need to communicate expectations of behavior and share experiences freely back and forth. Parents need to understand how they can help the teachers, and teachers need to know where they can find help when things aren't going as desired.

The boundary waters where families and school people form partnerships is the all-encompassing stage that must be set to foster the respect and high expectations that will create school *climates* and classroom *conditions* favorable to teaching and learning. To prevent bullying and other undesirable behaviors, a supportive, inclusive, respectful climate is essential, and we have known for a long time that *positive relationships* keep our youth connected to a civil community. If they feel excluded from positive activities, they can find inclusion in "gangs."

Functional communities know how to work cooperatively to put this type of knowledge to work. Dysfunctional communities and their schools have demonstrated by their very existence that they do not and cannot put knowledge into practice without help. So we can think about a community education organizer located outside the boundaries of the school institution working to poke holes in existing structures to allow a freer flow of communications and services.

Creating safe schools that are conducive to respectful attitudes and self-discipline can't be treated like just another job in the school setting; it needs to be a community position. Safe and disciplined schools issues deserve attention in and of themselves. The problems that our young people are bringing to school with them can't be solved strictly within the institutional walls of a school. Delinquent youth behaviors are the ultimate of community issues and must be approached at that level. Coordinating efforts inside the school with those out in the community is essential to success.

Successful efforts to address issues related to discipline, community improvement, and the resultant *school improvement* appear to have several elements in common. They include:

- bringing caring community members together,
- assessing the needs of the community,
- setting goals,

- assessing the effective services available,
- targeting unmet needs,
- and evaluating the results against the targeted goals.

These steps are done on an ongoing basis, and goals are adjusted as indicated by the ever-changing needs identified by the community. Communities have paid consultants to come in and conduct these types of programs. Others have done it themselves or have been fortunate enough to work with an organization set up to do this very thing. You don't have to wait.

The process for *community and school improvement* has been well studied and our government provides "tools" to help guide community's efforts. Community assessments are an essential first step. "Find Youth Info" (www.findyouthinfo.gov) can provide guides, mapping instruments, and ways to "identify and track partners and programs." Communities That Care is another useful program our government owns, which assists in identifying risks and "protective" factors in a given community (http://preventionplat-form.samhsa.gov). And StopBullying.gov can also provide ideas.

One element that is essential to success in these communities seeking to improve themselves and their school systems is the ability to communicate facts, ideas, goals, and expectations to the schools and the general public alike. Communication is essential to helping ensure the success and sustainability of any community plan. As Jack D. Minzey and Clyde E. LeTarte explain in *Reforming Public Schools through Community Education*, a community education organizer, which is commonly called a "director" in the original community schools, "acts as a broker, relating problems to resources and making referrals to the appropriate sources" (1994, 86).

A community education organizer position may first need to be used to function as a catalyst in stimulating interest in the *improvement process*. Developing within people the will to act is more often challenging than not. An understanding of the *change process* is essential. These are concepts that could and should be brought to a community in depth.

Briefly, in the early 1900s, Edward L. Thorndike was credited with defining education as the production of change in people. Much later, the *Concerns-Based Adoption Model* set the stage for new teacher professional development models based on the philosophies outlined by Susan Loucks-Horsley (1996). Her working theory emphasizes that education leads to change. Change brings different levels of concerns to people. Those concerns need to be addressed in order for *people to progress* to the action phase.

Recall the Theory of Action developed by the National Science Resource Center (see Fig. 3.1). That model emphasized that, as your basis for change or action, you have research findings on which you develop a *shared vision* for your community. Common sense and research both tell us that a plan has a better chance of succeeding when those that must carry it out have a say in its development. These two models (Adoption and Action) can to be applied to safe schools issues.

Bringing knowledge of research to community members, using the research to develop a vision, and moving a community into action requires coordination. And the communication, necessary to make this happen, needs to be of both the research on which a vision should be developed and the developed vision.

The goal of a community education organizer, in this case, can be seen as similar to that of the original American Lyceum. The American Lyceum was founded in 1826 by Josiah Holbrook. It was a system of *adult education* that used lectures, debates, and readings to reach out to the public with the *goal of disseminating information* for the betterment of *community schools*. The lyceum was dedicated "to procure for youths an economical and practical education and to diffuse rational and useful information through the community generally" (*Encyclopedia Americana*, 1999, vol. 17, 878). The official organization died shortly after the Civil War. The precursor to the original American Lyceum is considered to be the Junto, which was established by Benjamin Franklin. The Junto was where books were shared and ideas debated. In turn, the lyceum is given credit for being the basis of the idea behind the current university extension system.

I tend to believe that, had the lyceum stayed in existence and brought current information to our community on safety and discipline issues in 1999, many of the problems associated with our gangs, bullying, and general delinquent behaviors, and the resultant classroom disruptions, could have been alleviated. A community education organizer could now serve to facilitate bringing pertinent up-to-date information to foster improvements in *school climates*. It is a function that could serve a variety of community and school topics from health issues to academics—addressing the needs of communities and their children.

## THE THREE RS AND THE RIGHT WAY—BALANCE AND EXPECTATIONS

One-fourth of the students who applied for college admissions around 1862 did not have "a good common school education" and the colleges found it necessary to establish preparatory departments. . . . This also has bearing upon the present controversy over the past and present effectiveness of the schools in teaching the Three R's.

—H. G. Good

We need to look at both the past and the present debates about teaching the Three Rs. The optimist wants to say that we are doing a better job in many ways, while the realist is still seeing twenty-eight children in first grade classes without the help needed to attend to their personal learning needs. The realist still sees children leaving first grade without the skills they need to sufficiently progress. The optimist thinks we will learn from the past, this time.

It seems the debate on how to teach reading, writing, and arithmetic has been raging since the beginning of U.S. history. In the early years of our country, before it was ours, our schools were modeled after those of the countries of origin of the people who settled a particular area. The teaching methods of different regions followed the *teaching philosophies* brought over by immigrants. Between the settlers spending their time concentrating on the necessities of life, working on establishing a new country, the influx of different people with varied philosophies, and the intermittent general *public neglect of the importance* of education and its funding, the United States has *lost its philosophical footing* repeatedly when it comes to teaching the Three Rs.

Understanding the philosophy behind how the Three R's are taught is important. An educational philosophy is a statement of beliefs about teaching and learning. It serves to help us define our goals or objectives, and our beliefs do guide our actions. In developing policies, the philosophical basis should help ensure that our actions support our goals. What you teach and how you teach depends on your *philosophy of instruction*.

Philosophy is also defined as "a particular system of principles for the conduct of life" (*Webster's*, 1976). It should serve as a guide. Another way of looking at the importance of philosophy in education is to look at how it presents itself in the reality of the school setting. For example, when you see "sight word" only methods being used to teach reading, as a parent, you should ask your school district about its teaching philosophy toward phonics. What do they *believe*?

Since most parents are currently not a part of guiding their school's curriculum and instruction, understanding what beliefs your district bases its decisions on is useful in lending some *consistency* to your child's education and is helpful in more quickly detecting deficits or glaring differences with your own beliefs or what your child needs.

To bring the idea of the importance of philosophy full circle, we need to ask the universities and colleges that produce our teachers: Are they preparing teachers to follow the philosophies and principles that we in the United States believe will *best serve our children*? "The failure of schools and colleges to co-ordinate their work has resulted in enormous waste of time, effort, and money" (Aikin, 1942, 126).

Do you know what our U.S. teaching philosophies and principles are? What have we, as a people, decided are the principles on which we wish to effectively teach the Three Rs? This is not the same as asking about national standards or a national curriculum. This is asking for clarification about *what we believe works best*. After all, "teachers, like the rest of us, are a product of how they have been taught" (Sarason, 1993, 182). After over 20 years of working closely with education reform, it is not clear what pedagogy (instruction in teaching methods) our teachers are being taught.

Throughout the years, it seems that the philosophies have changed many times over in keeping with the latest educational fads, often swinging dramatically from one side of the belief spectrum to the other—a pedagogy pendulum. Historically, that is also true, but recurrent themes throughout the history of American education seem evident. Many of those recurrent ideals look to be good starting points, excellent middle ground on which we could build understanding of what we as a nation value in education.

In talking about colonial Americans and their lack of knowledge about the science of language, H. G. Good concluded that "their greatest mistake was the failure to understand that speech is the real, the living language and that writing and print are only its lifeless symbols" (1956, 33). Many much-admired men in the field of education believed that drawing should come before writing and the art of conversation before reading. As mentioned previously, the art of conversation in the United States is waning. With this next generation growing up with the technological substitutes for human interaction that they have available, we might want to pay close attention to focusing on the elements of conversation: thinking, speaking, listening, and questioning.

Conversation is not a focus of the No Child Left Behind (NCLB) law. Reading is and does deserve the spotlight. It appears that our brush with success in reading instruction occurred back in Delaware around 1640, as described by Edwin E. Slosson. Slosson explains how the Swedes had settled that area and at the time it was said that "there was not a peasant child in Sweden who had not been taught to read and write" (1921, 38). However, as this segment of the colony became incorporated into a more diverse community, its "education left no traceable mark on the later educational history of Delaware" (39).

We have ignored the teaching successes of other countries as well, including the Germans, who have consistently been teaching reading through a combination of word and phonics methods. The belief is that we are doing this now, again, also. The belief is that we have found a *balance* between using word and phonetic instruction. Is that our current philosophy about reading instruction? What about our expectations?

Teachers have been taught, and we have accepted as fact, that children must learn to read by third grade. Yet observations show us that kids know by second grade if they are behind and they begin to compensate. Later on, that compensation is called cheating. We may have until third grade to turn the majority of children into *independent* readers. That isn't the same thing as accepting that letting them leave first grade without *mastery* of basic essential reading skills is acceptable. We need to question the conventional wisdom that we have until third grade to teach them to read.

And what is our philosophy and expectations of writing instruction?

Writing has two elements to it that deserve particular attention: the mechanical part that is of course not necessarily tested on NCLB and the grammatical part that is tested to some extent. With well-established mandatory testing, we shouldn't have to worry about sentence structure not being taught. What we as a nation should be discussing is the importance of writing itself, because an emphasis on writing has been shown to be a common factor among high-achieving schools.

Writing is not just grammar lessons that can be tested by multiple choice questions. It requires multiple thought processes that train the brain in a way very different from memorizing word patterns. And the mechanics of cursive are just now being associated with the ability to take quick and accurate notes. How important is that to us?

The same question should be asked about spelling. As mentioned previously, spelling is very important in many workplaces. When you receive a written message that you cannot decipher because of words you don't recognize, it's a problem. Workplace efficiency decreases. When that same issue arises in medical records, the problem becomes potentially dangerous.

Frustration with the inventive spelling concept is one thing; its potential detriment to society is another. How we teach spelling deserves more consideration. Using spelling lists and tests to "drill and kill" is not the only way to accomplish the task of producing adequate spellers. Spelling can be taught differently if we decide to approach it with a different philosophy.

History provides another option to consider; it is that you learn to spell words correctly as you use them. It has been suggested that the schools create a correct-spelling *habit* and correct-spelling *conscience*. That means we need to provide multiple *opportunities* for children to write, opportunities that need to span the length of their K–12 careers. Providing those opportunities requires that time is allowed for those activities in the curriculum. With only so much time in a school day, it seems that knowing what we citizens value and agreeing on teaching philosophies would be helpful in making decisions on how best to have our children spend their time. That same idea should be applied to arithmetic instruction.

Math has gone the way of multiple directions of emphasis. An interesting concept was one developed around 1900 called the "social use principle," which used as its guide to teaching those things that had "a clear link to usefulness in life." In one investigation, a survey was done on arithmetic concepts and practices needed in occupations: "Everybody agreed that pupils should learn to perform the four fundamental operations with whole numbers and small fractions, confidently, rapidly, and accurately; and that they should be taught to check their results" (Good, 416). People in various occupations would wholeheartedly agree with that assessment of needed math skills, but our expectations are now higher due to the high-tech nature of manufacturing. If we had been using the "social use principle," we might have met our current needs in manufacturing for the new "shop-math" skills that our current generations lack.

From store-owners to medical professionals, when you no longer have confidence in your staff to do the math correctly, you do it yourself, taking away time from your work and decreasing your efficiency. Our education system must set an expectation of mastery. It is a reasonable request. Many other math skills are relevant, but people have not agreed on their importance. Those discussions need to continue, be heard, and we must decide the question of how to teach.

Balance between philosophies would serve our children well. To balance the conceptual with the practical, we need both hands-on manipulation of learning materials to solidify concepts and rote memorization of math facts to ensure the desired accuracy. Is that the philosophy behind which we wish to develop our instruction? We have options; let's choose wisely. Let's put our knowledge to use.

## SCIENCE EDUCATION: CALLING ALL SCIENTISTS

The greatest deficiency of the teachers lay in the lack of a thorough scientific education. It is a great mistake to suppose that just any one can teach even the simple elements of science. To have a smattering of something is one of the greatest fallacies of our time.

—Edward Austin Sheldon

Many of our children are only receiving a smattering of science education. This is a result of allowing wide variation (between the states, within states, and within districts) in the emphasis of what subject matter we consider important enough to teach in the United States. With the lip service given to the importance of math and science, particularly as it applies to the economy, you wouldn't think making a case for teaching science would be needed. The fact is the need is huge.

To begin, we have different definitions of science. The study of science should include knowledge of nature and the physical world plus an understanding of the principles and methods of scientific study. To understand those principles and methods, critical thinking skills become essential.

Critical thinking skills require careful analysis, good judgment, and the ability to ask good questions and seek their answers. For children to understand science, they need to observe accurately and master the principles of science, not just cover what's in the book to later regurgitate facts on a test. Mastering *principles* requires the time to question the "facts." As Marion B. points out, teachers "need to be freed-up for projects." The education system needs to understand that concept and how important it is to *nurturing* a child's natural curiosity.

Children learn instinctively through all their given senses. They imitate the people around them, learning by example. As they grow, if allowed, they question all that surrounds them. That is inquiry-based learning; that is hands-on learning. For thousands of years, we humans have understood that concept. Aristotle has been quoted as saying "Nothing is in the mind that is not first in the hand." If we understand this, why has it been so hard to keep quality science education in the elementary schools?

A couple of things need to be clarified before proceeding. First, some of you may be questioning the necessity of science education in the earlier grades. Probably the two best arguments in favor of elementary science education are that (1) a student needs many years in order to allow complex science concepts to become solid thoughts, and (2) quality science instruction incorporates reading, writing, and mathematics, and provides hands-on, inquiry-centered learning to add relevance, stimulate interest, and in turn increase a student's effort in active learning. That is a philosophy we should consider establishing.

Second, many of you may be assuming that science has been and is taught in the elementary grades. For most districts, that may be true; for many, it is not. And a smidgen at this age doesn't pass as *quality*. For example, our district has taken the Open Court reading program and aligned reading of science facts. Teachers that understand and love teaching science find ways to supplement those lessons with hands-on materials. Experiences of the past tell us that it won't be consistent. In dysfunctional districts, whether a single child receives quality science instruction throughout the primary and secondary school years is left up to luck.

If people realized how important it is for children to learn an adequate amount of quality science, they wouldn't be leaving that opportunity up to luck. The importance of science education is obviously being misunderstood. We can fix that.

Many citizens of the United States have been talking about the need for more able scientists for many, many years. Corporations, institutions, and professions are considering, or already are, importing more scientists or out-sourcing where that is possible. And technology is making more things possible. Many of these jobs are good jobs that our students, being unprepared, don't even consider. We can change that.

The goal is not to make everyone a scientist. We need to develop citizens able to understand the complex issues of our society today, many of which are based in one branch of science or another. That is what you hear referred to as "scientific literacy." It means we want everyone to have the science background they need to function well in our society. We must accomplish that.

Our solutions start with knowing what we value. Then we must ask what we can do as a nation. I focused on elementary school here but the students in our secondary schools (middle and high schools) badly need community scientists and other members to step forward and help teachers add relevance to their lessons. Students need to see how to use what they're learning.

One belief of the schools reported in the *Eight-Year Study* was that "the spirit and practice of experimentation and exploration should characterize secondary schools" (Aikin, 1942, 19). There is no reason why we can't offer such *opportunities to all* students. Wise Services is one example of a non-profit (http://www.wiseservices.org) that assists in developing a "school-based experiential learning program." High school students "design projects that include internships with local community agency members or business people, intensive research, or cultural, artistic, or performance-based pro-jects." We do not have to reinvent wheels; we need to use the practices we know work and that we have available. We must face our problems.

Historically, the problems associated with sustaining science education in the elementary schools have included:

- Inadequate scientific education of the elementary teachers, which leads to decreased enthusiasm for teaching it,
- Heavy schedules,
- Large class sizes,
- Lack of administrative support,
- And inadequate supply of tasks and materials to do hands-on science.

This sounds like an all-encompassing list of problems in a chapter devoted to solutions. But remember, for every problem, there is a solution. Educate teachers, administration, and the community about the realities; give them the facts. Let the community know what materials and other support is needed to provide quality science education to those not currently receiving it. The reality of the state of science education in our schools must be revealed; this is a call for transparency. The science community and institutes of higher learning need to join forces and do what they do best, put out the innovative solutions they have been incubating. Let the extension of those ideas go out into practice. There is not one item on that list of needs for which one of the richest, most powerful countries on the planet can't provide, if so desired.

## OTHER DESIRABLE SUBJECTS, NOT LESSER

> The education of the many in the practical affairs of life is no substitute for the cultivation of high genius for mathematics, physics, chemistry; and it is also dangerous to neglect the humanities—for what shall it profit a man to save his life and lose his sense of values?
>
> —H. G. Good

That you will find no chapters devoted to social studies, humanities, or the arts is not because of viewing them as lesser subjects. They definitely are not less significant for a well-rounded education. These subjects are many times seen as "other" but should be considered desirable, necessary, and deserving of their rightful place in all school curricula.

Edwin Slosson talked about Benjamin Franklin's theories on mental and moral education. He discussed Franklin's desires for the teaching of history: "It is universal and comparative history that he wants, with special reference to customs, politics, religion, natural resources, commerce, and the growth of science. History, thus properly taught, would naturally lead to the study of ethics, logic, physics, oratory, debating, and journalism" (1921, 70). Benjamin Franklin was a man who knew through experience what it took to be an inventor and a fine statesman; this was a man who embodied the American spirit of *resourcefulness* and *initiative*. We should listen and contemplate his, as well as others', ideals concerning education.

Others have talked about the need to first teach history about your local region and visit local historical sites to connect kids to the history in their own backyards, thus stimulating interest in the subject to further a student's effort to study and learn. "Study of the community often creates a strong desire in young people to do something about the conditions which they have discovered. Usually, however, they find their hands tied—they can discover no way in which they are *permitted* to act" (Aikin, 1942, 64). Time to unbind the hands of our youth? Once upon a time America expanded west, now we have trouble getting into our own community. It's time for opportunity expansion.

Teaching foreign languages beginning in elementary schools was seen in this light by the National Commission on Excellence in Education: "We believe it is desirable that students achieve such proficiency because study of a foreign language introduces students to non-English-speaking cultures, heightens awareness and comprehension of one's native tongue, and serves the Nation's needs in commerce, diplomacy, defense, and education" (1983, 26).

These ideals will only become a reality for all children once we decide to: set our focus on clarifying what we value in education; quit wasting time changing gears with every new educational fad; and bring stability, balance, and fairness to the governing philosophy of our system.

## THE BIG THREE IN EDUCATION OR COLLECTIVE LEADERSHIP

School people are to the last degree impatient of criticism and suggestion. They resent them as a reflection on their personal character. As one man, they rush to the defense. The better among them excuse the worst and the worst grow abusive.

—Nicholas Murray Butler

Over the years, when thinking about how to address the problems created by the Big Three in education (administration, the school board, and the public), no solutions or ways to change the system could be found. Trying to analyze the problems would draw you into a never-ending circle of thought. It felt like being caught up in a whirlpool.

After much effort to break free of the vicious cycle of thoughts, some reasonable conclusions were made that could be deemed helpful: the administration should at least know the basic research findings on any issue before making a decision; the school board members should begin by reviewing their state code governing education and their own code of ethics in order to function; and the teachers and parents must *unite* to stimulate interest in education within the general public.

They aren't bad suggestions, but they do demonstrate our tendency to want to dissect the problem. We want to break up our problems into small pieces that we feel are doable. It's what scientists tend to do. It's the way government bureaucracies are set up, in divisions. But, in doing so, we continue to fail to fix the bigger problem. Something is always missing.

On August 15, 2007, the day the writing of the first edition of this book began, the intention was to offer the idea of the community education organizer (called a coordinator in that edition) as *the* answer to help correct the failures witnessed under my dysfunctional local control system. As others know, local control does not work 100 percent of the time. In underachieving states, "local control will remain little more than a guise through which the states can shirk its responsibility for ensuring that all students have access to quality education" (Noguera, 2003, 101–2).

If underachieving districts lack the knowledge, skills, abilities, resources, and motivation to improve, they lack the *capacity* to act. Under those circumstances, local control does result in school district's failing—no question. The Big Three must share some of the responsibility when schools underperform. They must become part of the solution.

A community education organizer working through already existing education agencies could help a local school board achieve the function for which it was intended. This position could function to help to bring information to the board and assist in educating the public. That position could be used to foster the development of the essential intimate, barrier-free relationship of the community and school. It could promote the cooperation necessary for us to listen to one another.

But what I now doubt is whether or not this type of "reform" would be enough. I, like Seymour Sarason and others, question the existing structure that currently governs education, from top to bottom. The Big Three have been so strongly influenced by state, federal, and local politics that, alone, they may never break free of the single-minded reforms that lack the backing of research and defy commonsense. This reasoning is possibly why, where schools are chronically "failing," the federal government is currently encouraging the "take-over" of school governance by city mayors or "education managers." But there is another *choice*.

The idea of a community education *council* has been recommended, developed, and used effectively in a variety of settings from small schools to larger districts. It is a structure of governing that brings together local "experts," educators, and a variety of interested community members and leaders. As Minzey and LeTarte explain, "To ignore the formal leadership structure is to ignore the wealth, the traditional community power sources, and the vast majority of the citizenry in the community. To ignore the informal structure is to ignore the voices for change—the alienated, the concerned, and the minorities" (1994, 200). This council type of structure makes for a more collective, democratic decision-making process.

## ACCOUNTABILITY DONE RIGHT

> Only a limited number of us can become scholars . . . but we can all become good citizens.
>
> —Theodore Roosevelt

We ask for "accountability" without seeming to understand that "account-ability" is a word that is interchangeable with "responsibility." But respon-sibility carries *a human obligation*. It hits on our core *American values*. To "do" an accounting of the education system is to take a cold hard business attitude toward "it." That's not to say that parts of the system don't need close scrutiny but if "reform" is be centered on children, we need to be *responsible* to them. That means the adults guiding the child are the endpoint of an accountability system for *school reform*. We know that the vast major-ity of individuals working directly with children are responsible.

If everyone were true to the universally accepted moral values of honesty and integrity, we wouldn't need laws to "enforce" accountability. We would have people doing their jobs to the best of their ability, and if they didn't, they would have to explain their actions and face consequences. That is what accountability means. Because of the reality of human nature, *oversight* of the government *institutions and systems* that deliver vital services to people is necessary. *Systemic accountability* is essential.

Accountability begins with an accounting of the situation. "The system" is based on trust (accreditation) and vigilance (local control) with monitor-ing, guidance, and support from our government. Systemic accountability has many parameters on which to be judged. In the development of a func-tioning education system, the purposes for its existence are determined and the indicators of success should be set. Our nation needs to set those goals and parameters for the people to understand before the people can hold them accountable.

In our current accountability "paradigm, two-way accountability does not exist: Although the child and the school are accountable to the state for test performance, the state is not accountable to the child or school for providing *adequate* educational resources. . . . If education is actually to improve and the system is to be accountable to students, accountability should focus on ensuring:

1. the competence of teachers and leaders,
2. the quality of instruction,
3. the adequacy of resources,
4. the capacity of the system to trigger improvements" (Darling-Ham-mond, 2010, 301).

To choose the easier route is to choose the wrong route. "Pointing fingers and assigning blame are typically easier than accepting responsibility" (Noguera, 2003, xi). Basing accountability of schools on standards and testing is wrong and has repeatedly proven itself to be the wrong road to follow in education. Standardized test scores can be "achieved" through the development of a test-based classroom *culture* or through the conditions necessary for *nurtur-*

*ing* learning; it's the difference between test preparation and true education. Test scores alone, or in large part, cannot be used to fully judge where we are not meeting our responsibility to the student.

For *"systemic changes* to improve student achievement," Ratner points out that we must "hold states and districts accountable for *implementing* key structural improvement . . . putting the emphasis of *school reform* directly where it needs to be; on *helping schools improve*" (2007, 34).

In the local school system, in the trenches, accountability must take on new meaning—a new direction. The teaching and learning *conditions* need to be evaluated. They are the things that local communities can have an influence on and are obligated to maintain vigilance over.

As Monty Neill explains, there were places in this country that refused "to reduce learning to what can be easily measured on standardized tests" and they worked to find alternative "models" of assessments and accountability. His organization, FairTest, worked with the Massachusetts Coalition for Authentic Reform in Education (CARE) in developing plans based on three sources of information (summarized here):

1. Classroom-based information as evidence of learning including student work and teacher observations of the learning processes, noting strengths and weaknesses of the student,
2. Standardized testing of literacy and numeracy as one "check" on school level information but not as the sole determinate about students or schools,
3. School quality reviews done by outside reviewer at least every five years with more frequents reviews for schools having "difficulty." (Meier et al., 2004, 110–11)

And some professional organizations took it upon themselves to take a professional position on accountability. The National Science Teachers Association "believes that individuals are accountable first to those directly affected by their actions and second to all other interested parties. Thus science teachers are accountable primarily to students and parents." These scientists also understood that the *cultural setting* or *environment* where this accountability would be expected should be based on "mutual trust and support." They laid down "the *conditions* under which accountability needs to take place." Here is a summary of their declaration (http://www.nsta.org/about/positions/accountability.aspx):

Teachers must be given:

• The appropriate resources,
• Access to quality educational opportunities,
• The time necessary to develop skills,

- The opportunity to participate in development of accountability measures,
- Information about the plan and timeline for compliance,
- And the opportunity to address accountability issues within a local network.

We need an accountability system where there is local responsibility, true state accountability, and a federal duty to monitor progress for the purpose of providing guidance and support. So if we want to continue to look at the issue of "improvement" in terms of "reform," school reform is a local responsibility. States are charged with an accounting of inputs and outcomes to provide meaningful oversight. And the federal government oversees the broader topic of "education reform" as it applies to the necessities of maintaining a strong republic. They must monitor, support, and guide.

Everyone should know by now that top-down education *mandates* for accountability tied to higher "achievement" scores has only furthered our resistance to change, made a bad situation worse for many, and escalated the education wars. The scholars are fighting over issues the people can't understand, while citizens are growing frustrated and walking away. This fighting must end.

We have all the tools we need to thoughtfully evaluate the classroom conditions we have created and to test the boundary waters to see if they are sufficiently warmed to allow growth of the mutual trust and support needed to build a safety net for children. "Reform" doesn't happen to us; it happens because of our actions.

We know enough now to proceed responsibly in addressing the needs of underperforming schools and in improving the quality of learning conditions for all. We have the answers.

We must use what we know. Pyramids are built to last because of a wide base of support. In an *educational improvement process*, we can now explore and choose from a deep body of knowledge about what has "worked" and what hasn't for any given issue. We can apply the Theory of Action (Chapter 3) to any instructional subject or educational issue.

Once an issue has been identified, the only way to build a broad base is to be open to engaging, educating, and opening the doors of communication, casting the widest net, so as to include as many people as possible in working toward the next step of developing a vision on which to move forward. It can, and should, be done at all governing levels if we wish to develop a true system. "Top-down" guidance and support with a "bottom-up" school improvement process is a winning combination with the potential to finally make the words "equal opportunity" become a reality for America's children.

## USING WHAT WE KNOW

Whatever other characteristics societal and institutional revolutions may have, they share the characteristic of altering traditional power relationships.
—Seymour B. Sarason

Our political system in the past has worked with the people by using policy to move practices. That process is not working for our children, today. It's up to us. We must develop the *common understanding* and *common vision* to guide us toward the goal of equal opportunity that thus far has proven elusive to this nation's education system.

We need to understand where we have failed in the past, for we have been warned by our forefathers that "if we are not cautious to avoid a repetition of the error, in our future attempts to rectify and ameliorate our system, we may travel from one chimerical project to another; we may try change after change; but we shall never be likely to make any material change for the better" (*The Federalist*, no. 26, Alexander Hamilton, December 22, 1787).

We have failed to maintain lasting educational reform in the past and will again unless we understand our errors. "Reform" is not a bad word. It should not be associated with a political party. Reform means "to make better by removing faults and defects or to make better by putting a stop to abuses or malpractices or by introducing better procedures" (*Webster's*, 1976). But reform has failed.

Thanks to my son's interest and enthusiasm for history, which was a gift from an excellent teacher, I stumbled on the keys to the understanding of the failure of reforms within the pages of *The Age of Reform* by Richard Hofstadter. He discusses Josiah Strong's theory that "if public opinion is educated concerning a given reform—political, social, industrial, or moral—and if the popular conscience is sufficiently awake to enforce an *enlightened public opinion*, the reform is accomplished straightaway" (1955, 202). Hofstadter went on to point out through the writings of William Allen White that "the only *permanent cure* was in *changing the system*" (259). The reformers of the Progressive period made policy changes but failed to change "systems."

Hofstadter also stated, "History cannot quite repeat itself, if only because the participants in the second round of any experience are aware of the outcome of the first" (313). Unfortunately, he was wrong when that theory is applied to educational history. He seemed to have not envisioned a world in which the people didn't read each other's work or works from the past.

One of Hofstadter's conclusions was that reform required laws, and enforcement of laws required political *leadership* with *moral quality*. He wrote that others believed reforms could be upheld despite the "relaxed moral vigilance" of citizens, provided the people "choose men of the highest moral qualities" for political leaders. He points out that "it was assumed that such moral qualities were indestructible and that decent men, once found and installed in office, would remain decent" (202). Well, surly we know by now that "absolute power corrupts absolutely."

J. M. Rice was one person that clearly saw the need to tackle the issue of politics in education. In 1893, Dr. Rice (a pediatrician) wrote *The Public School System of the United States*. He suggested three things that were necessary to improve the city schools: (1) drive out the politicians, (2) train and keep training teachers so curriculum could be indefinitely broadened without detriment to the Three Rs, and (3) provide competent supervision (Good, 398).

More recent authors offer other solutions to our political dilemma. Kevin Phillips's book *Arrogant Capital* offers insight into how we might begin to *"reclaim the people's role* in governing our country." In the last chapter of that book, Phillips offers proposals that include the idea of "decentralizing or dispersing power away from Washington" (1994, 186). That particular proposal is well suited to address the changes needed in education. Education is not benefiting from the influence of lobbyists. Political influence is not an essential ingredient of quality education—the influence of the people is.

The negative influences of politics on education have been noted previously, with NCLB being our most current and striking example. Unfortunately, breaking the political stronghold on education is both necessary and a thought people are reluctant to consider. Change is difficult. It scares us. It shouldn't. A change for the better is called progress.

> The time is always right to do what is right.
>
> —Martin Luther King Jr.

## Chapter Seven

# Formula for Success: Simple, Not Easy

Let us think of education as the means of developing our greatest abilities, because in each of us there is a private hope and dream which, fulfilled, can be translated into benefit for everyone and greater strength for our nation.
—John F. Kennedy

When considering the complex interrelationships and the entrenchment of the parties involved in education, to break free of this whirlpool of thoughts long enough to move forward, we must focus on the nuts and bolts of what is right. "Our society and its educational institutions seem to have lost sight of the basic purposes of schooling, and of the *high expectations* and *disciplined effort* needed to attain them" (National Commission, 1983, 5).

To think through this concept of universal public education, the essential elements of education are easiest to look at and think about in the form of an equation. If we as a nation stay focused long enough, we can work through this equation. The formula provides focus and clarity for those whose vision has been clouded by the political complexities of education. The formula can serve to refocus our thoughts during times of confusion. And, like a compass, it will assist in redirecting our actions when we drift off course.

We have made this whole business of educating children way too complicated. The resulting cost to run this bureaucracy is detrimental to the education of the children that it is supposed to serve.

The formula for educational success is:

| Kids Ready to Learn | + | Teachers Ready to Teach | + | The Materials to Do It | = | Equal Opportunity for Education |

The pieces of the equation are what we see on the ground, in our classrooms. When I explained "Kids Ready to Learn" and "Teachers Ready to Teach" for the first edition of this book, I got lost. I failed to understand something very important to the *universal improvement* of public schools. It's because I had trouble seeing more specifically where the change must take place first—it's in the boundary waters.

Land boundaries are very distinct; property lines are easy to draw. Water boundaries are not always so clear. They change with the erosion and sediment of the changing current. The "boundary" isn't as neat and tidy as a writer, reformer, or the public would like. These boundaries are where "parents and schools interact on behalf of children" (Price-Mitchell, 2009, 9). If "reform" is to focus on children, this is the place to start.

And if we expand this concept a bit further by taking to heart the suggestion that "education reform should focus on the goal of creating a Learning Society" (National Commission, 1983, 13), the boundary widens to include communities. A compass is essential.

## KIDS READY TO LEARN

The secret of right education consists in respecting the pupil.
—Ralph Waldo Emerson

When we think about kids coming to school ready to learn, multiple things come to mind. Do they get enough sleep? Are they hungry? Are they emotionally ready to learn? Do they live in a nurturing home? Do they have a home? The recipe for "Kids Ready to Learn" is a long and varied one based on our consideration first of needs of the "pupils"; to show consideration is to show "respect."

What children need to be ready to learn isn't just about early childhood education. The topic needs to be seen as a spectrum that addresses the issues that the teachers are seeing in the classrooms. While the sleepy first graders' parents may need to know about sleep requirements for that age, the "zoned-out" teenager, or one that is acting out, may need sex education, physical education, focus on learning deficits, or counseling to rein in emotions and get back to learning. Just like discipline issues having underlying causes that need uncovering, the classroom teachers and school counselors are a vital source of information and guidance to assist in revealing what is required to have our children ready to learn.

In a book called *Central Park East and Its Graduates: "Learning by Heart,"* David Bensman describes the investigation he conducted through interviews of the students and their parents years after the kids had graduated from this elementary school. One of the key things he found that contributed to this school being successful (as judged by notably high graduation rates, college acceptance rates, and personal satisfaction of its graduates) was the *consistent respect* shown for children, parents, and teachers.

Bensman also noted that time and again former students would tell him that they felt supported and encouraged. They also felt that, among other things, they came away from this school understanding the ideal of "respect for the human spirit's creativity and the American citizen's *communal responsibility*" (2000, 8). And one of his conclusions was that "children quickly learned that their family and school were of one mind not only about the importance of learning, but about *what children had to do to learn*" (103).

Back in Chapter 6, under the heading "Safe and Disciplined Schools: Creating Community Civility," you will find a list of suggestions by Bosch that apply here as well. When we create civility in communities, we have a better chance of creating civility in the boundaries surrounding our public schools; we then have a better chance of developing the *personal relationships* that become partnerships with our schools, ultimately benefiting children.

Children need us to form partnerships. "The more people tie together socially and interconnect because they value children's success in school and life, the greater potential for productive outcomes. If a teacher and parent know, trust, and respect one another, there is a greater likelihood that one will initiate contact with the other when needed to help the child" (Price-Mitchell, 2009, 18). Partnerships aren't a way to shift responsibility; they are a way to share it.

Parents and families are a child's first educators. It is the responsibility of parents to care for their own children and to prepare them for school and their place in a larger community. But the reality is that many do not or cannot meet that responsibility at this point in time. Our economy and our changing values have been detrimental to the family unit; that is a fact, not a pass.

There is no excusing the fact that too many parents have not made education a priority or understand their responsibility to send their children to school ready to learn. But we must show restraint in assuming that they don't care. Have we seriously "educated" parents about classrooms, schools, and their roles? And have they been given ample and consistent opportunity to engage and participate? We need to stop thinking about ways to "deal with" parents and start thinking about ways to "work with" parents.

Ruby Payne stresses the importance of support, insistence, and expectations in her book *Working with Parents: Building Relationships for Student Success* (2005). She stresses that in order to clarify your expectations of parents and students; you need to understand how to communicate with the group you are trying to educate. Her experiences point out important differences between our *economic class cultures*. Dr. Payne explains that the "societal rules" are different depending on which economic class you experienced in childhood. We can't expect or take for granted that everyone follows or even understands the rules by which we govern schools. She states that, for many children raised in poverty, "schools are virtually the only places where students can learn the choices and rules of the middle class" (62).

We shouldn't take for granted that everyone has the same meaning for even the word "respect." We need to teach and reteach our behavioral expectations to the children, to the parents, and to the community. And all people need to model those behaviors—*educating by example*.

As mentioned previously, one definition of "discipline" is that it is the process of training a child so that the desired character traits and habits can be developed. It is not a matter of domination or strict "classroom control"; it's the *development of personal character traits* that act to serve our students well throughout life. Those desired traits and habits need to be defined and communicated so they can be modeled at home and in the community and need only reinforcement in the schools. This process requires much more than just listing what we want to see developed, handing it out, or mailing it home. It requires open discussion about what works, what doesn't, and what we as a community can do short-term and long-term to accomplish what we desire.

We need to coordinate the effort to work with educators and the public on developing their message of expectations and getting it out to the community through *existing adult education agencies* such as our cooperative extension system. The basics of any issue are not so complicated that everyday people can't understand them if we would just translate them into words that can be understood. We can educate the people. It will build consistency.

Inconsistency leads to confusion and frustration on the part of the child and parents. For that reason, it is important that in addition to the schools making known their expectations, parents must be able to discuss the expectations they have of the school. The school does have some responsibilities in helping children to be ready to learn.

The schools should not fail to reinforce lessons that decent parents try to instill in their children nor fail to provide children with the essentials for learning. To be ready to learn, children need access to water, bathroom facilities, proper nutrition, fresh air, and recreational exercise to help facilitate a fresh view on learning. If parents value fairness, acceptance of others' views, the development of good study habits, and a strong work ethic, schools should reinforce those values.

Children getting mixed signals are confused, not ready to learn. Inconsistencies make the job for parents more difficult; it makes the teachers' job more difficult. Open discussions and common goals go a long way in preventing difficulties. Sara Lawrence-Lightfoot has these bits of insight to offer in *The Essential Conversation: What Parents and Teachers Can Learn from*

*Each Other*: "Beginning with the assumption that all children have 'special needs' is a kind of catalyst for bringing parents and teachers together 'on the same side'" (2003, 158). And she discusses "the essential ingredients of *empathy* and *respect* that define successful parent-teacher encounters" (243). It seems we humans, young or older, just want to know that others care enough to consider our concerns. Successful partnerships make the waters pleasant and the sailing smoother.

When parents fail to do their job as parents, great communities step up to support the children that are least fortunate. Supportive communities see raising children to become informed and responsible citizens as essential for the greater good of society.

In his article "Advisory Programs to Restructured Adult-Student Relationships: Restoring Purpose to the Guidance Function of the Middle Level School," Howard Johnston said the following (bulleted for emphasis):

> Good children are raised by communities of adults:
>
> - who share common beliefs and values about what constitutes reasonable and appropriate behavior,
> - who accept responsibility for sharing the wisdom of their years and experience with children, and
> - who share a common commitment to all the children in the community and nation. That is how we were raised. That is how good, successful, achieving, happy children are raised today.

A voice from the past will tell us, "In every community there are many men and women able and ready to serve the cause of education. Schools are learning through experience how to draw upon these rich *human resources* for *counsel* and *support*" (Aikin, 1942, 40). Is it time to ramp up the Volunteers in Support of America (VISTA) program to help us address the wisdom gap and provide effective advisors and mentors? Hard-working, frustrated parents need help.

Parents, teachers, and community members, in a collective process, need to guide the education of dysfunctional parents to ensure that we are all on the same page in serving the needs of our local children. To serve as a framework in building a guide, here is what the National Commission on Excellence in Education had to say to parents (*A Nation at Risk*, 1983, 35):

> You have the right to demand for your children the best our schools and colleges can provide. Your vigilance and your refusal to be satisfied with less than the best are the imperative first step. But your right to a proper education for your children carries a *double responsibility*. As surely as you are your child's first and most influential teacher, your child's ideas about education

and its significance begin with you. You must be a *living example* of what you expect your children to honor and to emulate. Moreover, you bear a responsibility to participate actively in your child's education.

You should encourage more diligent study:

- monitor your child's study;
- encourage good study habits;
- encourage your child to take more demanding rather than less demanding courses;
- nurture your child's curiosity, creativity, and confidence;
- be an active participant in the work of the schools;
- exhibit a commitment to continued learning in your own life;
- help your children understand that excellence in education cannot be achieved without intellectual and moral integrity coupled with hard work and commitment.

As communities, we can do a better job getting our children ready to learn so that our teachers can better educate them. Some "business minded models" have been looking at the "economy of time" as it relates to the classroom. They would be wise to pause a moment, look back at the work of their predecessors, and then consider through a new lens how we can best make more time for teaching. If children don't become major distractions in the classroom setting, don't teachers have more time to teach?

## TEACHERS READY TO TEACH

Teacher and child are the leading characters in the educational drama. If the child is to play his part well, the teacher should be well prepared.

—H. G. Good

Teaching became a profession during the middle 1800s. The criterion on which it gained status as a profession was that the need for *special preparation* was recognized and developed. Teachers became recognized professionals. "Professionals" are defined as "engaged in or worthy of the *high standards* of a profession" (*Webster's*, 1976).

Having no formal training in the field of education, I don't claim and won't pretend to know the "what and how" of teacher preparation. What can be claimed is that I have been through training for a profession; I am a professional. Before entering the profession of veterinary medicine, the expectations of the profession and the concept of "standards of practice" were made very clear and those same ideals reinforced repeatedly throughout the preparation process and through continuing education. A consistent message about maintaining a standard was upheld.

As professionals know, maintaining high standards requires constant vigilance on an individual's part to keep up with current information and practices. As a professional, it is that person's responsibility to maintain high standards. That is what professionals do.

What differs greatly between my profession and teaching is that in the veterinary medical profession across the country, we have a clearer, more consistent teaching curriculum that our universities follow in our education. The knowledge of the sciences, practices, and procedures that veterinarians receive is reliable. Our preparation and continuing education is based on what we need to know to practice the art and science of veterinary medicine successfully.

In the art and science of teaching, that does not appear to be the case. Maybe our teacher preparation programs fail to use what we know. Maybe they fail to acknowledge that addressing the needs of each child requires a *personalized* approach, just like a medical or surgical case. That's why veterinarians are required to learn way more than most will ever need to use in practice. In vet school, we joked about all the "zebras."

This discussion is not to point blame; it's to help us face the facts. If society hasn't decided our philosophy of instruction for the Three R's, science, and "other," how can we possibly know what to teach our teachers? Experience points to the fact that the pedagogy (teaching technique) pendulum has been swinging for so long, it is difficult to know how colleges and universities are setting their aim on what to teach to teachers. And how do you truly "personalize" instruction if you only know one way to teach, one philosophy to follow?

The words that follow are not meant to tell teachers how they should teach; the intention is to share some ideas, some research, and some best practices. The public shouldn't tell teachers how to teach. But, rather, through public discussions, the public's views should be used to establish our *guiding principles* that drive teacher instruction.

Curriculum, in the case of the educators themselves, should not be left up to the preference of an individual or vary so wildly between states and institutions within the same state or from year to year that education is left up to luck. What to teach, how much emphasis to place on a subject, and how we would like our children educated should be decided based on the direction society needs its education system to go.

Boards of education are set up to guide curricula, but, again turning to experience, the tendency would be to conclude that they have not served us well, consistently; many do not want "the collective voice" involved in their decisions. The result is the same as what we see occurring in our government in general; the system reacts too slowly when it isn't listening to the voice of the people. The result is too often a chosen direction that does not meet the people's needs.

As Emery and Ohanian put it, "an authentic debate over what constitutes 'real quality in education'" must occur. "This is not an easy task and requires that teachers, parents, nonprofits, and businesspeople look at their own assumptions about what they believe is equity and quality, look closely at what is happening in schools because of high-stakes testing, recognize the legitimacy of multiple goals of education, and then be prepared to make compromises" (2004, 202). That process would make review of our current work on teacher evaluation and preparation much more responsible and relevant to our needs and prevent problems in the future.

But we must start where we are with the existing structure and the terminology most commonly used: pre-service teacher instruction, in-service teacher instruction, and teacher evaluation.

Pre-service instruction is the teachers' preparation. Once more we turn to Seymour Sarason for his expertise on the subject, as he provides noteworthy advice in *The Case for Change: Rethinking the Preparation of Educators*. Sarason states that "preparatory programs inadequately prepare educators (teachers and administrators) for what life is like in classrooms, schools, and school systems," and that "preparatory programs unwittingly contribute to the manufacture of problems." And "there has been little educational leadership to inform the general public about the whys and wherefores of prevention" (1993, 4). So, let's talk about prevention.

## The Expectations of Professional Development

Doing research and writing for the science professional development grant mentioned in Chapter 3 was confusing, as was writing about teacher education in my first edition. If the public is being asked to treat teachers with the respect we do other professionals then the assumption is that they *are* professionals when they step into their first classroom. The expectation is that their "professional development" has occurred. They should continue to grow through experience and continuing education as all professionals do. But at this moment in time, I advise we see teacher preparation as the coursework and practice necessary to develop a professional teacher.

From classroom observations and comparisons comes the assumption that teacher development should include defining their obligations as teachers, developing their understanding of how children learn best, honing their skills in recognizing learning difficulties or differences, and expanding their subject matter (content) knowledge base.

Their general obligations as classroom teachers should emphasize principles like those set down by David P. Page in his 1847 book *Theory and Practice of Teaching*. He emphasized that the teacher is "responsible for the morals, health, intellectual growth, and study habits of his pupils" (cited in Good, 321). If there are "issues" with that statement, they are exactly the things we should hear about in open debates.

During past exchanges of ideas, the reference to teaching morals has produced huffing and eye rolling. The reaction probably stems from the meaning of "morals" being greatly misunderstood and having a sexual or religious connotation. "Morals" means "dealing with, or capable of making the distinction between, right and wrong in conduct" (*Webster's*, 1976). We know teaching morals is a responsibility of the home and community, but it must have been obvious back in 1847 that it needed to be emphasized in classrooms and therefore in teachers' education.

Page also emphasized that the teacher "must teach pupils how to study intelligently, how to *master the principles* of science instead of preparing for a recitation or covering a book" (Good, 321). Science is the example in that statement but each topic has its own best ways to be taught, "best practices." Being informed about researched-based best practices would make for a solid foundation (Theory of Action; Chapter 3) on which to build toward the goal of preventing problems.

Teachers and parents alike should understand how children learn best. That knowledge should be guiding decisions on subject matter and technique. Scientific knowledge of brain development has helped identify what is developmentally appropriate to teach, meaning that we should recognize when a student is able to best comprehend a concept. Research has identified successful techniques. But the art of teaching is harder to understand so it must be harder to teach to teachers.

In veterinary medicine, some of the art of practice was in being able to read the body language of your patient. At times, it is a skill that can save a veterinarian's life. So stumbling on the children's book *Learning How to Learn* by L. Ron Hubbard (1992) felt like my lifesaver. It was a moment in time that brought some welcomed clarity for our son and us.

As a parent, finding a book designed to help children, parents, and teachers understand the basics of learning was exhilarating and fun. It was a discovery worth sharing. Mentioning the book to several administrators and teachers in various situations over many years, not a glimmer of interest was noted. Not one of "them" was curious enough to want to hear this perspective. That was not the case when mentioning it to other parents. This was back in 1995 and, having loaned the book out to parents until it didn't return, what is recalled here is from memory and the notes our son took.

In a section written for adults, L. Ron Hubbard instructs the parent or teacher about the basics of recognizing the cues a child gives, what they might act like or their facial expressions, and how they feel when they are failing to learn. Most attentive mothers and fathers, like good teachers, probably already know this instinctively. That is part of the art of teaching; it's about reading children's signals. Hubbard then goes on to explain that, when they are having difficulties, it means they are experiencing a *barrier to learning* and only three barriers exist. They are: (1) lack of mass, meaning they are being presented with a concept they can't touch or see or conceptualize; (2) the missed step or too steep a learning gradient; and (3) the misunderstood word, the most commonly occurring barrier not only to learning but to communications in general for all of us.

The major portion of this book is the picture book itself designed for children. Hubbard teaches the child these same concepts in simple words and pictures. In each section, it has some mental exercises that include drawing and writing to illustrate and review the concepts he's teaching. The purpose of the book is to explain to children having trouble that when they experience confusion or difficulties learning they are still normal; they have just run into a barrier.

He teaches that a barrier is something that stops you. In the case of learning, it stops you from achieving understanding. It's a simplistic way of teaching about learning how to learn.

In the education field, it seems they are trying to explain the concept of "lack of mass" by saying children learn best when taught a concept "in context." However, after using this terminology of "taught in context" in a discussion with a college counselor, her confused look and the conversation that followed confirmed that it is not a universally understood concept or the terminology is not universal. The simplistic explanation that Hubbard gives helps the child, parent, or teacher to understand that, if lack of mass is the difficulty, they need to find a picture, a thing, or a demonstration or relevant explanation to put a concept into a context that the child understands.

The missed step or too steep a teaching gradient clarifies that children need to learn things step-by-step or they may become confused. Hubbard compares it to following a recipe where, if you miss an ingredient, it doesn't turn out right. His suggestion is to go back and find out where you went wrong, what step you missed. Thinking about what this concept of a missed step means in an education system, if you are expecting middle school or high school teachers to go back and try to figure out the missed step for their students, the importance of teaching things right the first time and *expecting mastery*, should be clear to all.

For the misunderstood word, Hubbard explains that you need to ask questions when confusion sets in and it may help clarify what word you have misunderstood. Or go back in your reading to where you last understood and reread until you come across the word that has tripped you up. He instructs to never go past a word you do not fully understand and gives the steps you should follow to "clear" the word. Clearing a word may include using a dictionary.

It was comforting and helpful to know of ways to assist a child having difficulties learning and, remarkably, the troubles always seemed to fit into one of these three barriers, in children with normal learning capacities. They weren't always something that could be fixed, like lack of phonics or a missed step in reading instruction. But others were doable, like finding or making a model of an atom when lack of mass was the barrier to understanding.

The greatest barrier, the misunderstood word, affects all our lives regularly. Look at the language barriers in medicine and education and the ongoing debate about English being our official language. What about the word "welfare" with a capital "W" and its use twice in the Constitution, or the word "preemptive"? Do we understand how those words were meant to be interpreted? Preempt can mean "to seize before anyone else can" (*Webster's*, 1976). The misunderstood word is a huge concept particularly when professional educators themselves have not settled on common terminology.

If this book by L. Ron Hubbard, or something similar to it, could help adults in understanding a child's learning difficulties, thus helping us more quickly come to a remedy for their confusion or failure, shouldn't we be using it in teacher education? In education they talk about remediation or remedial classes, but it appears to be a concept that has not been fully or consistently taught to teachers.

Recognition of problems is best done as soon as possible. If you compare it to training an animal, it's always easier to make the correction of a teaching mistake immediately rather than let bad habits develop and have to totally retrain. Or compare it to any disease. It is always best to treat early in the course of the disease rather than wait while the disease causes further damage. Whenever possible, prevention is preferred.

Recognition of learning difficulties, differences, and the development of an understanding of both verbal and nonverbal communication is important in recognition and prevention of learning failures. In preparation to practice veterinary medicine, we considered recognition of nonverbal cues to be a basic element of *successful clinical practice*. My observations in the classrooms did not lead me to believe the same was true of the preparation of teachers. So, if that essential piece of educator preparation is missing, that fact probably explains why it appears that many teachers seem unaware of the nonverbal cues that they are sending out to children. This may be in something they do, or how they structure instruction.

Children are like small animals—no, they are animals. We all are, but children are just less domesticated than we adults. Children seem more in tune with their instincts and, therefore, more sensitive in general to the influences of others, especially those they look up to, as all young learners do their first teachers.

All first grade teachers need to be specially trained. It has been all too common a practice for first-year teachers to be placed in first grade classes. Some may do fine, but are steps missed? Would they do things differently, better, the next time around? If a child only does first grade once, can we risk potentially creating a problem and expecting the next teacher to figure out what went wrong? We must do things right the first time.

First grade is critical. First grade must be a successful experience for all children. The only way to ensure success "happens" for all is with proper guidance and *personalized* attention to the learning and developmental needs of the child. That will only be accomplished through exceptional, specially trained teachers in small classes. First grade teachers must be taught to ensure that things are done right the first time.

I spotted a reader board that said: "To fail to prepare is to prepare for failure." First grade is our children's ground zero. Teacher preparation programs are our prevention of future failures.

Other specialized teacher instruction is important, too. Not enough educators appear to be properly trained in middle school instruction. This partially explains the specific "failures" of our middle and high school curricula and instruction.

The Trends in International Mathematics and Science Study (TIMSS) report concluded that the United States was doing a competitive job in the early grades with math and science instruction but our students would then start to lose ground by eighth grade (Valverde & Schmidt, 1997–1998). Combining that conclusion with the fact that we have large dropout rates in many of our schools has led us to conclude that something is amiss in our middle and high schools.

This phenomenon is not the fault of teachers; they have not been given the information they need or proper support. Teaching the importance of the functions and purposes of middle schools and high schools appears to have been swept out with the tide of standards testing. Our middle schools or junior high schools were supposed to function as the bridge between the elementary school and high school. The purpose of the middle school was to help the student stay on the bridge to avoid falling into the turbulent waters created by the adolescent period. That work requires the collaborative effort of family, church, and community to be successful. And the need for professional, well-trained counselors guiding the professionally recommended number of students is an essential and apparently neglected piece of the story.

Consistency is a must at this stage. Specialized instruction of teachers, counselors, administrators, and parents about the unique developmental changes of the adolescent period would go a long way toward fixing and preventing the special problems associated with adolescence. The same story holds true for the high schools.

The high schools' function is to finish the preparation of students to transition into the "real world." It is the final step in preparation from schools to careers. This may mean preparing them for college or a vocation. This dual function of the high school is why prior student assessment and *proper guidance* is important in making the high school function as intended.

The extreme importance of an *effective* counseling program can't be stressed enough. Neither can the importance of continuing and intensifying the involvement of the community because, at one point in time, the purpose of a high school was to act as the center of a community and serve as a center of activity. In functional communities, it still does.

These ideals and ideas are not new and have been explored in depth, along with other relevant issues, in the previously referenced Cooperative Study of Secondary School Standards. This study's findings have not been taught to all secondary school teachers, administrators, and counselors or drawn any widespread public attention. Instead, we are blindly looking for the answers to the woes of high schools when our government has already studied the subject intensively. The current powers that be may not even know of the existence of this information, for war had disrupted the progress of this project as it had similarly with the American Lyceum and other worthwhile projects.

The purpose of "the study" was to improve functioning of secondary schools (the middle or junior high and high schools) through an "active self-improvement process." The importance of the counselor's role in secondary schools was prominently emphasized, as was the importance of community. The *school improvement process* that was the focus of the original study was based on: what the *characteristics* of a good school are, how you evaluate a school's *effectiveness* in relation to its objectives, how a good *school becomes better*, and how to stimulate schools to continue to *strive to become better*.

When talking about high schools, one particular group of schools in Providence, Rhode Island—referred to as the Met—deserves mention in that they have shown improved graduation rates and have earned high marks from parents. On a measure for parental involvement that was designed to assess how involved parents feel in the school and how comfortable they are with teachers and *school environment*, the 2006 Rhode Island State Report Card statistics show 80 percent of parents had positive responses compared with 42 percent for the state.

Their instructional plans are based on learning through internships. The first of these schools was the subject of a 2002 book by Eliot Levine, who explained that "learning happens best when tailored to each student's needs," thus the title *One Kid at a Time: Big Lessons from a Small School*. Many aspects of these Met schools deserve consideration, including the ideas of interest-based learning, a balance of needs and interests, learning through doing, small student-to-"advisor" ratio, community involvement through mentors and internships, a set of expectations that includes personal qualities, and a view that "parents are essential partners whose input shapes the student's learning activities" (2002, 97).

The aspects of the schools that make them successful were not things that were put in place through a program. Rather, it appears to have begun with a person with a vision. That vision was then more clearly focused, and continues to be focused, based on the exchange of ideas between administration, educators, students, parents, and community members. Through this ongoing process, the staff has developed a shared vision and has attempted—it appears, successfully—to build a community of learners that includes all but is *centered on the value of each student*. It sounds like they model what it means to have *respect* for each other's opinions and what can result when *high expectations* for learning are set, for real, and in real-life settings. How many of these basic philosophies about how children learn and the processes for school improvement are taught in our teacher, counselor, and administrator preparation classes?

In talking about teacher preparation, we have jumped from first grade to high school. But the idea is to clear up the misunderstanding that what you see happening in ineffective classrooms is *always* the fault of the teacher. The experimentation in teaching techniques that were expounded on earlier as being less than successful were not a reflection on the teacher. It wasn't a bad teacher; it was inadequate teacher instruction. It's the difference between a well-educated and not-so-well educated professional.

Our colleges and universities must take teacher training programs through an improvement process with the aim of preventing the large inconsistencies and "gaps" in teacher education that are currently occurring. Our children's education system deserves an effort greater than that of other professions to make "professional development" what it should be. After all, "creating a strong profession in education is not a task that can be tackled school by school or district by district. And creating uniformly strong schools cannot be accomplished without a strong profession" (Darling-Hammond, 2010, 197). This is a systemic issue. This is a national issue.

This effort to improve teacher training is going to take collaboration of government with public higher education institutions, teachers associations and organizations, the business world, and the public. Common ground on our collective needs and desires must be established to proceed effectively and efficiently. And a balance in the education of our teachers must be found, just as it must for our students.

Overall, teachers "should be steeped in subject matter, but they should be no less be steeped in what makes that information digestible to children. It is a dual obligation that makes teaching as challenging as it is difficult" (Sarason, 1993, 152).

While teacher development is restructured to become more dependable, "in-service" education can be used more effectively. As alluded to previously, "in-service" is many times called staff development. In other professions, it is continuing education.

## Continuing Education

From my perspective as a veterinarian, when I attend large continuing education conferences, I spend some time preparing by evaluating what I feel are my areas of weakness in techniques, what topics I feel I should know more about, and what I feel would be beneficial to the practice (patients, clients, and employer).

The process for developing effective continuing education of existing professional educators must include assessing their deficits in understanding and filling those gaps. Those words make the job sound easy. But the required time and money to do it right, particularly in "failed" districts, make the effectiveness and efficiency of staff (teacher, administrator, counselor, and support) education extremely important. It must be well planned, focused, and doable, with all involved parties in agreement on the direction or at least acknowledging common interests. Now it sounds complicated.

As with most fields of study in education, many experts and much information abounds. It is worth sharing again that the Theory of Action and the Concerns-Based Adoption Model can serve us well to take individuals from whatever level of understanding or proficiency they are at and bring all to a higher level.

Teacher continuing education should always be done with the concerns of the teacher in mind and with adequate *time for adaptation* to the philosophies and ideas presented prior to any changes in the classroom. The idea is not to tell them how to teach but to help them teach in their own way, only better.

Unfortunately, many teachers now think of "professional development" as time spent in learning about a new program that is changed with a change of administration or on the whim of a new fad. Our efforts need to change to focusing education of existing teachers, counselors, and administrators on:

- The educational principles we value;
- How to identify and remedy problems they are seeing in their classrooms;
- The elements of how children learn best specific to their population of learners;
- The content knowledge of the subject or subjects they teach;
- Updates on what resources are available within a community to help with remedies; and
- The building and maintaining of essential partnerships.

Dr. Lawrence-Lightfoot in *The Essential Conversation* expressed her concern that most teachers "had not been adequately prepared in their professional training programs to build relationships with families as a central part or their work, nor were they getting support or guidance from their administrators and colleagues" (2003, xviii). She offered this solution:

> Three specific skills that teachers need in order to have productive interactions with parents:
>
> 1. Trained in the art of observation,
> 2. Trained in the skills of record keeping and documentation,
> 3. They must learn to listen. (105)

If parent-teacher conferences were less about test scores and more about discussing the child's strengths and limitations that need special support and individual attention, conferences would become "about collaborative problem solving using the insights of the teacher and the wisdom of the parents" (195).

Can you imagine how much further ahead the teacher would be each year if the observations, solutions, and strategies that proved successful or failed were recorded and used? These things aren't always measurable, but they matter. Less time spent in using trial and error to find out what others already knew about how the student learns best means more time advancing. For the student, it is one more step added in the name of "consistency."

## Judging Our Teachers

Until we find consistency in the professional development and continuing education of teachers and address all the issues that dysfunctional districts face, the discussion of evaluation of teachers is perhaps a moot point. If the *standard of practice* for teachers is not set, taught, and monitored properly, trying to develop a "standard" way to judge individual teachers individually and competitively makes no sense. If we aren't equally providing the necessary resources for teachers to do their jobs, judging them in a standard way is certainly not fair.

We need to remember that most school districts in this country have settled the question of what to teach and how to best go about it. So in the 43rd Annual Phi Delta Kappa International (PDK) poll on education issues done in conjunction with Gallup, we shouldn't be surprised that 71 percent of Americans say they "have *trust* and *confidence* in the men and women who are teaching in public schools." This year's poll, titled "Betting on Teachers," also found 73 percent of Americans preferred education policies that "give teachers flexibility to teach in ways they think best" over those that "require teachers to follow a prescribed curriculum so all students can learn the same content" (Bushaw, 2011).

In any given classroom, the teacher becomes their own manager. They plan the lesson, guide the students, and evaluate themselves and their students. As James Lewis Jr. explained, "The highest form of self-management is intrapreneurship" (1986, 172) and "if teachers are to become intrapreneurs, they must be given the freedom to act on their own" based on the principle that "organizational management should be based on observing problems from the bottom up and not from the top down" (173). This is a business model lesson we must learn to use. I believe the American public would agree.

If the American public is right, or even close, we are looking at roughly 70 percent of the time that teachers are "performing" to a satisfactory level. So if the majority of the country sees the majority of the teachers as competent, why have we started a war against the teachers unions? We should be focusing our efforts on improvements for the 30 percent that need it. It is not to the benefit of our students for us to continue fighting. Stop, look, and listen; we are closer to solving our problems than we seem to know.

Carrie Mathers and others wrote the research-based paper "Improving Instruction through Effective Teacher Evaluation: Options for States and Districts," leaning heavily on the work of the Midwest Regional Education Laboratory and other experts. It was written "to provide state and local policymakers with a comprehensive understanding of the measures used in teacher evaluation." You can't say the experts haven't tried to inform lawmakers.

This "brief" outlines the tools that can be used in teacher evaluations as well as the *strengths* and *limitations* in their uses. The tools include; lesson plans, classroom observations, self-assessments, portfolio assessments, student achievement data, and student work-sample reviews. The report also discusses *recommendations* and *realities* as well as who typically does the evaluations and how often. These factors are more *human variables* in the equation.

Before they started making "performance-based" laws, our lawmakers should have been asking, how do we "efficiently" and "reliably" measure teacher performance? If they did not know how, they put the cart before the horse, again, when they passed "pay-for-performance" laws; they made *uninformed decisions.*

To make evaluations "matter" to teachers or to hook it to accountability, the view presented in this "brief" was that "a good starting place is to consistently connect evaluation results to investments in teacher continuing education. Teachers may feel empowered and supported by the evaluation process if they see that it is designed to sustain their growth" (Mathers, Carrie, et al., 2008, 14).

Their overall conclusion was that "without a *careful review* and *inclusive dialogue* at the state and local levels about how to improve approaches to teacher evaluation, opportunities to truly influence changes in *teacher quality* are mostly empty promises" (17). In other words, we must use research and our collective experiences and expertise to best ensure our choices are informed and reasoned.

One thing has been constant over the years, "improving the quality of teachers should be the *top national education priority*" according to the American people (Bushaw & Lopez, 2010). And as with any profession, there must be ways to handle the individuals who do not meet the standards of the profession. To handle it through laws that impact the whole country is to throw out the whole bushel because of a few bad apples. Wasteful.

In veterinary medicine, when a client feels a violation of the standard of practice has occurred, a complaint is lodged and an investigation by a state board of our peers takes place. If the complaint is found to be valid, punishment ensues. The punishment could include continuing education in the area of practice where the violation occurred, but it can also mean removal from practice. The processes are in place. Those charged with oversight must do their jobs.

Our *leaders* must *ensure* proper professional development, relevant continuing education opportunities, personnel trained to *effectively* and *reliably* evaluate teachers, and the mechanisms for dismissal when necessary are in place and used responsibly. And for it to be an equitable process for teachers, the students must have equitable opportunities. Please consider that even excellent teachers, by whatever standard you make that judgment, can have their efforts thwarted if they don't have the resources to do their jobs.

## THE MATERIALS TO DO IT

The time has therefore come when a plan of universal education ought to be adopted in the United States.

—George Washington

Failure to provide the materials for all our students to succeed in school is a long-standing problem. We as a nation should be ashamed of the fact that we have not addressed it. We pontificate about our children being our greatest resource. We talk about investing in our future, our children. We say we value education. We state that we understand its importance to the future of our democracy. But we don't put our money where our mouths are.

Materials always cost money. And, to spend money wisely, you have to have a plan that helps you identify the materials essential to reaching your goal. Even without a plan, we know that material support for education consists of everything from the buildings themselves to books, paper and pencils, science and technology equipment, educators' pay, and, of course, the currently overshadowing cost of testing. This is the place for the business world to help the education system. We need help conducting a serious review and evaluation of the spending throughout the educational bureaucracy; we need to streamline this "system."

Smaller government is not better government when we make *uninformed decisions* that leave essential services crippled. Our government systems need to develop the efficiency and effectiveness that are currently only buzzwords. These words are being applied to the classroom when they need to be applied to the wasteful governing structure that we have created.

The building of school buildings is a perfect example. Over the many years of attending school board meetings, the board has spent countless hours discussing a building's features and aesthetic appeal. They never spent that kind of time debating whether it is time to reduce our first grade class sizes to fifteen students to ensure that we begin the job of educating by doing it right from the start. They never spent that much time discussing whether we have a sufficient number of books in our secondary schools to teach proper study habits.

Instead, the school architects happily presented yet another new design for our board to proudly attach their names. Over the years, as a watchful taxpayer, it has been unclear at times whether the essential elements of a healthy, efficient building were foremost in the decisions. In the animal industry, we have used science to determine the required elements of efficient buildings and have *disseminated that knowledge* through the Cooperative Extension System for producers to use, in the handbooks mentioned previously. But in this "system" we call public education, local boards continue to independently spend taxpayer dollars on architecture and design fees unknowingly spending dollars that could better be spent elsewhere. And now with the charter school movement, more buildings are going up independently, at taxpayer expense.

A duty of the U.S. Department of Education as outlined in the Smith-Towner Bill was to "conduct studies and investigations in the field of education and to report thereon" (1920, 577). All these meetings, all the individual school building plans, and the national report on the essential elements of healthy school buildings has not been discussed. Does it exist? Has no one considered our local tax dollars important enough to assist us in using them wisely?

It isn't just ill-informed school boards that are so costly; there are multiple issues with the way we fund and govern schools that are costing us dearly. Darling-Hammond addressed this topic in saying, "An important role of the state is to evaluate the outcomes of programs and strategies to inform the decisions of localities about where to invest most wisely" (2010, 102). If we have 70 percent of our schools performing well, shouldn't we be looking at providing material support to those lacking it? Yet "during the Reagan administration, some federal data collection and reporting that allowed analysis of inequalities was discontinued" (104).

I can tell you with certainty that there are inequalities nationally—between states, within states, and within local districts—school-to-school within the same district. And if we lack the capacity to evaluate those inequalities, we cannot correct them. The states that cannot meet their responsibilities themselves need federal guidance and support.

It was President Reagan that appointed the commission to study excellence in education. *A Nation at Risk* stated, "Excellence costs. But in the long run mediocrity costs far more" (33). To accept mediocrity anywhere, to refuse to face the facts, is to accept the cost of failures.

This subject of materials is all about money. Unfortunately, it is a fact we cannot circumvent, nor can we get around the fact that currently money spent for education and the politics tied to that money cannot soon be separated. In observing the politics of my time, it has appeared that our government would cut education dollars whenever *financial panic* arose. That panic has more often been caused by our overspending on wars and we can now say, by financial speculators dependent on government bailouts, our dollars.

When reading about the history of education through H. G. Good, one should be taken aback to hear him make the same observation of the past and his time. His book was published the year I was born. His conclusion was that this society does not sufficiently support its schools. And he offered a cure. It is "to be found in *fuller information*. To doubt this is to doubt that the public is genuinely favorable to good education" (1956, 17–18).

From the past to the present, we seem to understand that it is essential to our society that we be informed and support a public education system. As Angela Engel says nicely in *Seeds of Tomorrow*, "Those students denied opportunities are at the greatest risk to become dependent adults, exacting costs to the taxpayer tenfold in the long run. Prisons and unemployment compensation are substantially more expensive than the cost of providing quality public education to all children" (2009, 90). Will we now stop fighting, work together to inform the public, and let them decide if quality public education is something they value enough to pay for?

# THE PLUS MARKS, COMMUNICATE AND COOPERATE

It takes a great man to be a good listener.

—Calvin Coolidge

Communication and cooperation—they aren't small words. They are huge words that, when their impact on the educational formula is considered, function as the stir stick in the beaker; they become essential to the mixing of the elements of success. Another way to see their importance would be to look at them as really, really big sticks in the boundary waters surrounding our school communities.

As Minzey and LeTarte point out, "there is more than a verbal tie between the words common, community, and communication." In true communities, there is a "common understanding" of "aims, beliefs, aspirations, knowledge—like-mindedness" (1994, 52). This is our commonality. It doesn't just happen; it is built through communications with one another.

For immediate impact in the schools that need our help, we need to look at "the people side of schooling" (Lewis, 1986, xxi). As Lewis points out, "In some cases, the school district has never even bothered to articulate its values or set forth a philosophy. This is an essential first step if people within the district are to understand how they should act and why" (31). This communication of expectations is the foundation for building *a cooperative culture for teaching and learning* in the classrooms, and support in the wider community.

And, in thinking about these words—communicate, cooperate— the ability to listen to one another is an element common to both.

Do governing boards, politicians, administrators, and professional educators with rigid ideologies find themselves unable to listen? Did they not learn that skill in school or at home? Or have they just chosen not to listen? The unwillingness or inability to listen is a major factor contributing to not only our problems in education but other social problems as well. The wars won't end until listening begins in earnest.

Civil unrest is surfacing in a variety of public arenas over issues from pollution of local land and water, to control of our media by monopolies, and the disproportionate influence of money in politics; the stories all sound the same. You, the public, go to public meetings where the voiced *consensus* is the same as your own. But you later hear that the final decision is not what you heard voiced at the public meeting. This type of blatant disregard for public opinion demonstrates a lack of respect for the democratic process, a lack of respect for the people. It's time we come to an understanding of what it means to work for the public. Too many "public servants" aren't cooperating. They are allowing their "cult of professionalism" to get in the way of serving the public needs.

A solution may be found in the words of Jaime R., "Individually and as a species we must get better and better at being human beings. This is the thought for the new educational paradigm: to get better and better." I believe if people are given the right tools they will make things better.

We should and we can teach others how to listen. And we can educate about the cult of professionalism and its effect on our ability to listen to one another. We all belong to a cult. You don't have to be labeled a professional to join. Parents do it: we know best. Philanthropists, corporations, and politicians do it: they know best. Expert educators do it too.

Barriers to listening must be understood to be overcome. Both communications and cooperation are improved from learning about and coming to an understanding of why we build barriers around ourselves. Ultimately this means you come to recognize why you don't want to listen and that you must do so in order to *respect* and consider the other person's opinion.

In *Fahrenheit 451*, a novel by Ray Bradbury about book burning, the character Faber says, "I saw the way things were going, a long time back. I said nothing. . . . Nobody listens any more" (1953, 82). You can't make people listen but each of us can recognize that we should and begin to practice listening regularly. Of course, that alone does not increase our chances of communicating effectively—other things need to occur for information to make a difference in people's lives. Through the character Montag, the wise old man, Bradbury makes clear the importance of "1) the quality of the information, 2) the leisure to digest it, and 3) the right to carry out actions based on what we learn from the interaction of the first two" (84). And if people are not using terminology you are familiar with, the quality of the information is lost right away.

Educators and scientists are well known for not being trained to communicate well to the general public. They tend to use words or acronyms common to their own areas of expertise but unknown to ordinary people. This can leave the general public feeling dim. In veterinary medicine, we were trained to communicate in terms that the person we are addressing can understand. Educators are aware of this situation, but consistency in practice of good communications skills is lacking.

The necessity to develop *effective* communications, with the intention of creating an informed public in order to build cooperation, can't be stressed enough. If we ever hope to build "civic capacity"—school-community partnerships—where it is lacking, we must be able to communicate and cooperate. To illustrate what taking "an active role in supporting schools" might look like for public and private organizations and institutions, a discussion on developing *civic capacity* by Noguera is summarized here.

These are capacity building activities other communities are already doing:

- providing community volunteers as mentors and tutors,
- developing work-related internships and support of career academies,
- assisting and supporting continuing education for educators,
- coordinating health and social services to fulfill students' needs. (2003, 98–101)

A community education organizer could help in bridging the many "gaps" encountered in building relationships by working toward clarifying language usage, improving communications, and coordinating the use of existing resources. But the ultimate solution to our lack of cooperation within our government, with regard to education, can only be found when an open discussion of their role in education is defined and clarified by the people. What do we expect from our "public school system"?

## THE EQUAL SIGN

> Equality, in the American sense of the word, is not an end but a beginning. It means that, so far as the state can do it, all children shall start in the race of life on an even line. The chief agency for this purpose is the public school system.
> —Edwin E. Slosson

In the education equation presented, what would the equal sign represent? What is the equalizer? Those are the questions I asked myself in order to write this section.

The first answer was easy. On a day-to-day basis, that would be the principal of the school. The principal needs to know the students, the teachers, what materials are needed, and have a clear vision of the goals of each grade level or subject, in addition to understanding the teaching process; receiving input from teachers, students, and parents; and communicating with all stakeholders. And in the end, it is the principal that can best evaluate the school's effectiveness.

The principal is the most important administrator in the hierarchy of school administration. This person sets the tone for the *school culture* and is responsible for establishing *the conditions* under which teaching and learning will occur. And when it comes to partnerships with parents, they are front and center in the boundary where improvements happen. "School principals can lead grassroots efforts toward partnership by creating opportunities for joint activities, problem solving, and dialogue in which parents and educators can learn and understand their different perspectives . . . nurture partnership formation" (Price-Mitchell, 2009, 21). Our success in schools depends on them, thus making their preparation and continued education of extreme importance. And they must know and follow the policies and laws governing their school.

Laws would be my second answer to what should act as an equalizer. This is a harder answer to discuss because it isn't holding true in our republic today. We are supposed to be a land of law-abiding citizens, but multiple examples exist of laws we choose to ignore. Some laws are detrimental and other laws we know nothing about. But there are many examples of laws that attempted to serve us well.

The Smith-Towner Bill of 1918 sought to establish the U.S. Department of Education and the position of secretary of education. The bill came into existence to encourage the following:

* Removal of illiteracy,
* Americanization,
* Physical education,
* Improvement of educational opportunities through

    * improved teacher preparation and in-service,
    * increased teacher salaries,
    * extension of public libraries and other opportunities.

* Research and reporting on these areas in such other fields as in the judgment of the Secretary of Education, may require attention and study (1920, 577).

In order to participate in the funding, this law set as requirements that a school would be in session at least twenty-four weeks, that all children ages seven to fourteen had to attend, and that the English language would be the basic language of instruction.

The debate at the time in favor of the nine-page Smith-Towner Bill was that it was seen as the only way to improve the illiteracy rate, nationally. The argument against it was that it would expose the states to the "potentially" corrupt influences of national politics. How far have we come with that debate?

But, "the department" went in and out of favor and law with the swinging pendulum of power; centralized to local. The emphasis of the law and our purposes in education shifted as much as the idea of a national department of education.

In 1979, Congress created the Department of Education as we know it. The purposes for its existence are to:

* ensure access to equal educational opportunity;

- supplement and complement the efforts to improve the quality of education;
- encourage involvement of the public, parents, and students;
- promote improvements through research, evaluation, shared information;
- improve coordination;
- improve management and efficiencies;
- increase accountability of federal programs to the President, Congress, and the public.

Another law whose purpose has been ignored is President Johnson's thirty-five-page 1965 Elementary and Secondary Education Act. It attempted to make right the wrong that is being done by *state* and *local* education agencies in *neglecting* educational needs of children in low-income communities. As judged by then secretary of health, education, and welfare, Wilbur J. Cohen, local districts appeared to be using the funds appropriately. His opinion was that the money was going to "activities most directly serving *the student's needs*: improving the quality of instruction and offering such services as medical care, guidance and counseling, and food" (*Congressional Quarterly*, 1969, 711).

That was then. Now we have our thousand-page No Child Left Behind (NCLB) bill that even I don't care to read, so I'll never understand how it can act as an equalizer, if that is its intention. It is time for the *Federalist Papers* to be required reading for lawmakers. They must note Alexander Hamilton's words in *The Federalist*, no. 25, where he said, "Wise politicians will be cautious about fettering the government with *restrictions, that cannot be observed*" (December 21, 1787).

How can the NCLB law serve the people as a guide? How can the people have any part in enforcement and *accountability* of laws we don't understand? It is time to question the wisdom of our politicians. It is time to make the law right (see Addendum 1). And it is time for inward reflection because we have obviously grown out of touch with our roots, our beginnings, our purposes, and our own laws. Laws are not serving as the equalizer that they should be; neither is money.

Unfortunately, money is the third answer as to what could be an equalizer. Money has been discussed in talking about providing the materials necessary for educational opportunity. Our funding formulas and the hodgepodge granting systems we have devised have led to greater inequalities and lost dollars in administering programs and granting grants. As Stephanie B. explained her situation in teaching children who come to school having never used a coloring book or held a pencil, these kids need extra resources so "why the need to apply for what they should have." We must be "granted" essentials.

What H. G. Good had pointed out, in reference to philanthropic monies, can be applied to the federal granting system: grants have created a situation where we are "offering a full meal to a fortunate few but only crumbs to the many" (1956, 141). This is another place where the great business minds of our country could really help by devising a way to gradually change funding procedures without disturbing the functioning of our schools in the process.

With insight and vision, together, we could provide funding aimed at ensuring equal educational opportunity. My faith in the innovative ways of Americans is intact. "Innovation is not in short supply in American education. More rare are the *systems* that proactively construct the *conditions* under which high-quality teaching and schooling can be widely available" (Darling-Hammond, 2010, 162). We can build such systems, I'm sure of it. We can provide equal educational opportunities if we set our minds and hearts on that goal.

## EQUAL EDUCATIONAL OPPORTUNITY

The democracy which proclaims equality of opportunity as its ideal requires an education in which learning and social application, ideas and practice, work and recognition of the meaning of what is done, are united from the beginning and for all.

—John Dewey

What does equal educational opportunity mean? Equal education does not mean the same education for all. Perhaps we should think about it as relevant education. Perhaps we should consider equal opportunity to a relevant education as our goal. We need to answer the question, for it is the overriding question whose answer should guide all our plans. To take aim, we must identify the target. The target has become blurred by our insistence on standards and testing.

The Cooperative Study of Secondary School Standards clearly stated in their chapter on guiding principles what they determined to be the desired results of *the learning process*. They felt it should include factual information or knowledge, meaning and understanding, an ability to combine knowledge and understanding with skill, desirable attitudes, worthy ideals, purposes, appreciations, interests, and resultant intelligent participation in general life activities. Are these still our guiding principles?

Look closely and you may find we all want the same things and they are stated for us in these guiding principles. If you don't agree, let's at least agree that the time has come for us to make known our desired direction for education—our "reform" goals, not standards but guiding principles. It's our duty to act given the fact that education professionals seem incapable of changing their system. It appears that a catalyst has become a crucial ingredient to making this reaction produce.

## THE CATALYST: THE PUBLIC

All measures designed to promote education must depend for their success, in this country, on the hearty cooperation of public opinion. It is only by enlightening and concentrating that opinion that powerful effects can be produced.
—Horace Mann

I believe that the majority of people here in the United States do care about education or would care if they understood the situation and *believed* that hope for improving and maintaining the system exists. Understanding starts with knowing the facts. We need to analyze, discuss, and face the facts; then, question the facts to get to the truth.

Without the truth, the public can't provide the check and balance they should to see through a plan for *creating an effective education system* that provides equal educational opportunity. It deserves repeating: it is our *duty* as citizens to get all pertinent facts and pursue the needed improvements. Change will only come about through people, both in and outside the system, who have the desire in their hearts to do what is right. And as Eric Hoffer notes in *The True Believer: Thoughts on the Nature of Mass Movements*, "Fear of the future causes us to lean against and cling to the present, while *faith* in the future renders us receptive to change" (1951, 9). We must think we can; we must believe in our strength as a people.

Fear should not hold us back; we have the answers. We have a compass. We now need some direction. The process for laying down a plan has been started many times before by many presidents.

In 1955 President Eisenhower called the White House conference on education. According to an account of it by H. G. Good, "Connecticut reported her problems were the universal ones; the shortage of teachers, buildings, and finances and the lack of effective ways and means to gain and hold a lively and well-informed public interest in the schools. The conference members concluded that they should deal with: (1) the need for school construction, (2) the educational aims/what the schools should accomplish, (3) economic and efficient organization, (4) recruitment and retention of good teachers, (5) financing of schools, and (6) maintenance of public interest in schools" (1956, 558). It was felt at the time that *stimulation of public interest* in schools had been an achievement of the conference, and it was reported that the participants walked away feeling that "if local and state conferences were continued as planned in some areas, the White House Conference will have been a success" (558).

In the Western Historical Manuscript Collection through the University of Missouri–St. Louis, a trace of that conference can be found in a report of the St. Louis–St. Louis County White House Conference on Education that boasts to have "established *effective communication* among lay citizens, educators, and legislators; and its recommendations have served as guides to developing policy, public understanding, and legislative support." In addition, they claim to have brought in "experts to speak on vital issues in education." It can be done.

To keep the public interest in the forefront of our decision making on public school support—transparency, public knowledge, and open dialogue are essential.

The hope is that by now these ideas are sounding familiar and that you can see that there is more than ample evidence to say, we have the answers. Now the time is upon us to pause and think hard about the road that led us to this point and the direction we now wish to take. Our children need us to choose wisely this time.

We need systemic change; we need a vigilant public. We all would like to elect the person to solve our problems for us. We would like that person to have vision, principles in line with our own, and integrity. That we must participate fully in the political process ourselves, and remain vigilant, seems to be something we don't care to do. Some think we have no way out of this political mess that we have created, which is blocking our progress in education and on multiple fronts. Others just know it is essential that we do find our way.

When you believe in acting thoughtfully, with common sense, with an *exchange of ideas* and *consensus* as your guides, change becomes desirable. No harm needs to come to the American children that we have promised to provide with equal educational opportunity. I have tried to live my adult life and practice in my profession by following the first law of medicine—above all else, do no harm. We can do the same for all the children of the United States. We must *act as the catalyst*.

The radical changes inflicted on us by our state governments test-based education "reforms" and nationally through the dictates of No Child Left Behind harmed generations of children by wasting their instructional time and not giving them *equal access* to the promised opportunities. Where were the leaders who are charged with looking out for the greater good of the people? Where were the people?

This time, we must answer the call for equality. And as we use the formula for educational success, consider it to be an algebraic-type equation. It has variables. It can never be standardized but it can always be solved.

# Chapter Eight

# What's Next? Starting in the Trenches

> The great keep the poor from the knowledge of their rights; and it is knowledge alone, diffused through the whole body of the people, that can preserve them from tyranny.
>
> —John Adams

Parents can offer insight into how their child learns best. Parents want to have a say in how and what their child is taught. Teachers want to have a say in what and how they teach. Local communities must have a voice in letting their needs of the education system be known.

By failing to inform the public of the knowledge we have gained through research in the education field and about the change process, we have failed to use that knowledge to its fullest benefit, for all children. Too many communities appear to not know how to take the next step.

Top-down mandates for "school reform" ignore the human element. People must be given the information and time to prepare themselves for change. We need to develop the capacity to change within ourselves. Human capacity is based on trust, respect, and a willingness to accept feedback and work toward improvement.

To fulfill our local responsibility to improve our schools, it's time to engage community members in the process, allow a free flowing exchange of information and ideas, and encourage further action by offering opportunities to participate. This process takes us from the foundation of best practices to the next levels of developing a shared vision and progressing to the actions necessary to improve our schools.

Ordinary Americans see the need for school improvement. They "get it" but they still haven't taken the reins and moved forward. It is that crucial first step that is always so difficult; we must face the facts. As Michael Jackson sings in "Man in the Mirror," "And no message could have been any clearer: If you wanna make the world a better place take a look at yourself and then make a change."

## WHERE TO BEGIN?

You have to begin where you are and you have to face your reality with all its truths, acknowledging the problems with the pleasantries. Celebrate what you can but move on to tackle what you must. When problems seem too difficult, don't skirt around them; meet them head on knowing that others have faced them before.

A note written to myself in the back of a notepad said, "What have we learned? If something isn't 'clicking,' don't move on; go back." In every experiment, failed or successful, a lesson is to be learned. In the analysis of a problem, go back and review the arguments. Let's go back and see if we can begin with a better *understanding*.

Knowledge, no matter how good and relevant, does us no good if we can't or won't put it to work for us. Muriel Lester talked about "the sin of being negative instead of positive . . . we theorized and argued, but we did not act . . . we had no clear aim" (1940, 15). Our "leadership" has failed to assist in diffusing knowledge about our ability to create *positive conditions* for change. We cannot wait to act until the day those leaders finally understand; we have children here in the trenches that need us to serve their educational needs today. Our aim should *focus* on what's best for children. Positively!

Our local responsibility requires us to make our best effort to collaborate. That responsibility begins with setting the stage for *improved school climates*. If there are local "adult" wars raging, they must end. Take this advice from Pedro C., "It's not about winning or losing; it's about being informed and getting involved."

Think about the formula for educational success: kids ready to learn, teachers ready to teach, and the materials to do it. Think about the elements that complete the formula, making it work for students: communications, cooperation, effective principals, and policies that support public schools. Then, listen and think. What have you heard yourself and others saying? Can you hear our *common* desires?

While lurking in the muddy boundary waters, I've been keeping a journal. What I know ordinary people understand is that children need a *solid beginning*. Teachers, children, and their families need a broad *support* system. We want our children to be schooled in a *safe* and *nurturing environment*. And we want them to have every *opportunity* available to realize their personal best.

For the system to assist in providing excellent education for all, we must begin by asking the center of our existing education system, our colleges and universities, to provide us *guidance*. They have been the constant strength and pride of our American education system. They have the researchers. They have the experts. And they are producing our next generation of teachers.

Rhona Weinstein likened the sequence of schooling to a pipeline, indicating that universities are "the last station in the pipeline." Liking the analogy but seeing through a different lens, consider the perspective that universities are the first station; they control the spigot. As Seymour Sarason wrote, "If and when educational theorists, researchers, and policy experts in our universities participate in the discussion, we have reason to be somewhat hopeful" (1993, 269–270). They hold the potential to help prevent problems in our system as well as in assisting communities in solving their own problems. There is reason for hope.

This is a time for hope but hope is not a strategy. Currently, higher education personnel don't appear to have an obligation to spread their knowledge in order to help us develop a broad base of support for school improvements. These highly intellectual individuals seem to lack the ability to reach the common people with their research. They won't turn the spigot unless we ask. Maybe they don't realize that the common people are the ones needed to drive improvements in "our system." We need to tell them.

The researchers in education know research continues, results vary, one study contradicts another, but they need help coming to the realization that we must *forge on* using the information they have, combined with our common sense, in deciding *what is right for our children* and what practices will help us move toward providing true equity in learning opportunities for the children in our respective communities.

As Minzey and LeTarte explain, "knowledge is necessary to find good solutions. The involvement of many people, motivated to obtain the best answers to *community problems*, will result in better solutions than those made by a limited number of like-minded persons with status" (1994, 191). If you see "your community" as local, *Reforming Public Schools through Community Education* has a chapter devoted to "organizing a community for process." Decision making is a process, as is change.

As Francis Keppel pointed to in *The Necessary Revolution in American Education*, "The problem here is not what the precise policy shall be but rather how shall decision on that policy be reached" (1966, 60). School policies drive practices, ideas are plentiful, and the best fit for your own schools will be found when we put our heads together.

Many successful practices have been presented to demonstrate the fact that we have answers, hopefully not so many that they seem overwhelming. Remember, go back to the formula for educational success if you get lost, and grab it to use as a compass. To illustrate how we can put these concepts into a plan that moves us into action, let's go through a few easy examples.

## HOW IT WORKS

To begin, let's imagine that we are in a community that appears apathetic, seems uninformed, and "wars" are raging between a handful of citizen "reformers," administration, school staff, and the school board. Easy example, right? But good fortune has been bestowed on this community; a community education organizer has been hired. The turmoil within this community necessitates that this person first act as an ombudsman and investigate the citizens' complaints that have been documented.

This person is then able to go about gathering and recording statistics, surveying the stakeholders, assessing the available relevant resources, and developing a plan of attack for communications. The topics of interest and concern to the community center around classroom discipline issues, unequal expectations for the poor and minority students, and lack of learning materials and opportunities as well as unequal distribution between schools and classrooms.

A recurrent theme voiced by a variety of community members and teachers is the need for respect both in the schools and in the community in general. Suggestions are gathered and exploration produces a local expert willing to come, present research on the topic, and lead a discussion. The expert is politely given instruction on communicating in simple terms, defining words where needed, and asked to keep in-depth statistics to a minimum.

The expert does an excellent job of reminding us that respect is essential to the functioning of our society and that children learn using their senses. The audience agrees that children must come to school with the knowledge of what it feels, looks, and sounds like to be respectful of themselves and others, particularly their teachers and classmates.

We as a "learning community" (parents, teachers, administrators, and the public) learn together about recognizing and really *internalizing* for ourselves what respect looks like, feels like, and sounds like so that we can *teach it first by example.* We come away from the evening with a deeper understanding and mutual agreement of how respect is demonstrated and how to recognize when a child or ourselves crosses the line to disrespect.

It is at that point that the conversation moves to the bigger issue of discipline. A suggestion is made to look into a program called Sound Discipline, whose work is based on experience and "evidence from the scientific literature." They provide programs for both parents and teachers with the belief that "discipline should be both firm and responsive" in order to "promote healthy development" and decreased "social risks" (sounddiscipline.org). The community education organizer leaves with plans to move forward on this next area to research while the other adults go on their way with an eye on the issue and with plans to explore more opportunities and resources. Plus, they will try harder to be respectful of each other.

As discussed by Robert V. Bullough in *Professional Learning Communities and the Eight-Year Study*, this process is in line with what researchers associated with the Southwest Educational Development Laboratory have identified as five "dimensions" of professional learning communities (2007, 176). Our process demonstrates:

1. Supportive and shared leadership—we come together because we care and are willing,
2. Shared values and vision—respect is seen as essential to increased civility in our community,
3. Collective learning and application of that learning—we shared information and we will use it,
4. Supportive conditions—we listened and participated,
5. Shared personal practice—we will share our knowledge with others and build support.

If the topics of discipline, bullying, or "respect"—school climate issues—are your area of focus or interest, a gathering like this is your opportunity to bring your views on the subject to the table, ask your questions, and share your thoughts on how best to accomplish the task of creating climates more conducive to learning using the research base the experts provided and the available resources within your community. This provides the opportunity for an *open exchange of ideas* from the higher education institutions to the local district. It allows the experts the chance to transfer the knowledge produced from research to parents, school systems, and the community. The community gets to take part in planning the next necessary action, thus giving the plan a better chance of being successful.

The ideas discussed or plans decided on would be communicated through a variety of routes to the part of the public that was not in attendance. The research on the idea of respect, how we can all work toward building respect, and the plans to move forward with tackling the larger topic of discipline would be presented in a way that all could understand.

This type of process helps in establishing guiding principles in our education system based on research and public input, helps shape our vision, and becomes self-perpetuating in that the knowledge originated in a higher education institution and, if the ideas meet public approval and are successful, they are taught to the next generation of teachers, counselors, and administrators. If we value an ideal or principle, it circles back into the teachers' curriculum. This is a vicious cycle, a process, in which we should want to get trapped.

The same process can be applied to the complaint that children in the district are being treated differently depending on their socioeconomic or minority status. This complaint is directed at the terminology in our district handbooks saying we will hold "high expectations for all students." It is supposed to be a principle that has been widely accepted already. The problem currently is that these are only words on paper until their application in our classrooms, homes, and communities is realized.

Those simple words, "high expectations for all students," are commonly seen in schools' vision or mission statements, or in state and national education propaganda. If the process described in the first example had been used, that complex concept of "high expectations" would have been fully explained, the research presented to the public and school staff, and its significance to local curricula explored in depth by the stakeholders. Instead, it appears that "setting high expectations" has wrongly been put into practice by first laying out a list of knowledge standards. Then we expect the teacher to drill those into the student and expect the student to perform their regurgitation ritual on tests. We call that "educational achievement."

The true complexity of expectations and their effect on students is explained in depth in *Reaching Higher: The Power of Expectations in Schooling* (Weinstein, 2002). It is a subject that is deserving of an evening lecture, especially since the impression is that the public and many educators do not understand what is at the heart of "high expectations." It is a topic that is useful for parents as well as teachers and has the potential to make a huge difference in people's lives.

For the purposes of this example, let's assume that no local expert was able to deliver the topic satisfactorily. Instead, we were able to get a faculty member from our local college to moderate discussion and provide an introduction of the topic. We had access to video conferencing that we used to connect to an expert in another part of the country who agreed to provide answers to our questions.

The introduction *clarified the concept* as something that is not necessarily a new one. Many an adult may recall overhearing parents talking about their belief that, if you keep telling a child that they are "bad" and "will never amount to anything," the child starts to believe you and what you are saying more likely becomes a reality. In other words, what you are expecting to happen becomes the truth; it is the phenomenon of a "self-fulfilling prophesy." It has both positive and negative aspects. On the positive side, if you tell a child they are capable of accomplishing a task, it is more likely they can.

To apply this concept in a classroom setting, educators would need to be made aware of the verbal and nonverbal cues that we adults relay to kids. An example of a verbal cue was encountered when one of my son's math teachers told him that he would "never be good at trigonometry." Nonverbal examples include things like putting young students into ability groups, especially when they are labeled as "high" and "low," or designated in any way that can be deciphered by kids. Kids in the low group aren't *expected* to be able to accomplish the same work as those in the high group. Placement in special programs for the "slow" kids is another nonverbal cue, as is "faster" kids getting to go do more interesting things. These nonverbal examples are getting at the very structure and content of what we teach (the curriculum). Children are made aware of their shortcomings by our actions and reactions to their work. Our actions in educational settings tell kids what we expect of them and that has an effect on their academic outcome.

The good news is there are "resilience pathways" for kids to avoid falling prey to negative self-fulfilling prophesies. With the help of my dad's old math books, just such a path for my son was provided. He was told that we thought the problem was that the book he was given to use and the way the subject was presented just didn't "jive" with the way he learns. We didn't do much. We showed him how the material was taught in the past; he did well in the class and the highest score on his ACT was in trigonometry. The expectation was that he could do it, and he did.

The effects that high academic expectations can have on students' educational outcomes would be impossible to fully evaluate in any type of humane research. The debate on the subject may continue. But ask yourself: Is there harm in creating what amounts to a positive nurturing learning environment where all children, no matter their "status," are provided *challenging opportunities* and *expected* to do well?

Shouldn't we want all children to be given the opportunity to demonstrate how high they can reach when we don't limit them by words or actions? If this is what we want, what we value, shouldn't we be working with our teacher preparation programs to ensure that the next generation of teachers fully comprehends the principles of high expectations and self-fulfilling prophesies in order to prevent problems in the future? And really, how much would it cost to put together some community information pieces?

This subject of high expectations is as important for parents to learn about as it is for the teachers. We need to be able to recognize when the educational system is not holding high expectations for our students, plus we need to become more sensitive to the cues we send to our own children at home. The understanding of the concept of high expectations needs to be spread throughout our communities.

In our hypothetical community, the teachers' and administrators' input to the community education organizer included multiple requests for the topic of materials support to be brought to the community's attention. In this instance, the educators were specifically referring to the lack of science materials in some elementary schools and hands-on opportunities for older students to apply relevancy to their education and for exposure to career opportunities.

For information on science materials support, we can turn to neighboring states and other local districts that have science centers. Some of them have arranged for community volunteer organizations to help put together science kits for easy use in classrooms. Others have purchased kits and called on volunteers to help keep them in order or help with hands-on projects in their classrooms. Nonprofit and for-profit organizations are available to come and explain how they work and present choices so a community can determine what works best for them.

To convey the need for learning opportunities to the community, we looked again at the schools referred to as the Met. At the Met, all students have opportunities to do internships based on their interests. Through his observations and experiences there, Eliot Levine got to see "hands-on" applied in a way much bigger than just in science classes. He made a statement in his book that really hits home at this moment in time. He said, "Learning through doing is as old as humanity. The artificial rift between classroom and hands-on learning is a modern invention whose fallout is becoming apparent" (2002, 43).

We can reverse the effects of the fallout and prevent the rift in the classrooms in the future if we bring to our own communities the information and the inspiration of those that have been successful in implementing community projects that hold students' interest and keep them in school. Community members need to be made aware of what they can do to help, and they don't have to chart new territory to do it. Research and the experiences of others can guide their actions.

Bringing research to the people, for their use, is a course of action that can be applied to the many teaching principles and basic beliefs in human behaviors that need to be examined in the process of deciding what we value in education and how we can use what we know to improve our schools. The point is to have you consider *the process* used to decide what we value, how to use those valued principles in the formation of our goals, and how to foster action.

This same process could be applied by the stakeholders at each school, keeping the developmental stage of the learners and their interests in mind. And this is where a strong and reasoned principal makes a school function. It comes back to *trust*. For us to allow this level of local control "across this country," Deborah Meier explains that "there are at least four critical steps on the road to trust: 1) build a community-wide consensus about the essential purposes of schools and education, 2) agree on what to do about minority view points, 3) select key educational leaders honoring the view of both families and professionals, 4) provide equal resources to the rich and poor" (2004, 76–77).

As you can see in the examples and the process that they were meant to demonstrate, our success in school improvement depends on coordination, cooperation, and communication.

## THE INSTITUTE FOR DIFFUSION OF KNOWLEDGE

Transfer of pertinent information is an essential piece in fostering informed decisions. Information must be communicated in understandable language, yet nobody is currently responsible for that piece of the equation. If elections are any indication, it should be painfully clear that getting and deciphering the facts has become too time-consuming for the working class. We need a better way. Knowledge should be the key to any "reform" decisions we make. It is essential to the responsible use of the process that I have been describing. "The process" itself is extremely important. It is the democratic process.

Seymour Sarason asked, "How can we justify our belief in the democratic principle elsewhere and then go back entirely upon it when we come to education?" (1993, 121). If we are to be successful, we can't and we shouldn't continue this practice out of habit. It's irresponsible. It's time we changed. Many believe the time has come for a more participatory democracy.

We must keep in mind that the downfall of a democracy can come about when the majority is wrong. It does happen; the majority is not always right. That is why an open exchange of ideas becomes so important. It can allow the *voice of reason* to enter the debate, if people listen to one another. The Junto and the American Lyceum were designed to provide information and foster that exchange of ideas.

We don't have to reinvent the wheel to set in motion the communication component of the equation. We have an excellent *adult education agency* in place that could serve the function of helping supply continuing education for teachers, counselors, and administration, and organizing opportunities for education on educational issues for parents and the community.

That agency prides itself on following these principles:

1. Fostering cooperation between the funding of its programs and other aspects of its work, including cooperation with other existing organizations (such as parent and teacher organizations in this example),
2. Always directing its programs based on stakeholder input (parents, children, teachers, administrators, and the greater community in this case),
3. Providing programs that are research based,
4. And always evaluating its programs to provide accountability to its own system.

That agency is the Cooperative Extension System of our land grant university system.

Extension services aren't just an outreaching of information. You shouldn't expect results if all you do is deliver information. Single lectures, publishing articles (or books), or making handbooks isn't enough. Ordinary busy people need "on the ground" assistance to put ideas into practice. We need experts that extend information into communities with personal delivery and are there to follow through, follow up, and be there for the public to consult with. That's what extension was designed to do—put research into practice—make knowledge work for people.

The Reagan administration report, *A Nation at Risk*, held this service high as an example of America's can do spirit. It recognized that "Despite the obstacles and difficulties that inhibit the pursuit of superior educational attainment, we are confident, with history as our guide, that we can meet our goal. The American educational system has responded to previous challenges with remarkable success. In the 19th century our land-grant colleges and universities provided the *research* and *training* that developed our Nation's natural resources and the rich agricultural bounty of the American farm" (1983, 33).

Many people wrongly think of the Cooperative Extension System as an institution solely based on agricultural education. It's not; it has many divisions depending on the needs in a county and includes family and consumer sciences and community development branches of service. It should be the logical extension service for education, given its heritage going back to Benjamin Franklin's Junto. But my impression is that schools of education have chosen not to use this system.

It appears that many schools of education have chosen to remain within their own cult. For our education system to function as a system, people must lower their walls, come down from the ivory towers, and work together. The institutional or personal barriers that have been erected must come down. Higher education cannot act in isolation.

Remember the components of communication and cooperation? They represented the plus marks in the equation. They bring the elements of success together and they should bring the people together so that they can act as the catalyst for change. Each of us must realize what we need to do to foster understanding and the process of change itself. We can make "change" work for the benefit of children as long as we keep their needs in focus.

For the formula for educational success to work, we must use our heads, our hearts, and our history. We must recognize what reform is and remember that it has been tried before, repeatedly, and with the same result of not changing the system, not completing the equation, and never, to date, reaching the goal of equal educational opportunity. We must resist our temptation to take the small, relatively easy pieces only and not tackle the bigger picture.

## WHERE THE GOING GETS TOUGH

The toughest element to tackle within the formula for educational success is the "Materials to Do It." We looked at an easy example, without details, without looking at the bigger piece. This money issue most certainly: (1) requires the most effort from the public to provide that much-needed catalyst for change, (2) is the hardest concept to understand the complexity of, and (3) without a doubt is the most controversial.

The material support for education comes in many forms. Much of the support for education costs the system nothing, or little, if it is done in a spirit of cooperation with community members, nonprofits, or volunteer groups. Those things are totally dependent on community efforts. That support is of extreme importance, but we must face the fact that the schools that most need our help in an improvement process are most likely to lack the resources to do so. In the trenches, we need *the country* to have an open discussion about governmental support for the material needs of underserved children.

Some may argue here that equality in funding has not led to equality in educational opportunity. I agree. But we must get our minds around the idea that equality in funding is not the same as adequate and equitable funding. This is where we have to keep our goal in mind and be very careful not to take funding, as a separate entity, out of the equation for educational success.

That may be where funding "reforms" have failed to demonstrate themselves as the "cure" in providing better student outcomes. School improvement requires all the pieces.

It appears these reforms in funding didn't work in consort with defining equal opportunities for a quality education and what efforts that entails. In short, some schools require more effort and therefore more money to get them up to a satisfactory quality.

Adequate financial support for education should not be dependent on where you live. Financial *support* for education should be a *national priority* never again to be tampered with because of the cost of war. In the United States at this crucial moment in time, we can't afford to waste the potential talent of any of our children, rich or poor.

Appropriate material support for education is financial support, is taxation, is supposed to be dealt with through representation, is married to politics, is directed by big business, and has failed our children. This is the part of the equation that continues to resist reform of any kind at the national level, where it must start—but not with reform.

We must insist on revolutionizing our governing structure of education, from top to bottom, to provide us the freedom to adequately support our schools financially. We need a system. Dysfunctional needs to become functional. Inefficient needs to become efficient. Ineffective needs to be eliminated. *Effective practices* must become *the standard* we expect. We are the catalyst for progress. It is time we all do what is right for the children of the United States.

I understand that many people want to "put on blinders," as Conny J. would say, and stay within their own boundaries where they are comfortable. But now is not the time for comfort. It's time to come out of the comfort zone, out of the trenches, and into the streets. We must *demand* our country *invest in our future*.

I know what ordinary people have to say about money. We understand that more money will not make an ineffective reform approach "work." As Jennifer L. put it, "money issues are of both support and waste." We get it. And her mother, Anna Lou, will remind us what those in power presume, "As long as you do nothing, we will assume you are satisfied." It's up to us.

The present is the time to invest in the future of our country, and no better way exists than investing in education. It is education's time to rise up above the rubble that greed and ignorance has created. Will we stand in support of our public school system? Will we demand that our representatives honor our desires?

The choice is yours; what's next is up to you. History and the experience of others tell us that we must unite behind a *common purpose* to make our voices heard. Is there any more worthy common purpose than educating the next generation of our children? Shouldn't we arm them with the knowledge and skills they need to pursue their happiness and improve our democratic society? Shouldn't the American public education system offer quality education to all children? We can.

> What is absolutely crucial in replication is that the assumptions, conceptions, values, and priorities undergirding what you seek to replicate are clear in your head and you take them seriously; you truly accept and believe them, they are non-negotiable starting points.
>
> —Seymour B. Sarason

# Chapter Nine

# The Road to Educational Quality and Equality: A Story with No Ending

Values and goals are not maps; they are beliefs, imperatives, and stimulants on the basis of which we plan our actions.

—Seymour B. Sarason

Ideally, our plan of action in education "reform" should be guided by our values and goals. For the public education system to excel, the questions Americans must answer are: Do we value a public education system? Do we believe it should be available to all children? If so, what are the expected goals of such a system? And, what actions will we take to reach our goals?

Tests have always demonstrated that when it comes to educational attainment, a socioeconomic and racial inequality exists in this country. Some children "have not lived in a world of books, or of ideas" and consequentially, "they have not understood concepts in tests devised for the majority of the children of our schools" (National Advisory Council on the Education of Disadvantaged Children, 1966, 1). These tests better measure "the results of the child's *opportunity for learning* more accurately than his capacity for present or future learning" (2). Federal education law set out to offer opportunity, equally.

## WE WERE HERE IN 1965

Education is too important to be left solely to educators.

—Francis ("Frank") Keppel

Appointed by President Kennedy in 1962, Frank Keppel became the U.S. commissioner of education at the Office of Education and is credited as the architect of the Elementary and Secondary Education Act (ESEA) (Hanna, 2005).

ESEA aimed "to strengthen and improve educational quality and educational opportunities in the Nation's elementary and secondary schools." This law attempted to bring social justice to the education system by (1) deeming it imperative to put in place within the system the *dissemination* of "promising educational practices" to better ensure their use; (2) designating funds for school library resources, textbooks, and other instructional materials; and (3) funding supplementary educational centers and services making sure to use the *existing* "cultural and educational resources of the areas to be served" (Elementary and Secondary Education Act).

The lawmakers recognized that *disadvantages of various kinds* led to the inequalities in educational opportunities and that these inequalities were not being addressed sufficiently by the state and local officials under which the inequalities occurred and were ongoing.

It was a prevailing belief that "the ability of our children to learn, whatever the limitation of their environment, is limited only by our skill as educators." With that in mind, to improve educational quality, they urged universities to *improve their training* for both *counselors* and *teachers*, stressing that those two groups are the ones most likely "to gain insight into the problems of the disadvantaged" (National Advisory Council, 1966, 14) and they are in "an excellent position to *help parents* realize the importance of the role they play" (15).

To aid the state's education departments, the law supported such things as identifying "educational problems, issues, and needs in the State," supporting "programs to improve the quality of teacher preparation" plus "training and otherwise developing the competency of individuals who serve State or local educational agencies."

The 1965 ESEA clearly prohibited several things including "any direction, supervision, or control over the curriculum" or "program of instruction" by the federal government.

What does all this mean? It means that, as a republic, we saw the value in improving the quality of education and believed all children in America deserved access to opportunities, equally. We believed education was a "hand up," out of poverty, and that we were capable of delivery on the ideal of equal opportunity, at least to children. And we saw a way to do it through materials and services that support teaching and learning, better university training of teachers and counselors, and better distribution of "best practices" to states and the communities who need them most.

We saw the need to clearly define the role of the federal government along with that of state and local officials in cooperation with parental responsibility and wise use of community resources. And Keppel's comment about education "being too important to be left solely to educators," reflects on his belief in the inclusion of people from outside the field of education in helping improve schools.

The clarity of vision that produced the ESEA of 1965 came about while civil rights were foremost in the minds of Americans. We understood that all children deserved the opportunity to learn and that with the proper resources, human and material, we could provide access to quality education for all. We intended to try to *even the playing field* for our nation's youngest citizens.

## WHAT HAPPENED?

Nations have recently been led to borrow billions for war; no nation has ever borrowed largely for education. Probably, no nation is rich enough to pay for both war and civilization.

—Abraham Flexner

To understand where we are now, we have to go back a bit further in our history to 1896 and the Supreme Court decision in *Plessy v. Ferguson* that was based on the doctrine of "separate but equal" thereby allowing legal segregation of public schools by the states. It stood for 58 years until the *Brown v. Board of Education* decision in 1954, which stated that "separate educational facilities are inherently unequal." Many believe this case opened the door for the civil rights movement and the resultant Civil Rights Act of 1964.

As part of that Civil Rights Act, a national survey was commissioned to assess the degree of segregation of students and teachers, and its relationship to student achievement. The findings were discussed in a report titled *Equality of Educational Opportunity* by lead researcher James S. Coleman. It is infamously referred to as the Coleman Report. And as then Commissioner of Education Harold Howe II stated in the July 2, 1966, summary, "My staff and the consultants . . . do not regard the survey findings as the last word on the lack of equal educational opportunities in the United States" (Coleman, iv).

The findings of the Coleman Report had a profound effect on both policy and practices, as the dominant "take-aways" that you will frequently see quoted from this seven-hundred-page report are: (1) that family background and socioeconomic status have more effect on student achievement than school resources, and (2) that disadvantaged blacks show higher achievement in racially mixed schools. The first fed the "funding has little effect on achievement" argument, and the second led to forced busing to racially integrate schools. But reporter Mike Bowler probably got it right in 1995 when he stated, "Dr. Coleman went to his grave last week at the age of 68 believing that the report had been widely misinterpreted by the media and education policymakers."

To examine the extent of segregation of our schools and its effect on student achievement, the study used "indicators of educational quality." This study was heavily reliant on the use of surveys as a research tool. They looked at both "school inputs" such as curriculum, facilities, practices, and teacher and student characteristics as well as "outputs" as judged by standardized achievement tests. They did so with the warning that a "statistical survey can give only *fragmentary evidence*" of a school environment (Coleman, 3).

Coleman used a research model called "an education production function or input-output model." As explained by Adam Gamoran and Daniel A. Long, what this means is that Dr. Coleman, for purposes of research, considered schools like "black boxes" and focused on the inputs and outputs for statistical analysis. This is the type of model economists use to assess "how an *economic process* works in a particular firm." It "allows for aggregate analysis without requiring an examination of the details of what happens within a particular firm or school" (2006, 6).

The summary of the Coleman Report emphasized that the research analysis was concentrated on the equality of opportunities offered by schools. It went on to acknowledge that the emphasis *neglected* "important factors in the *variability between individual pupils* within the same school; this variability is roughly four times as large as the variability between schools" (Coleman, 22).

The emphasis on "pupils" in that statement is in keeping with the *focus* of the Elementary and Secondary Education Act (ESEA) of 1965 and the conclusions of the National Advisory Council on the Education of Disadvantaged Children. Yet, the ESEA of 1965 is written in history as the first federal "general aid to education" law in our nation. It directed funds, through Title I, *to help needy children*, not schools. And the advisory council repeatedly stressed in numerous ways that these funds should not lose sight of their objective of *helping children* from low-income families.

The money appropriated through this law's formula funding could be used in "endless" ways for programs and projects to "meet the special educational needs of educationally deprived children" (Congressional Quarterly, 1969, 710). The law stipulated that "appropriate objective measurements of educational achievement" would be used to judge the effectiveness of all programs and projects federally funded to meet the needs of these *needy children*.

The original formula funding used each state's average dollar per student as its base. It was changed in 1966 to the use of the national average in order to better help the "poorer states." However in 1968, the formula funding was made "conditional upon *availability* of sufficient appropriations" (Congressional Quarterly, 710). So, in reality as the number of students covered was going up, the number of dollars per student was actually declining. This coincided with the Tet Offensive of the Vietnam War, which marked the peak of our involvement there.

In addition to the competition for federal funding between war and education, administration of ESEA faced opposition by those that saw it as "government interference in local matters" particularly when that "interference" was desegregation. And that is where the Coleman Report finding "that the [racial and economic] composition of the student bodies has a strong relationship to the achievement of Negro and other minority pupils" (Coleman, 22) came into play on the overall outcome of the execution of ESEA and the struggle with desegregation and "white flight."

And with each reauthorization, the law was modified further, and further from its original *focus.*

As recalled by Marshall ("Mike") Smith, the 1972 reauthorization "overlegislated against a misuse of funds" resulting in the creation of pull-out programs with "aides who were often less well trained than the teacher." So Smith and others who rewrote the legislation in 1978 dedicated funds for "a whole school program that would improve the overall quality of instruction." Smith also worked on the 1994 reauthorization and explained that "the fundamental idea was that in order to have an efficient system, it was necessary to align resources around some goals, and that the standards would set the goals so that some measure of progress could take place" (Hanna, 2005).

That's one part of the politics of this story!

## IN THE FIELD

It doesn't matter who gets the credit as long as the job gets done.
—Frank Manley

Frank Manley is credited for being the "Father of the Modern Community Schools Movement." With an idea planted by his college professors at Michigan State Normal College, he did what he could to actively pursue the use of *schools to meet community needs.* He formed a "sportsmen's club" during noon and after-school hours that included regular "business meetings" to catch up on how the students were doing in their classes. What he found was that with attention, these "troubled" children improved (Decker, 26). From that humble beginning, with leadership skills and luck, the *concept of community education* bloomed and multiplied.

In 1935 true to his philosophy of "involving people and using a democratic approach to problem-solving" (Decker, 7), Manley was spreading his ideas at the local Rotary Club, where he caught the attention of Charles Stewart Mott. Mott was a General Motors industrialist and philanthropist whose family motto was "Let us be known by our deeds." Together, Manley and Mott spent the next thirty-seven years developing, enacting, and spreading the community education philosophy based on their shared belief that "*the 'spirit of teamwork'* could be used to solve community problems using available community resources" (Decker, 8). The guiding principles they developed were:

- Community schools help people to help themselves,
- Community schools focus on prevention and education rather than charity,
- Leadership development programs must provide encouragement to people, who have ideas, initiative, creative ability, and the necessary "feel" or touch,
- Wise administrators combine sound business judgment with sound vision,
- Start at home. After your neighbor has been cared for give nationally and internationally based on a proven model of "helping people help themselves." (Decker, 9)

These principles still guide community education around the globe because these two men put into practice their belief that community education was a *continuous process* and they learned much as they went. They expanded and improved on the programs offered to Flint's youth and adults and saw to it that leadership development programs were put in place to spread the concept. They developed programs in cooperation with numerous universities during the 1940s and 1950s as well as internships and workshops in Flint. As hundreds of graduates of these programs spread out across the United States, they embedded the philosophy in teaching colleges and universities as well as using it in the establishment of other "community schools."

By 1963, the idea was spreading internationally, and in 1964 Manley presented the Flint Program of Community Education to the U.S. Office of Education. With the continuous financial support of the Mott Foundation and thirty plus years of experience and evidence of success, political support for community education was mounting, as was evident by the urging of President Johnson for the expansion of community schools in Washington, D.C., in 1966.

At this same time, spawned by the 1966 Coleman Report and increasingly convinced that "the characteristics of schools are an important determinant of academic achievement," school *effectiveness researchers* in the 1970s and 1980s were studying schools where minority and low socioeconomic status students were achieving at higher rates than expected and the "achievement gap" was narrowing. These schools were labeled "effective," and researchers concluded that effective schools had "essential" characteristics common to all; they called them "correlates."

Ron Edmonds has long been credited as the lead researcher of effective schools. Edmonds team revealed that *the effective schools correlates* are:

1. The principal's *leadership* and attention to the *quality of instruction*;
2. A pervasive and broadly *understood* instructional focus;
3. An orderly, safe *climate* conducive to teaching and learning;
4. Teacher behaviors that convey the *expectation* that all students are expected to obtain at least minimal *mastery*;
5. The use of measures of pupil achievement as the basis for *program evaluation*. (Edmonds, 4)

Edmonds also noted that when it came to the common characteristics of the *school improvement "programs"* that were used in these schools, their common characteristics were that they all saw the local school as the focus of analysis and intervention; they all assumed all children to be educable; and all focused their design on more *efficient use of existing resources* (Edmonds, 10).

## UNDER THE INFLUENCE

. . . as a wheel turning in revolutions, moving as it turns. American education is on the move in this sense also but there is need to be certain that its movement is forward, the direction purposeful.

—Frank Keppel

To contemplate what weight the work going on in the field had on policymaking, you have to look at the influential. In addition to Keppel, the most influential people associated with the writing and implementation of the 1965 ESEA were John W. Gardner, the residing secretary for health, education, and welfare; Wilbur J. Cohen, who succeeded Gardner in that position; and Harold "Doc" Howe II, who followed Keppel as commissioner of education.

These men and others formed the educational "brain trust" of their time and they wrote the 1965 education law with purpose. Its *goal* was clearly to move toward *improved quality* of education and *access to it for all*. Education for all was highly valued, and these men knew it could not be achieved if we took our eyes off the children and communities that needed support. Continuing education was seen as being as important for the elderly as it was to keep people employable. And this "wheel" had been set in motion by educators themselves, who were calling for change and improvement in their ranks. "Education, the institution that can do the most to prevent the accumulation of an unskilled labor force, has not met its responsibility." And the way forward was envisioned and laid down in law based on the belief that "future schools and colleges must become truly *community education* and cultural centers" (Keppel, 1966, 26).

It was deemed imperative for the country to address both "the abolition of the conditions of neglect and the improvement of the schools" (41), *together*, because "full national development, in an economic sense, cannot be based on pockets of poverty and social neglect" (43). So with a commitment to focus on educationally deprived children, planners began the task of implementing the law based on their belief that "children's capacity to learn is a greater factor in their eventual success" and that the education system could deliver on the promise of both excellence and equality. The way forward was not seen as "aid" by Keppel but as "federal *support* for special purposes . . . an *investment* in education . . . *investment* in people and therefore in the nation" (71–73).

Phrases that express the *community education philosophy* can be found throughout the writings of these people, within the 1965 ESEA, and in the words of Ron Edmonds as he described effective schools. These great men of their time have all passed from this world, but the *values and goals* espoused within the concept of community education lives on, at least partially, under other names including community schools, full-service, extended-service, and promise neighborhood schools. As Minzey and LeTarte expressed, "most new ideas are old thoughts with new titles or the idea of others who were not given appropriate credit" (1994, xii).

## A SLIPPERY ROAD

Some leaders may be quite gifted in solving problems personally, but if they fail to institutionalize the process, their departure leaves the system crippled.
—John W. Gardner

When it comes to discussing education reform, you often hear the words "wrong road," "wrong track," or "wrong path," but there is another way to look at our systemic problems in education. The road the 1965 ESEA paved was one whose foundation was the goal of attainment of quality education for all. And Mike Smith's explanation of the 1972 reauthorization that focused funding on whole school "programs" and the idea of setting measurable "standards" as the goal made sense, in a way. If the goal of the law was to produce a federal accounting of one educational outcome, test scores, this would make sense. This is exactly what Coleman used as a research tool for statistical analysis, thus setting the stage for the "outcome-based" or "business-model" of education reform. Unfortunately, laying down curriculum standards was like the formation of black ice—an invisible danger.

Our modern-day standards movement can roughly be marked by the release of *A Nation at Risk* in 1983. The standards movement crept into ESEA with the help of Assistant Secretary of Education Diane Ratvich, under George H. W. Bush, who promoted the use of "academic" standards. This wasn't the first time our country has faced the danger of "standardization."

Around 1913, the industrial "efficiency movement" focused public attention on outcomes, but when educators attempted to "routinize teaching," or standardize it, it didn't work (Marzano & Kendall, 4). And as mentioned previously, by the late 1930s, research was completed by the Cooperative Study of Secondary Schools Standards concluding, among other things, that instruction would need to be adjusted according "to *conditions* and *needs* of pupils as a group and as individuals" (1993, 47).

The plans that were made for moving forward with the findings of that study were set aside. And we moved on, it would seem, unaware of what had come before.

So by the 1994 ESEA reauthorization, the areas of change to the law included a focus on higher standards and on teachers better trained to teach to high standards. The focus on "outcomes" was firmly cemented into law. And by the 2001 reauthorization that we call No Child Left Behind (NCLB), the law focused all of our attention on accountability for *all* schools based on student outcomes as judged by standardized test scores. Not only was the road slippery but, in addition, we took our eyes off the road; we slid off. We broke through the guardrails of *excellence* and *equality* in educational opportunity that had been constructed for us.

There were no villains in this story, to this point. We just didn't see the danger; we lost control and our trajectory landed us in the ditch, stuck. When our actions focused less on the child's needs and more on the statistical outcomes, when we picked a few research findings on which to base a very *narrow* set of beliefs in dealing with this multifaceted issue of public education, the *conditions we created* turned the road of progress into a treacherous one. Our forward movement was brought to a halt.

Remember, Coleman was asked as part of the Civil Rights Act to assess the degree of inequality of educational opportunity based on race, color, religion, or national origin. He applied an economic research model that is used to study economic processes in order to answer the questions asked of him. That's fine, for research purposes. But when it comes to educating children, schools are not empty "black boxes" and an "economic process" does not equate to "a learning process." In other words, *a research model* does not equate to *a reform model*.

When it comes to education reform, our actions have followed our goals. We made tremendous progress in the sixties and seventies. The gains made toward desegregation of schools peaked in the 1980s and a narrowing of the achievement gap, "however modest, occurred during the 1970's and 1980's" (Gamoran, 5).

In a September 2007 report, *How the World's Best-Performing School Systems Come Out on Top*, McKinsey & Company looked "inside the black box" of schools in other countries and took a peek at our overall outcomes as a nation. They found that our spending per student, adjusted for inflation, had increased by 73 percent between 1980 and 2005 while our "student outcomes," as judged by our own national tests, "stayed almost the same" (1). And during this time, many states reported accounts of having "achieved" scores that did not correlate with other *indicators* of quality and equality of opportunity. Standardization attempts have proven costly.

This road that we have been on for so long led us to consider what *effective* schools look like and how *indivisible* communities and schools should be if we are to ensure our children's commonwealth. But as we passed by these ideals for what seemed the easier road to travel, that of standards and testing, we turned our heads, we lost sight of the children—the original focus of the law. The cost has been enormous.

It's not the wrong road; it's the wrong focus. We need to admit that we were driving recklessly and our eyes shifted off of the service of educating children and on to the business and politics of the influential in education without regard to what was happening in our communities and schools. We changed but in the process, we did not make progress.

## STUCK IN THE MUCK

> Even now, we—in the community, in the university, in the school system—are not all ready to take the road he [Frank Manley] pointed out and on which he traveled so far. It's too hard a road. We are looking for panaceas. But there is no panacea.
>
> —Ernest O. Melby

Are we now stuck because we don't see the urgent need within our public education system, or, as President George W. Bush has said, is it "the soft bigotry of low expectations"? Or is it because we switched drivers and can no longer follow the map?

We replaced individual "performance" standards with state "curriculum" standards; we supplanted the idea of expecting that every child is capable of being educated and is *expected* to master a set of skills. Now we risk setting national curriculum standards instead of recognizing that children need us to *identify their individual strengths and weaknesses* and work with them to attain a level of mastery of the classroom curriculum as outlined in a locally agreed upon instructional framework. This isn't a philosophy that gets away from being held accountable to a standard; it's one that is responsible for meeting the needs of the individual student along with educational standards. This is a *philosophy* that can take us from a classroom culture of test preparation to a culture of educating each child to the fullest extent of his or her talents—meeting *the standards for American excellence and equality.*

We spun our wheels and dug ourselves in even deeper when we not only set curriculum standards but tied them to standardized tests. Standardized tests are *one indicator* of equality of opportunity, not necessarily the quality of education. They were not what the 1965 ESEA meant when it stated "appropriate measures" of student achievement. Quality education was to be determined based on the intention of the program of instruction and its targeted population of students; success was to be defined by how well "a program or project" *solved* an identified problem. The law intended to use testing to judge the effectiveness of federally funded programs targeted for the educationally deprived, only. The federal role in testing stopped there, until the development of the National Assessment for Educational Progress (NAEP).

We aren't progressing because we are undermining the public trust in teachers rather than investing in the teaching profession. We have continually professed our belief in having a qualified teacher in every classroom but have not acted to ensure that they are more highly educated within our own public system. The system of accreditation of teachers colleges and universities is not functioning under any well-professed or publicly accepted "standards." And for continuing education, we have allowed private providers to sell us services for a variety of "training" without holding them accountable for results.

We aren't moving forward because we continue to give lip service to the idea of parental and community engagement. We fail to provide the knowledge, leadership, and resources to bring the practices that have been proven to work to the people who could most benefit. If we truly believe that parent and community support for our youth are essential to their success, we have to do more than write laws and depend on volunteers or charity alone to put them into practice. We have to plan purposeful actions that take methods proven to work in highly functioning communities and help seed them in less functional ones. We have to understand that these "proven" practices will not work in dysfunctional school districts without firmly cementing support services within the communities.

We are stuck because we have not laid out the expectations for each building block of the system and expected all individuals to fulfill their responsibilities in working toward the desired outcomes. And now, states across the nation are cutting education funding. We are making it harder for individuals to hold their own expectations high. It is *never* good enough to provide a high standard of education only when and where there is "availability of sufficient appropriations." It's a harder road to work cooperatively to make the existing community resources fill funding gaps.

We're stuck because our leadership, for quite some time now, has not expressed cohesive, coherent vision for the public education system. We're stuck because our focus, our funding priorities, and our personal beliefs and attitudes are failing to serve our country.

We know the right thing to do is to close the "achievement gap," but is it the sole goal of education or is it just one indicator of what may be a better goal—excellent education for all?

We are stuck in the standardization of children ditch because we set test scores as our goal—in law and in the minds of Americans. The modern standards movement politically overpowered, but did not destroy, the modern community education movement.

## PULLED FROM THE DITCH

> Often those on whom action depends must develop new attitudes and habits. Social machinery must be set in motion.
>
> —John W. Gardner

From the usage of words in the 1965 ESEA and knowing of the people surrounding this law, it's not much of a leap to see ESEA as an attempt to federalize an educational philosophy embodied in the *community education concept* and the ideals of quality and equality in educational opportunity. And given that the epicenter of the modern community education movement was in Michigan, and mapping some of the hundreds of leaders that became followers of the philosophy, it's not a stretch to presume that in Edmonds' original work with effective schools that many of the schools he studied, if not most, were indeed run based on the community education philosophy. It is a philosophy whose narrative goes back before the time of Manley and Mott leaving it embedded deeply in our educational history.

And the philosophy will continue on because, as one student of the concept, Larry E. Decker, explained, "while fads come and go, good ideas have a way of enduring, of turning up again and again, often coming back stronger than ever" (1999, 46). The modern community education movement did not die with its founders. It is, however, overshadowed by wrong-minded "reforms" because those currently governing do not fully comprehend the community education concept.

In the original Coleman Report, it was acknowledged that the "*pupil attitude factor* which appears to have a stronger relationship to achievement than do all the school factors together, is the extent to which an individual feels that he has some *control over his own destiny.* . . . Thus such attitudes, which are largely a *consequence* of a person's *experience in the larger society*, are not independent of his experience in school" (Coleman, 22).

Coleman's later research looked at differences in achievement between public and private schools. His findings supported the idea that "functional communities" surrounding the schools contribute to "social capital," which he once defined as "the set of resources" that are inherent in family relations and in community social organizations that are useful in childhood development. He "argued for innovations that would increase the *resources* of families or other actors interested in children" (Marden, 9).

Frank Manley believed "that basic human needs cannot wait—that our social institutions cannot compensate tomorrow for what they fail to do today" (Decker, 5). He built a vehicle in which to spread his *vision* of individuals participating in solving the problems of their own communities. That vehicle is the community education concept.

Frank Keppel believed that a revolution in education was well under way to provide *equality* of opportunity and that a revolution to address *quality* of education "must be next." He approached the problems knowing that "the greatest *challenge* for the future is to *reorganize* education into a more *responsive* and *responsible* governmental unit" (Keppel, 157). He drew a map directing us to the finish line of equality in opportunity and it pointed the way to excellence. That map is the 1965 Elementary and Secondary Education Act (ESEA).

And this is where the ideas and ideals of Manley, Keppel, Coleman, Edmonds, and all the others in the story become intertwined like the strands of a sturdy rope. They are bound together by an *understanding* of the importance of our *focus on the students* and the experiences they bring with them. This is the point in the story where they all comprehended the significance of having teachers and other staff who recognize the *individual needs* of each child and are able to focus resources on those needs. They grasp the worth in efficient use of existing resources and having the guardrail of "social capital" in place for our youth.

Who and what we equip our "black boxes" with does matter. The *climate* created in the box does matter. And the opportunities, expectations, and experiences both in and out of the box make all the difference in our world. Only we can turn change into progress—if only we can see our problems as opportunities, *grab hold of the problem solving process*, and use it like we have in the past.

## ON THE ROAD TO PROGRESS

A century of experience with land-grant colleges has demonstrated that Federal financial participation can assist educational progress and growth without Federal control.

—John F. Kennedy

The educational visionaries in this story saw an American education system that was a federal, state, and local partnership. They saw educating children as a school-community partnership that would find itself in need of support and guidance from time to time and in varying locations. They identified the roles and responsibilities of all the working parts and all the characters in the educational drama.

The federal government's involvement in education was to oversee our *progress as a nation* knowing that the landscape would be ever changing, pockets of need a moving target. Their responsibility was to be at the ready with support, both informational and material. The states were seen as the first responders in meeting educational needs but could only meet their responsibility if they possessed the *capacity* to identify their own states' weaknesses and be responsive to them. The federal government would be a partner in developing capacity where needed. The local community would always be the largest contributor to the experiences that would shape and determine the future of its schools' students.

These visionaries looked into the black box and saw the need for *excellence in education for leaders, teachers, and counselors* in order to pass on quality educational experiences to all students. They *set high expectations for the system* in recognizing the requirement of local schools to make school services fit the needs of their students rather than expecting the child to fit the school. The systems' standard of performance would be *judged by its responsiveness* to people's interests and needs.

These visionaries of our past saw the need to maintain the *integrity* of educational research and development through the use of our public institutions of higher learning and urged our lawmakers to ensure that integrity through law.

So as President Johnson addressed the issues of poverty *simultaneously* with those of the education system, he saw the need to provide services for children that would "be adapted to meet the pressing needs of each locality" and he urged that we "draw upon the unique and invaluable resources of our great universities to deal with national problems of poverty and community development." And it was envisioned that the *university extension system* could help the people meet their needs. In order to do so, the government of the people would need "to help the university to face the problems of the city as it once faced problems of the farm" (Johnson, 1965).

So as envisioned by the main architect of ESEA, a network of regional educational laboratories was written into law. As Keppel expressed, they were "designed to serve education much as the agricultural experiment centers long served and stimulated the development of agriculture (1966, 123). Meeting the goal would require "coordination with state departments of education, and the availability of research personnel from the academic world and industry." This would bring together schools and school systems, *link proposal to practice*, to provide "a missing link that is in good part responsible for education's reputation for resistance to innovation" (125). As with much of the original law, war and politics changed the direction of progress.

Today we have ten regional educational laboratories, but, to be similar to Cooperative Extension Centers in funding and function would mean beginning as federally funded public facilities that would progress to federal/state/local cooperatives with "extension" of information from universities and research facilities to every county in the country. Nationally, that would take a system, a far reaching network, of trained individuals. That is how the Cooperative Extension System is set-up. It is an existing community resource.

The regional educational laboratories we have now are run primarily as nonprofits through a competitive federal granting process in addition to lists of outside funding. Their work is many times done in conjunction with public universities and personnel. They have many excellent professionals on staff and they continue to do useful work, however the goal of forming a network to *freely disseminate information* and assist in training at the *local level* was never fully realized.

The regional educational laboratories were intended to provide the basic research and development of *practical solutions to the issues facing schools*. They were to serve as the *bedrock of excellence*. The information they provided was then to be disseminated to the schools and the general public— free of charge, for the most part. They would be supported by the public system. Flow of information needed to be in both directions to ensure the researchers were addressing what the stakeholders needed to know and be able to do.

## UNDERSTANDING THE SIGNS

Our security depends on the enlightenment of our citizens . . . our freedom
depends on the communication of ideas through many channels.
— S. Douglass Cater

In 1966, the first annual report of the Advisory Council on the operation and
administration of ESEA, Title I, explained that "what is necessary is for each
community to study its own problems and resources on the basis of which it
can devise programs that are likely to attack at the roots the problems found
there, utilizing the resources that can be brought to bear there" (33).

It's hard to know how well communicated the ideas expressed in ESEA
and the reports that followed may have been. The 1960s were tumultuous
times, and the attention of the country was focused on a variety of social
issues. And time and again, politics has proven itself to be an irresponsible
driver of educational progress.

Douglass Cater, an advisor to President Johnson, explained, "I think one
of the major problems of politics is that one takes a fairly *recognized crisis*
before the government is able to come to grips with an area, *a problem in a
policy area*, and then if it's anything of a major nature, just passing a law and
appropriating money is only the beginning of a long, hard process" (1981,
15).

The process that was to bring excellence in education to the steps of every
school house began with ESEA.

The road signs were erected:

Title I—*Education of Children of Low Income Families* to provide financial assistance to local education agencies in support of *children from
low-income families.*

Title II—*School Library Resources, Textbooks, and Other Instructional
Materials* to provide for access to educational materials *for all students* in the State.

Title III—*Supplementary Educational Centers and Services*, available to
the *entire community*, to provide services not currently offered but
deemed vital to educational improvement.

Title IV—*Educational Research and Training; Cooperative Research Act*
to provide research, training, and dissemination of information *aimed*
at improving the quality of teaching.

Title V—*State Departments of Education* "to stimulate and assist in
strengthening the *leadership* resources of State educational agencies."

With values and goals as guides, Howe was then charged with overseeing the first attempt at implementation of ESEA. About it he said, "I doubt that anyone could have dreamed up a series of education programs more difficult to administer . . . but ESEA was not designed with that in mind" (United States, 38).

Title I, the touchstone of ESEA, is a particularly complex idea made both difficult and now clearer, in a way, by the original terminology of the law, the reports that followed, and the words chosen by its architects. The federal formula *funding* was distributed directly to the *counties* for assistance of *"children of low-income families"* and it was directed from there to the school districts. Once at the district level, the directive was to *address the needs of "educationally deprived children,"* which the architects understood would include more than just the low-income children, given that the schools where the most funds would flow were "inherently unequal." Potentially all students in those schools are at risk for being underserved. Thus, one piece of the national approach, through Title I, was to address the disadvantages children face—economically, educationally, mentally, or physically "disadvantaged"—that were being ignored, or in some cases created, by state and local agencies. Oversight of the management for improvement measures, or *accountability*, was seen as a continuing *state responsibility*.

When you add in the other educational supports of ESEA—material resources, additional applicable services, proven practices, teacher and counselor development, and responsive state leadership—you do improve the quality of education for all but it begins with addressing a known disadvantage, *poverty*. Equality of opportunity is what the writers had in mind and the focus was children with services radiating out from them, weaving their social safety net.

Attitude and training were key; understanding the concepts essential.

## READING THE MAP CORRECTLY

Inevitably, reaching for social or economic change is a slow and complex process.

—Harold Howe II

ESEA was written based on values and goals with the purpose of guiding and focusing our actions. Its architects understood more work needed to be done in the education field. President Johnson felt the issues to be faced included "how best to fuse national interests with private, state, and local responsibilities . . ., how best to give proper weight to innovation and the views of scholars and other experts in the areas of knowledge that should be taught,

and how best to strengthen the machinery of government to relate educational policies and programs to other needs of the society" (Keppel, 1966, 68).
Our actions were to move us down the road of progress, as a nation.

Keppel spoke with a focus on the quality of education. He acknowledged
that standards varied widely between schools and that the variation was
"*controlled by attitudes*" and "*influenced by a variety of sources.*" "If the
curricular policy was too important to be left only to educators, as many had
long agreed, it had now become too important to be left *only* in local hands"
(118).

Today, when we look at the map, we have trouble reading it, particularly
at the point where we should be finding *the road to excellence*. The ink is
smudged from so many fingers going back and forth over this area of conflict. The marker is blurred.

The "standards marker" has been the most misinterpreted portion of the
map. We use descriptors of every kind when we talk of standards: academic,
performance, process, content, curricular, core, opportunity-to-learn, and always "higher." And as we should understand by now, as explained in "To
Standardize or to Customize Learning?"—"If not properly conceived, standards can do far more harm than good" (Reigeluth, 1997, 202).

As Charles M. Reigeluth explains, we can use standards in two ways,
"they can be used as tools for standardization—to make all students alike. Or
they can be used as tools for customization—to help meet individual students' needs" (203). He also reminds us of *basic skills* that we should expect
all *students to master*, which is in keeping with what Edmonds found in
"effective schools." And to achieve the quality of education set by learning
standards, students have to be *engaged in the process*. "Perhaps the two most
important conditions for active mental engagement are the intensity of motivation to learn and the quality of the instructional support for learning . . .
*uniform* standards are actually likely to be counterproductive with regards to
both of these conditions" (206).

The process for using standards is not simple. It seems reasonable to have
content standards developed in cooperation with experts in the content areas;
that is where "experts" can help "locals." And after that, "standards-based
approaches must be tailor made to the specific needs and values of individual
schools and districts" (Marzano & Kendall, 1997, 11).

The Mid-continent Research for Education and Learning (McREL) regional educational laboratory has developed a data base of content standards
along with advice on how to use them to develop classroom curriculum to
meet the needs of the community.

So what this controversial and divisive topic of "standards" comes down
to is the fact that we can take a "content" standard, which is a description of
what the student should know and be able to do, as defined by experts in a
given subject, and turn it into a "curriculum" standard which takes into

account how a subject is *best presented* along with *suggested activities.* This produces a *usable instructional framework.* What is "best" for students in any given classroom can ultimately only be decided right there, in real time, with much prior planning. This is one starting point in the travel toward excellence.

James Lewis Jr. can take our thinking further. He put forth the "success-emulation" theory where he clearly stated that "the important feature of my concept of excellence [in our schools] is that the standards selected, whatever their nature, must be stated in writing, *mutually agreed to* by a *team* of school and community people, and disseminated throughout the school and community" (1986, xiv). This portrays the *philosophy* that the best "programs" are those that can be reinforced in schools and in the community. And if we are to adopt anything from the best the business world has to offer to the public education system, it should be that "the best-run companies start with their people, trusting them as human beings and trusting their capability and their potential. In essence, they are *people sensitive*" (xvi).

To be "people sensitive" starts with individual attitudes. The *process* of educational improvement begins in the minds of those that desire to do what is best for the nation's children. It requires being *open-minded* and *cooperative.*

There is no standard way to drive; there are rules, there are guidelines, but when it comes to getting behind the wheel, it's an individual thing with decisions made based on variables. "To use a travel analogy, standards for manufacturing are comparable to a single destination for all travelers to reach, whereas standards for education are more like milestones on many never-ending journeys whereby different travelers may go to many different places" (Reigeluth, 1997, 204). As long as we offer all of our education traveler's quality opportunities along the way, we have fulfilled our promise.

To teach to the test has taught generations of students that learning a chunk of knowledge is an endpoint. We demonstrated that a test score was the goal and once reached; the knowledge no longer had value and could be forgotten with *unforeseen consequences.* Individuals and society are now paying the penalty.

But we now have the opportunity to fuse our interests in education, uphold our responsibilities to the next generation, and be inclusive of scholars and other experts while addressing the needs of our society. To be successful, we have to understand that standards are necessary. As Dr. Reeves said, "My defense of standards is not a protection of the many *deeply flawed* standards and the egregious examples of *mindless* test preparation masquerading as rigorous academic standards" (2001, 2).

And we must be clear that standards for academic achievement are not the same as standardization of instruction. We can set national goals and define national guiding principles—an acceptable standard of practice—without promoting teaching to the test. We can have a system fundamentally standards-based in nature without the full weight of the accountability system being laid on the "outcome" of test scores.

The study *Beyond Test Scores: Leading Indicators for Education*, by the Annenberg Institute for School Reform, looked at districts that were leading the way in "data-informed decision making." The focus was not on using standardized test scores, which too often lag as indicators. Instead, they were looking at a way "to understand when (and whether) progress is being made *before* the results show up in indicators like student test scores" (Foley, 1). We have found ways to help students before they become just another number that indicates our failure to help them succeed.

The push to "fix" America's schools has, no doubt, been a complex and confusing process of change particularly for the general public. We have encountered some delays and multiple detours. We have even had a significant wreck with some major damage. But we have carried the ideal of equal opportunity very far from where we began. Now, we can easily pull ourselves up out of the ditch and we have the expertise to fix the damage and rebuild the guardrails.


## FOLLOW THE MAP

Freedom of choice places the whole blame of failure on the shoulders of the individual.

—Eric Hoffer

Equality of educational opportunity was seen as equality of inputs until "Coleman and his colleagues redefined equality of opportunity by focusing on results." Now would be a good time to consider the view of M. R. Olneck that, in addition to inputs and outputs, "two other concepts may serve as the basis for judgments about equal opportunity: *representation* and *participation*." We must have "participation in the process to have our ideas about what successful schooling is and how it should be judged represented. . . . In the absence of equal representation and participation, unequal outcomes are likely to persist since the terms of success are dictated by dominant groups" (Gamoran, 2006, 17).

The "terms of success" in 1965—the destination, the goal of the education system—as expressed by Keppel was that "American education must not only provide an education for everyone, but transmit the value of a democratic society and provide *equal access* for all to the best that education has to offer" (1966, 2). One thing was obvious then, racial segregation was limiting access. Simple accounting practices could measure success or failure in that category.

For people that see the tie of education to the economy and the greater society, they can see the other indicators of national educational success. The dropout rate, college attendance, unemployment of the undereducated, and the costs of incarceration versus costs of educating are some of the real life outcomes on which we can judge our system. These are numbers that can serve as national indicators of success.

ESEA was a national map. Currently, under No Child Left Behind, it has one goal—close the achievement gap. It stands on three pillars—"accountability, flexibility, and choice." The accountability mechanism has failed because it rests on false assumptions, was ill conceived, does not represent American values, and it set the wrong priority—testing outcomes.

"Flexibility" addressed the funding mechanism, which is the part of the education equation that most Americans would prefer an accounting of and in school districts most under pressure to "perform," flexibility in instruction was replaced with test preparation practices. And it is time for the country to consider what "choice" means when it is placed in the context of federal law and what its impact is on equal access to quality education.

If a national map is well conceived and functional in guiding and supporting local actions, our state and local maps could easily be overlaid to become mutually useful for all levels of the education system including higher education.


## FORWARD MOMENTUM

> People can think of any aim like one thinks of a bullet hitting a target; aim, fire, and see what happens. A more fitting analogy for the work I propose is Atlas holding the world on his shoulders. We each pick up a load, marry it, and carry it as far as we personally can.
>
> —John Jensen

For over forty-six years we have planned and changed plans while mostly moving forward, albeit stumbling over the wreckage of our values and goals. We have repeatedly heard that the education system is failing to keep pace with the rest of the world; it is a security issue. For over thirty years we have debated whether or not the educational crisis is real or created by politicians or others with a political or monetary agenda. If we won't act until we feel an educational crisis exists, what meets the definition of crisis? What are our "social indicators" telling us?

We instinctively understand the economic and social consequences of a poor education system—unemployable people, low income, dependence on social services, incarceration, higher health care costs, poorer health, and the list goes on. Given that it takes a generation to really evaluate a change in

education, we should face the fact that we have had almost three full generations of public school students who have emerged out from under a test-
based classroom culture.

We have high unemployment; we have job openings that can't be filled
by underskilled Americans. We have college graduates unable to find work
in their fields of study; we have misdirected, undereducated, and failed to
properly support our next generation. But have we associated our educational
shortcomings not with an "overall" poor system but with one that continues
to have pockets of inequalities, big and small, that accumulate like so much
sludge in the engine?

Education was seen as nationally significant and it was thought that as a
nation we should not lose sight of it as a whole system. From that point of
view, there is every indication, then as now, that "the system" is not functioning at a capacity sufficient "to yield a maximum of individual development
and national well-being" as President Kennedy stressed in his message to
congress on January 29, 1963. And, Keppel came to realize, "the problems of
education are too technical to be resolved by political response to public
demonstrations" (1966, 145). And Gardner knew "it is not enough to set
aside funds for an educational program. What may be needed most is a way
of treating individuals that provides them with the challenges that produce
growth" (1994).

To achieve excellence is going to take a cooperative effort from a variety
of experts in fields related to education as well as educators themselves. Each
must carry their load, meet their responsibility.

And there is more to the politics of this story!

## CAUTION SIGNS

The three R's of our school system must be supported by the three T's—
teachers who are superior, techniques of instruction that are modern, and
thinking about education which places it first in all out plans and hopes.
                                                                —Lyndon B. Johnson

"In the 1960's and 1970's, liberal policies were threatened by the (incorrect)
perception that 'schools don't matter; families do.' Meanwhile, conservative
policies were bolstered by the emphasis on families as the source of inequality. By the 1980's, when Coleman *did* find school effects, his results were
embraced by conservatives who favored vouchers for private schools, whereas liberals questioned the purported private school advantage" (Gamoran &
Long, 2006, 15). And in a variety of ways, that same debate is going on
across the country today!

Too many people are continuing to fight over who is right instead of using their energy to do the things that are right. Do we now move down the road with the belief that schools can't make a difference, or do we approach revolutionizing the public education system based on the expectations that all children will be educated to the limits of their abilities—period?

In this story, there are not any villains; no villains—education industry opportunists, yes. We are witnessing the rise of the education-industrial complex defined here as an alliance of education related organizations and government with education industries. Their politically powerful influence of money is now the dominant voice in policy decisions and appropriations of federal, state, and local tax dollars for education.

The privatization of this once world-revered system of *public* schools is quite advanced because, as with formation of the military-industrial complex, the education-industrial complex is fed by the greed of some opportunists and by visions of grandeur in some well-intended powerful individuals. The education-industrial complex is benefiting, too many students are being left behind, and the American tax-paying public is paying a high price with insufficient return on investment.

Education businesses thrive on fragmentation and dysfunction—on the privatization of services that could be provided within a *complete and functional public education system*, if it were developed to its maximum potential. If we were to truly "fix what ails us," we would no longer require many of the service providers currently profiting through No Child Left Behind.

That's not to say the system can do it all; it is to say that the true believers in community education concepts saw that the "wise" use of existing resources, public or private, was desirable in filling the community's educational needs. Public education should act in partnership with some existing private organizations but not without each "player" having a well-defined essential role that is publicly communicated to ensure accountability of the system. And where public education institutions can serve other public education institutions they should; it strengthens the system.

If villains are lurking along the roadside, they need to be rooted out. The only way to do that is to clarify our expectations of the American public education system, ask Congress to hear us, represent us, and act on behalf of this nation's children. We know what we want but we can't possibly know who the villains are, if they exist, until after we have taken *the social action necessary* in the process of giving our consent to the directives of our education laws.

# THE CROSSROADS OF OPPORTUNITY

We can, whenever and wherever we choose, successfully teach all children whose schooling is of interest to us; we already know more than we need to do that; and Whether or not we do it must finally depend on how we feel about the fact that we haven't so far.

—Ronald Edmonds

In this story, crossroads weren't apparent. The American public wasn't asked to *choose* between a road directed by free market industrial concepts or one paved with the concepts of quality and equality. The map showed no such major intersections indicating the formation of an *education-industrial complex* or the continued maintenance and improvement of a *free system* of "public" education. No single marker designated the road to privatization. The map was drawn based on our value in education and equal access to it; *"public" was understood.*

The vast majority of American public schools were performing well prior to our attempts to "reform" them all. Effective schools and vibrant communities don't need federal or state mandates to improve their student performance; they need to invest in continuous improvement and continue to be vigilant of individual children being underserved. But dysfunctional communities, those who don't see what their *full responsibility* to children entails, they need assistance, support, and the development of effective leadership.

Effective schools and community education concepts are not programs to be bought and sold; they are concepts to be understood and applied where needed. *Education reform* is not about a model or program; it's about *an improvement process.* Models and programs don't work; people do.

If there is any "blame" to be laid, it is on the whole of society for its negligence. Our desire for change indicates our dissatisfaction with the current system, but do we understand what is at the root of our unhappiness?

We are witness to the longest gap between reauthorizations of ESEA in its history. Ten years after its passage as No Child left  is too long. To think that the public education system can administer  1,000-plus page law in an effective and efficient manner is pure folly. We must now come to grips with what we have learned from this detour we call "No Child Left Behind"; you don't cure dysfunctional districts with data. "Accountability, flexibility, and choice" have not *strengthened* and *improved* schools.

The system no longer knows who the drivers are or where they are taking us. It is time to go back and rethink our actions.

Our actions in the name of "educational improvements" are a case where *the means must justify the end.* When it comes to educating children, to sacrifice the means to this end is to sacrifice a child's education, today. Have our values and goals changed so much since 1965 that the goals of quality and equality in educational opportunity are no longer worthy of guiding our actions?

We have over sixty years of experience with the modern community education concept, over thirty years of effective schools research, and over thirty years of research and practice with an outcome-only focus of "education reform." What do we now see as "reform"?

ESEA was a thirty-five-page law that allowed educators the freedom to choose what was right for their students while being held accountable for results. *Strengthening* and *improving* this nation's schools was central to its conception.

The 1965 ESEA didn't give up any "standards"; it *aimed for excellence*. It didn't lack accountability; it required an accounting of progress for the children it was designed to help. It funded a move toward equality of opportunity, not across-the-board testing. It did not shift the responsibility of educating children to any one stakeholder group; it emphasized a *shared community responsibility*.

For those that see NCLB as the federalization of the standards and testing movement, you should now be able to look back on the 1965 ESEA and see it as the attempted federalization of the community education concept with an aim at equalization of opportunity for underprivileged children as well as promotion of a school/community improvement process.

If you believe that all children can be *engaged* in the learning process and that we should approach teaching and learning with the *expectation* that all children are capable of achieving to the limits of their personal potential, then you understand that "excellence" will never be standardized nor will we be able to judge it in a "standard" manner. Quality education means different things to different people, as it should. Basic education essentials are common ground, a starting point.

Day-to-day accountability has to occur at the school level first and foremost. If we see educating children as a *societal obligation*, if the focus is children, our responsibility is to be responsive to them. To "get it right," changes to our laws must be preceded by *social change*, which begins in the minds of Americans—it's our democratic circle of survival.

While acting as the president of Carnegie Corporation, John W. Gardner laid out what functions were essential in order for social change to occur: the problems facing the group must be clarified, solution ideas formulated, objectives defined, widespread awareness of the objectives made, "and the will to achieve them" must exist.

If we can now build the will to act, it's time to take Frank Manley's keen "feel" for what is needed on the ground and in the trenches, combine it with Frank Keppel's keen political sense, passion, and revolutionary soul, and move the wheels of progress forward.

The relationships of these insightful men were interconnected in ways that we may not now be able to totally unravel. Perhaps it is this weaving of ideas and ideals that is our strength. Whether it is in communities or schools, it is *personal relationships*—the keystone of social capital—that make a difference in life, schools, society, and our world.

We have questions to answer, and more to be asked, until we are clear in our minds as to what we expect from public education. We need *federal education law to guide and protect us* but only if it is based on principles that hold true to our values. To find our way out of the confusing mess we have made of education "reform," we need a clearly written, easy-to-read map because only people can make a plan "work."

The country is stalled. The consent of informed citizens must fuel our progress. It's crucial.

As Frank Keppel put it, "American education, that great engine of the democracy, does not drive itself. It must be guided, not by one but *by many*, into a future of incalculable promise" (1966, 163). And those that knew Frank Manley, I'm sure, will hear him chime in, "Let's get on with it" (Decker, 17).

This is not the time to sit idling. The reauthorization of the Elementary and Secondary Education Act (No Child Left Behind) provides us the opportunity to progress as a nation, toward *the destination* once collectively envisioned for America's children—*excellent education for all*—by strengthening and improving all our public schools.

> Democracy must be consciously promoted and transmitted to each new generation. The freedom of a democratic society enables the school to promote greater democracy and the society to improve education.
>
> —John Dewey

*Chapter Ten*

# Democracy and Education:
# The Powerful Will Drive Progress

Perhaps the sentiments contained in the following pages, are not yet sufficiently fashionable to procure them general favor; a long habit of not thinking a
thing wrong, gives it a superficial appearance of being right, and raises at first
a formidable outcry in defense of custom. But the tumult soon subsides. Time
makes more converts than reason.

—Thomas Paine

Intuitively, the common people know the time is right to do what is necessary. Everyday people are feeling the urgency of their needs. Time is running
out. We aren't going to get many more chances to get things right. We have
continued to fail to *solve* the problems that are looming over us, threatening
to take us under.

It is time we face the fact that we do not have a large enough pool of well-
educated American citizens to fill all the essential jobs for a successful,
prosperous, democratic society: scientists, health care professionals, educators, and political leaders. Our leaders' actions do not demonstrate that they
feel any obligation to "the generations left behind." They are taking action to
import and give citizenship to better-educated foreign intellectuals, once
again leaving American citizens behind on our own soil. It is a plan that will
work to fill the needs of corporate America, not the needs of our children,
communities, and country. Of late, virtue and wisdom have not guided our
policymakers.

Unless we are ready to give up our sovereignty as a nation to the idea of
being only a part of a global union, we need educated American political
leaders to fill all our congressional seats. We need wise men and women that
know enough about science and economics, in addition to the Constitution of

the United States, to do the job that they are supposed to do. Congress does not comprehend that "the fabric of American Empire ought to rest on the solid basis of The Consent of the People. The streams of national power ought to flow immediately from that pure original fountain of all legitimate authority" (*The Federalist*, no. 22, Alexander Hamilton, December 14, 1787). Having the uninformed masses silent while school children and their families struggle is un-American.

Much of the country watched in 2000 as Michigan began to steadily lose auto manufacturing jobs—it was Michigan's problem. The country looked on as New Orleans' poorest couldn't escape Hurricane Katrina—they've always had a problem there. We heard reports in 2006 of the housing market taking a hit in Florida—we ignored it until it hit us all. In California, the education system once led the nation—did we care as it fell? Did we even look back as it was left behind?

Hurricane Katrina supposedly pointed to both bureaucratic failings and the state of poverty and ignorance within our United States. It pointed to a failed public education system that many outraged Americans vowed to get behind and fix. Have we? Some are trying and some "reform" is occurring, but, how the Katrina story ends isn't the point.

The point is—it shouldn't require an act of God to change a school district. And we can't just drown the problem in money. And we must quit looking the other way, allowing inequalities to go on in our public education system, when *we know* we can end them. Ordinary people know it's time to *invest* in the profession of teaching, in leaders skilled in applying *effective* schools principles, in the resources that effectively and efficiently support children's needs, and to truly *invest* in effective family and community engagement, not just "promote" it. I hear ordinary people asking for safe schools, safe neighborhoods, and quality education for their children. We get it!

Practical, proven solutions have gone unused because we, as a united nation, have failed to answer a question basic to both educational improvement and the ideals of a democracy or republic: Whose job is it to keep the public informed? We talk about the founding fathers and our Constitution's significance to us, but we failed to see the full worth in the words our first president spoke as he was leaving office.

George Washington was the first to experience the implementation of this great experiment to establish a republic different from the failings of other great republics. And, in his reflections on that experience, found in his Farewell Address to Congress, he spoke of promoting "institutions for the general diffusion of knowledge."

Being accustomed to the laundry list of wants expressed by our modern-day presidents, the context in which George Washington spoke about "diffusion of knowledge" is surprising. The call for knowledge was *the only* item that he promoted. It was what our first president saw as a deficit in our experiment to build a lasting republic based on our "free Constitution."

As stated in *A Nation at Risk*, "A high level of shared education is essential to a free, democratic society and to the fostering of a *common culture*, especially in a country that prides itself on pluralism and individual freedom" (National Commission, 1983, 7). We do understand the need.

Many great men that valued our union, and valued education's role in it, did not see through the implementation of a plan to provide *universal* education. It is not a radical idea. It is not a call for sweeping reform but instead a call for a necessary service. *Effective* changes in the *governing structure* are required to get what the public needs to improve our schools. Only a complete change from a fractured and dysfunctional bureaucracy to a functioning system will provide the services children need. Only a systemic change can provide equality in educational opportunity.

The second paragraph of the Declaration of Independence begins with: "We hold these truths to be self-evident, that all Men are created equal, that they are endowed by their Creator with certain unalienable Rights, that among these are Life, Liberty, and the Pursuit of Happiness—That to secure these Rights, Governments are instituted among Men, deriving their just Powers from the Consent of the Governed." The *"consent of the governed"* is the foundation of *our governing structure.*

And in the words of President Washington, education's link to democracy: "Promote then, as an object of *primary* importance, institutions for the general diffusion of knowledge. In proportion as *the structure of a government gives force to public opinion*, it is essential that public opinion should be enlightened."

Our founding fathers knew how important education would be to achieving a true functioning republic that would endure the test of time. H. G. Good summarized it best in writing that "the educational thinkers of the revolution and the following years" viewed education as "a means of preserving liberty, securing unity, promoting good citizenship and developing the resources of the land and people. Education would help maintain the union of states, a united people and a republican government" (1956, 81–82). If you believe in a republican form of government, you believe in the importance of education.

Education is key to economic development, essential to the practice of preventative medicine, paramount to quick change in our building environmental disaster, and is the backbone of democracy. The hope is that these are *concepts* every one of you thoughtfully considers the importance of and will now devote yourself to helping *strengthen* and *improve* our public education system.

We may not have the time left to only improve one school full of children at a time. We don't know from what geographical location or layer of society our best and brightest will sprout forth. We can't afford to let any of them wilt. We must do our best to ensure all our schools equally offer opportunity. There should be no doubt; it is "the governed" that must act.

An *informed public opinion* driving policy will have a very different outcome than an uninformed or misinformed public pushing the hidden agenda of those who stand to profit. It is *money driving policy* versus *people driving policy*; this is the real internal war raging in our country that has made its way to the schoolhouse steps.

## ASSUMPTIONS: REFORM THROUGH CHOICE, COMPETITION, PRIVATIZATION

"Choice" is the status quo, the current flavor, of school reform. Single-mindedness has left us offering choice as a method for "turn around" or "failing schools reform." The reason is that a portion of the public grew frustrated with public education. Not all schools provide the education that parents rightly feel their children deserve. Dysfunctional schools model entrenchment. When parents see they can't change their situation, it is easiest to leave these "failing schools" behind and start new ones, "charters."

Each time a new school is set up in a manner different from our current traditional public schools, it attracts and selects the best teachers it can find. Those teachers continue to leave the "old" schools, limiting the learning opportunities for the students left behind. Each time a new school is created, it attracts parents who care about education, effectively removing their influence from the old schools. Some children are helped while others may be hurt. We call this "choice" and the process is called "reform" even when it changes nothing in the old school. For some, the consequences are reality and they are foreseeable.

When parents feel they are forced to choose a school other than their local neighborhood school, it adds further to the break-up and deterioration of some neighborhoods. It may disconnect the children and their families from other families in their community. When school activities are no longer located in existing communities, local businesses suffer. Communities crumble. And schools are "public" institutions implying "institutional memory" of the important culture and traditions of their people. That stable knowledge base is dependent on neighborhood families. With "choice," the families are being shuffled around. Connections lost. How is this success when, "An *informed* and *engaged* community is one of the primary indicators of a successful school" (Engel, 2009, 100)?

As discussed in "Choice or Commonality," if educational responsibility remains solely on the immediate family, "'choice' may take place in a world of insufficient numbers of quality schools, inadequate information about the stakes and alternatives, and large numbers of people unable to use the choice system effectively. This state of affairs means choice for some and not for others, and whether a child's educational needs are met will depend on her parents' ability to choose" (Minow, 1999, 551). Does that road lead to equality and quality?

The assumption is that "choice" will lead to competition, which will lead to school improvement. The first charter laws were in 1991 in Minnesota. We now have two decades of experimentation with "charters" and what we know from research is that their *quality* is not consistent; they do not ensure equality in opportunity. There is no broad base of *proven effectiveness* on which we should take action. To act on this "theory," to replicate it widely, is irresponsible.

There is higher personal satisfaction with school choice than what research indicates there should be. The majority can be wrong; it happens. The PDK/Gallup poll shows rising approval of "charters." This may reflect what Eric Hoffer meant by choice putting the responsibility on the individual. It is hard to admit that a school you chose for your child is a mistake. That doesn't change the reality for the child, our focus.

The average American is having trouble judging the quality of schools. It is confusing, and most do not know what goes on in classrooms even when they have a child in them. But people may very well like the way they hear that charters are governed, less bureaucracy. That is a change in "governing structure"; we can, and must, do that without fracturing the whole system.

People with a variety of political ideologies, agendas, and beliefs in some rigid doctrines favor "choice." The powers that be listen to whom they consider to be the *powerful*, some of whom believe in *free-market* ideals for education and others who stand to profit personally from the full *privatization* of public schools. And competition, of course, can lead to lower prices for consumers. The major fault in this theory being applied to public schools is that it isn't the taxpayer who is the customer; it's children (Lewis, 1986, 76).

Taxpayers support public education as a societal obligation, the price for a civilized society, a way to promote our *common culture*, our unity. Taxpayers deserve to have their hard-earned dollars spent effectively and efficiently. So, what the public needs to consider is that education funding, although through three pockets of money (local, state, federal), originates from the same pair of pants—taxpayers. Beware the shell game.

With "choice" comes some increased costs not brought to our attention when the public was originally sold the idea of charters. School buses are crisscrossing the countryside taking children further from their homes, greatly increasing transportation costs. Legislation is at the federal level to fund building costs, because charters began with the promise of not affecting your property taxes. How many local buildings will stand empty while "they" take money out of your *other* pocket for new buildings? Who profits? Who's watching? Who's going to keep track?

Our schools have been moving toward privatization because of *policies* that have promoted excessive testing, "supplemental service providers," "approved" curriculum materials, charter management organizations, in addition to for-profit and not-so-ethical nonprofit charters. Now venture capitalists are coming into play. The vultures are circling. As we should know from experience, free markets are not always fair markets, and the culture of greed will eventually dominate. A free market carries risks. Will we allow the privatization of public education to be the last great frontier for corporate greed to rape and pillage? It should bother *everyone* that it's children at the center of this.

Who profits from a dysfunctional public education system? Does anyone have a vision for what the system will look like down the road when we achieve this "choice"?

And if we take the free-market model even further, once fully privatized, we would want to decrease labor costs to maximize profits, which in this case would mean fewer teachers and/or less pay. Since when is "cheap" an American value? It was not cheap education; it was quality education on which this country's public education system was founded and grounded.

After two generations of use, it is questionable whether we can depend on charters to deliver *quality* education to all and provide the *transparency* and *accountability* that the American public deserves—aren't those the same things we wanted fixed in traditional public schools?

Historically, we have had a strong and vibrant public education system—for over two hundred years—but the foundation is being eroded; it's in need of repair. Not by corporations, by the public. For now, the majority of our schools remain strong.

High-achieving schools have similar characteristics and function in similar ways; charter or traditional isn't the question. Low-performing schools have similar characteristics of their own. Among other things, the *governing* of our dysfunctional schools *does not allow its own people* to become part of the solution. That is a problem that charters have helped to solve, for individuals. It did not improve the schools that needed improving. Also consider that an "unintended" result of "choice" is that it pacifies many of us. If you are only looking out for your own child, this "reform" may work for you and yours. But it never "fixes" the cracks in the education system.

"Choice" should not be looked to as the answer but rather just a temporary step in the necessary *change process*. Consistently on multiple measures of achievement, Massachusetts and Minnesota are high-performing states.

They stand as the ultimate of research—they are living experiments. They respectively have 2 percent and 3 percent of their students in attendance at charter schools. If the proponents of charters want to say that charter school competition deserves credit for spurring the achievements of those states, fine. Consider yourselves "right"; we now need to get on with fixing the schools that need fixing.

What these states *have proven* is that we can improve our existing public school system. "Choice" should include the freedom to stay in the regular public school system knowing you can *trust* them to *cooperate* and *coordinate* efforts that will support and guide the community in making *your community's schools* the best they can be. This assumption must become our reality.

## CONCEPTIONS: THE GOVERNING OF REFORM

Like most words, the word "conceptions" has different meanings. When applied to the replication of *effective* practices in education, both a "formulation of ideas" and the "beginning of some process" (*Webster's*, 1976) seem applicable.

The governing of education is legally a state responsibility. The reality is that some states do a better job fulfilling that responsibility than others. Partially, it is because of differences in the way they are governed. For example, as the result of a lawsuit against the state of Massachusetts, a ruling was made that "all children must get an adequate education" and their 1993 Education Reform Act was created. The goals were to equalize funding among districts and improve all student performance. The state chose to use these instruments for change (as outlined by Minnesota): (1) increase state spending on education, (2) create *curriculum frameworks* that set *high expectations* for student learning, (3) create student performance assessments *aligned* with the curriculum frameworks (http://www.minnesotaspromise.org/publications/documents/Massedreformsummary.pdf).

But there was something else very important to Massachusetts's success, *the process*. In section 3 of their law, they set up *advisory councils* in the following areas: early childhood education; life management skills and home economics; educational personnel; fine arts education; gifted and talented education; math and science education; racial imbalance; parent and community education and involvement; special education; bilingual education; technology education; vocational-technical education; global education; and comprehensive interdisciplinary health education and human service programs. And the law specified "a reasonable balance of members," that they should "be broadly representative of all areas," and it described specifics for each advisory council (http://archives.lib.state.ma.us/actsResolves/1993/1993acts0071.pdf).

We must continue to remind ourselves that we cannot take one piece of the equation or one aspect of a successful "model" without considering all the other factors that contribute to success. Summaries or "briefs" as presented here can never do justice to the bigger picture.

Massachusetts used their available experts and a broad range of interested community members to form councils that established their *success factors*. It couldn't have been easy. Democratic processes never are. But "democracy is not attained through osmosis. It works because people recognize their responsibilities in it and *put forth the effort* to make it work through their actions" (Minzey & LeTarte, 1994, 88). And some states took note, like Minnesota, and followed suit. How their stories end, we can't know. What we do know is that too many states are making uninformed decisions, are not using researched practices, are not using "experts," are not adequately funding education, and are not using a democratic decision-making process. Some states fail to meet their responsibility.

Our founding fathers did not include education as a fundamental right under the U.S. Constitution. By default, it is covered in the Tenth Amendment, which states, "The powers not delegated to the United States by the Constitution, nor prohibited by it to the States, are reserved to the States respectively, or *to the people*."

The founding fathers did not give the U.S. Congress the power to legislate on the subject of education. They did give the Congress the authority to tax and spend for the general welfare. As the article "Constitutional Requirements Governing American Education" (education.stateuniversity.com) explains, "the content of education was a classic area of state, not federal authority." Yet we have been witness to and victims of Congress overstepping its authority, through No Child Left Behind, by holding states hostage with the dangling of the carrot of money leading to intrusion into our classrooms. And *we let it happen*.

At a local school board meeting shortly after one of its members had been to our State School Board Association meeting, one thing that was brought back to the group was the idea that "we must align our curriculum to the test or there will be punitive damages." Our curriculum, what is being taught (the content) and how, is being decided *based on fear* and standardized test results rather than on what our community's children need from the education system. Some local districts are failing to meet their responsibility.

Too many states and localities do not adequately meet their obligation. As a republic, it isn't acceptable. When states fail to provide for the learning needs of all their children, it is the duty of the federal government to provide the needed guidance and support. But federal policy and funding has gone from a focus on the *urgent needs of inequality* in opportunity to testing and accountability of the whole system. This is one pendulum that should swing back and then be cemented down. People who understand this must act to make it right.

As firmly as we believe in our individual states' rights and our local control of education, we must open our minds to the idea that we should and can maintain local control of our local schools' curricula while insisting on our federal government functioning effectively to provide protection and service *without* interference in the classroom. The U.S. Congress is authorized to tax and spend for the *general welfare* of its people. It is not authorized to intrude in the local control of curriculum content.

That does not mean we can't establish national values and goals as our guides and do a better job of disseminating practices and policies that are working. We can. And as we develop our educational philosophies and principles, we can work side-by-side with financial analysts charting the essential materials needed and planning a smooth transition to federal financial support of quality educational opportunity for all schools throughout the United States. At the very least, we must now look back at the ESEA of 1965 and follow its example of looking at money as *an investment* extended to needy children.

In either case, we must use what we know. NCLB results, if used properly and in conjunction with other statistics, identifies the schools our efforts should target first. And our guiding principles concerning what is appropriate for federal intervention and what isn't, should keep our actions from overstepping. Successful districts don't need federal interference. Dysfunctional districts need experienced experts to assist them in *evaluating their problems* and *their solutions*. Then this country will be positioned to make "strategic investments" in education.

There are common problems among schools that struggle to improve that would be best addressed by "a coordinated attack at the state and federal levels, it would be highly wasteful and inefficient to try to address these endemic problems through ad hoc remedies at individual schools. To develop these human resources nationwide, the federal government needs to lead the way so that state and local governments can focus coherently on actually carrying out the hard work of change in their own jurisdictions" (Ratner, 2007, 20). We need to face that reality and *the opportunity* it presents.

## OUR VALUES: SOME IN CONFLICT, MOST NOT

Equality, governing by the consent of the governed, freedom—these were values worth fighting for; they are the basic desires behind our independence. These ideals created a nation offering us all opportunity.

It's time to reawaken that American spirit. Remember, Americans not only settled a land, successfully staged a revolution, and established a new republic, Americans revolutionized the industrial world; we can revolutionize our own education system because we share common values in education. And I would hope we share a common goal.

We see the worth in a school like the one described here:

> The school provides an academically challenging curriculum *with flexibility* to meet the needs of *individual* students. The *faculty works* to instill a feeling of self-worth and self-confidence in each student while also requiring that he or she recognize the needs of others. The *atmosphere* is relaxed and informal with *a balance* between freedom and discipline.
>
> The program is geared to the *mastery* of basic language arts and mathematical skills and encourages individual creative expression. Teachers use a *thematic approach* to learning which gives students an understanding of the relationship between disciplines. Scientific and artistic exploration as well as physical activity are important parts of the curriculum. The computer is used *to enhance* the teaching of many subjects. Students *often visit the wider community* on field trips and for *service projects.* (http://www.sidwell.edu/lower_school/index.aspx)

This is the type of school that many a dignitary chooses for their own child; therein lies vision.

A school such as this honors individuality yet is able to balance it with teaching the student to think of others, seeing a common worth, demonstrating respect. No conflict of values in that, it's balanced. They expect mastery of basic curriculum while acting on the value in exploration, a balanced curriculum. And they value "the atmosphere," seeing the worth in it.

Meanwhile, the public fights over "competition" at the expense of "cooperation." They are in direct conflict in policy and practice. The toxic culture of politics has spilled into classrooms. And it makes no sense.

We value quality teachers yet are accepting that competition for "merit pay" will improve teaching. But in a 2000 Public Agenda survey, more than 86 percent of teachers and 73 percent of administrators "felt: *Student behavior* and *parental support* were more important than increased salary. Teachers require not only *fair and reasonable compensation*, but safety, fairness, and an understanding of the demands of their work environment" (Reeves, 2001, 134).

Parents want their children to enter classrooms where the teachers are happy about doing their job and they are enabled to do it well. It is *not acceptable* to allow government *mandates* from any level of government to have the opposite effect on *our children's* learning environment. Parents like President Obama will tell you, "When a child walks into a classroom, it should be a place of high expectations and high performance" (State of the Union, 2011). Plain and simple.

"To achieve excellence, one focuses *not* on the mission, but on the culture" (Lewis, 1986, xxi). And it is "freedom factors" that "are the foundation for enabling school people to satisfy their higher-level needs. Only when we are able to produce a *school environment* that meets these needs will we be able to *achieve excellence*" (173). This is not what we have created with a test-based, competitive culture. And parents that are out to "give their child every advantage" have added fuel to the fire of competition while modeling a culture of selfishness for their own children.

Equality, governing by the consent of the governed, freedom—these are basic American values. Education law must embody what we value.

Our founding fathers did not frame an education system for us. It is time we face that unmet challenge. Obstacles have been created by the modern economy, mobilization, globalization, and the resultant decline of the family structure and function. But Americans have overcome obstacles of the past that were far greater than that.

America is still known as "the land of opportunity." For that opportunity to be offered equally to each new generation, education must be offered equally to our children. It is an individual adult's responsibility to strive to continue learning to improve their own life. It is their responsibility. A child's education is quite a different matter. "Central to our collective future is the recognition that our capacity to survive and thrive ultimately depends on ensuring to all of our people what should be an unquestioned entitlement—a rich and inalienable right to learn" (Darling-Hammond, 2010, 328). We as a nation have an obligation to our nation's children.

## PRIORITIES FOR SCHOOL IMPROVEMENT

In this country, school improvement has a solid foundation of ideas and proven practices provided collectively by the wisdom of our people; they lie waiting to be used.

Yong Zhao will tell us that "*Personalized learning* recognizes that every child has different talents and different needs, and educational institutions and educators should be responsive to individual children instead of treating them as a collection of products that can be churned out like Henry Ford's Model T" (2009, 186). And he reminds us that what we do not want is "high scores but low ability" (81).

We know that educating children is not a "go-it-alone" type of endeavor. Dr. Joyce L. Epstein of John Hopkins University and the director of the National Network of Partnership Schools (http://www.partnershipschools.org) spent decades addressing these issues and concluded that, "Research shows that well-designed and well-implemented programs of *partnerships* improve schools, strengthen families, energize communities, and increase student success at all grade levels." It's been done; it's being done.

"But perhaps the most important condition for finding common ground and supporting productive engagement between parents and teachers is the frequency of their contacts with one another." And as Dr. Lawrence-Lightfoot went on to point out, "crossing the boundaries frequently and naturally certainly helps produce the conditions for better communication, but it is important to recognize that this does not necessarily require the physical presence of parents in the classroom" (2003, 74). It is doable in a variety of ways.

In *Realizing School Improvement through Understanding the Change Process*, Shirley Hord provides this insight, "when educational leaders understand and acknowledge that the *change process* itself is a factor to be accommodated in their school improvement efforts . . . and when they develop plans that take these factors into account, then they will be providing *leadership* that guides, manages, and supports change. Only then will the likelihood of school improvement be realized" (http://www.sedl.org/change/issues/issues11.html, 1990).

Individuals need to change. First, we must quit taking a narrow, rigid view of the solutions, fixing one piece while another falls apart. Then, we must move forward using what we know to work *cooperatively* to support the processes and practices that are proven ingredients of success. The *community education concept* provides the organizational structure that dysfunctional districts need. And my personal recommendation is that a *community education organizer* be instilled *outside of the regular boundaries* of school building governance. Based on experience in wading in the unfriendly waters inside the boundaries of "dysfunctionality," an organizer outside the *school power structure* offers the best opportunity for this person to act as an ombudsman when needed and keeps the position from being co-opted into the *entrenched existing structure*. With the position within an existing stable institution, such as the Cooperative Extension System, long-term sustainability of collective governance of schools is most safely kept.

Once structures are in place that can put a change process in motion, then we can work more effectively in using lessons we should have learned. Robert V. Bullough provides us with these lessons of importance to school improvement, among others: "school reform consists of *teacher education* and *capacity building*. Sustained school reform will require both a *foundation of trust* among teachers and life-enhancing relationships with one another and with young people" (2007, 178). And this is where our current governing structure fails so badly to recognize what "failed schools" need. They need assistance in building capacity.

"The absence of this staff and parental capacity is assuredly not a problem unique to individual Title I schools. It is a widespread problem resulting from common *policies* and *social conditions* nationwide. Rectifying it will require major improvements in teacher and administrator preparation, teacher and administrator staff development and enhancing parental literacy and parenting skills around the country" (Ratner, 2007, 22).

We also need to "recognize that the problems of failing Title I schools usually infect the *expectations*, *attitudes* and *practices* of all the stakeholders: the principals, teachers, parents and students" (30). The very *culture and conditions* need improving and if a community lacks the capacity to help themselves immediately, they need to be guided through an improvement process designed to help them help themselves.

Some localities and some states lack the capacity to support and guide school improvement processes and it is for this very reason that *we need effective federal education law*. But this time, unlike with No Child Left Behind, it must be driven by people to create workable, practical education policies in order to construct a system of public education able to deliver on the promise of equal opportunity.

Consider the effect in classrooms when we focus on these areas for legislation:

- educate teachers, counselors, parents, and principals to be more *effective*,
- provide support to families, educators, and communities to build successful *partnerships*,
- provide flexibility to stimulate local initiatives *coupled* with responsibility for results,
- support and facilitate *school improvement processes* for lowest-performing schools and states.

Consider that by focusing our efforts we can *create the conditions* to support students, teachers, and their communities *that enable* schools to govern and function based on *democratic principles* using *continuous improvement processes* that are monitored by *performance indicators*. This is a single solution, not a silver bullet; never a single way to use it.

# ENDING THE PRETENSE OF REFORM AND THE ILLUSION OF DEMOCRACY

In my first edition of this book, I wrote that our leaders lacked vision. I was wrong. They do know what quality schools look like; they can visualize them because they have seen them, been in them. Yet too many children are denied this same quality of educational opportunity. There is nothing acceptable about this state of affairs.

When No Child Left Behind (NCLB) was written, policymakers weren't listening, the people were uninformed, and those warning of foreseeable consequences were being brushed aside. Forgive the lawmaking ignoramuses, then, but within five years, good research was documenting the "unintended consequences." The very same people who pushed "the plan" now say they hear us and are calling for "waivers" while offering more slogans than solutions—providing the illusion of democracy.

The foundation for our great country was set by the Declaration of Independence. Its writers were experiencing the corruption and greed of an *oppressive* government and anticipated this country would see this destructive behavior again, for they went on to say, in reference to life, liberty, and the pursuit of happiness, "that *whenever* any Form of Government becomes destructive of these Ends, it is the Right of the People to alter or to abolish it, and to institute new Government, laying its Foundation on such Principles, and organizing its Powers in such Form, as to them shall seem most likely to effect their Safety and Happiness." This was the talk of revolution. Revolution is not only a founding right, it is our duty.

The need to revolutionize the education system was recognized long ago; that plan went unfinished, waiting to become a national priority once again. One meaning of "revolution" is "a complete or radical change of any kind" (*Webster's*, 1976). For the sake of children in classrooms today, recognize that "radical" change is not desirable. It upsets the climate.

The current climate is being disrupted by a multitude of wrongful and oppressive state and federal laws. NCLB should have been our modern-day Boston Tea Party. We should have been burning tests on our Capitol's steps. Instead, one consequence (intended or unintended) of NCLB was that it further fractured the people.

NCLB appeared to be giving us the freedom as individual states to decide our standards and spend our money on designing and testing tests. But, in the end, we were trapped into setting our curriculum based on NCLB rules rather than the needs of our population of learners. *This pretense of reform* effectively divided the states with busy work at a time when we should have united against the *irresponsible intrusion* of the federal government in our classrooms. Just as an administrator can choose to diffuse or ignore any single parent's concerns or issue without fixing the root of a problem, our governing structure in the education system has effectively *subdued us with reforms and choice* and successfully divided us with policy, both nationally and in many states.

"Officials" acknowledge NCLB as "faulty," but lawmakers have refused to change it. It is openly acknowledged that policymakers are not experts on education, and they depend on "briefs," which leaves us vulnerable to the details, yet, we have accepted having politicians lead "education reform." Top-down. These school reformers fail because "they" want a model and a standard that *fits all* schools; it won't work. And this lawmaking process is unacceptable.

We can't reform our education system to society's satisfaction because we do not have a true America education system. With the current "system," we can only piecemeal together bits of reform in the way of ineffective, unequal granting schemes. There is no democratic process, what has been *mandated* are not reforms; we do not have a republican form of government working in the best interest of children. America is weakened by political corruption. And the *safety net of vigilance* has a gaping hole.

To *strengthen* and *improve* the learning conditions in our schools involves changing an extremely entrenched educational bureaucracy that involves the apathy of the people at the bottom and the politics of our political system at the top. There should be no doubt; this is revolutionary thought. A change to the system is a revolutionary change. And success is the only acceptable option.

Our American Revolution was successful because fundamental changes were put into the political system to help ensure mistakes of the past didn't happen in the future—doesn't that sound like something our children deserve to have us do for them?

To ensure the general welfare of the common people through an informed public, revolutionary change is our only hope. Reform and choice satisfies some. It has satisfied the right people. It has satisfied enough of us to keep us from revolting. The time has come when pretenses and illusions must be revealed; the truth brought to the surface.

Our words speak of change; our inactions show our resistance to it. Our founding fathers indicated their understanding of this fact in the Declaration by writing that "Mankind are more disposed to suffer, while Evils are sufferable, than to right themselves by abolishing the Forms to which they are accustomed." They were speaking out to future generations, to us.

*A Nation at Risk* spoke, "Of the tools at hand, the public's support for education is the most powerful." And President Reagan commented on this fact when he said: "This public awareness—and I hope public action—is long overdue. . . . Our challenge now is to create a resurgence of that *thirst for education* that typifies our Nation's history" (National Commission,

1983, 16). In peace or at war, quality education for all children must become and remain *a national priority*. We must change our national education law to meet the nation's need for progress. *People must push policy*. The Tenth Amendment reaffirms that power.

And our Declaration of Independence ended with these words: "And for the support of this Declaration, with firm Reliance on the Protection of divine Providence, we mutually *pledge to each other* our Lives, our Fortunes, and our sacred Honor." Much has been sacrificed.

The ideals of democracy have not let us down; we the people have let down our republic. We need to listen to the words that were left to us, reflect, and respond. We must right ourselves, for we are riding on turbulent waters, teetering in our canoe, and holding on to the hope that we don't tip and go down. The crucial cry for balance must be heard.

As one, I am powerless to change the flow of the current. Together, our belief can overcome the barriers standing in the way of our nations' progress.

> Americans have a sense of pride in the immensity of the national endeavor to educate all the people. Partly this is the pride of the strong nation convinced that its way of life is better than anyone else's. But behind this pride is a hope—or, perhaps a belief. It is a belief in the idea of progress.
>
> —Frank Keppel

# Reflections: Finish the Fight

Ideals are ideas about what should be; at the same time we know and regret
that we will fall short of the mark. It is one thing to aim and fall short of the
mark; it is inexcusable if knowing you will inevitably fall short of the mark,
you do not even take aim.

—Seymour B. Sarason

In our education system, good people are doing good things every day. But
the system is not always kind to people, leaving them feeling powerless.
When a teacher's obituary reads, "It was her wish that everyone *could* and
*should* get a good education, but though she loved her students and colleagues, the pressures of the education system became something she no
longer wanted to fight," that should give us pause.

Why the fight? Getting my children through school felt like a fight. It
shouldn't have been that hard. Maybe it was tough because I never understood the fight, never knew the answer to the question: Who is my opponent?
Who has been working against me in the battle to provide my children, and
my community of children, with the best education possible? I don't want to
believe it is racists and devious elitists who have continued this war against
equal educational opportunities. I don't want to believe it is the ambivalence
or pure selfishness of the public in general that limits excellence for all. I
want to believe that "we know not what we do."

The dream of equal educational opportunity in the Great Society or ob-
taining the level of "excellence in education" as envisioned in the Learning
Society has not come close to a reality. Education has suffered terribly from
the collateral damages of wars. Neither political nor educational leadership
has been strong enough to overcome the forces against which we must fight.

Schools need improving; absolutely and always! The problems have always been the same—how to deal with discipline, how to provide quality teachers, better working conditions, and adequate pay, and how to stimulate public interest in education and its financial support. The answers have always been the same—educate parents and children about the rules of a civil society, better educate teachers, counselors, and administrators, and educate the public with the facts. The belief stands—an informed and educated public will act responsibly.

But for far, far too long we have closed the doors of our classrooms so as not to see the inequalities occurring within them. We closed the doors behind us as we met in our committees to argue the wording of our new plans. And our representatives closed the doors to the people and ignored the daily struggles of parents just wanting a fair shot at what they believe is best for their children, a quality education. The children are seated, today. That is the "fierce urgency of now."

What makes us think it is alright to cram students into overcrowded classrooms where maintaining discipline may end up being nothing more than making them sit like a dog? What makes us think that it is acceptable to offer some students activities that stimulate the love of learning and not offer similar opportunities to all? What makes us think that inequality in opportunity is acceptable for America's children? It isn't. Voices have risen and been ignored. It is time to stop accepting the unacceptable!

I have listened to the arguments: When the pedagogy pendulum swung, the curriculum sequence went out the window; we ended up with too many kids that couldn't read well and do basic math. Progressive education got a bad name and the "accountability" weight swung the pendulum the other way, hard! Progressive and traditional educators went to war over curricula. Business and political leaders took up arms against professional educators adding yet another dimension to public chaos. The noneducators are said to be ill-informed and incapable of directing our public schools. And the educators are accused of having failed to advance the public education system, instead clinging to the "status quo." The union bosses and moneyed bosses are in a power struggle. Children are collateral damage.

We quarrel, bicker, and squabble about who's wrong and who's right, letting our human emotions displace our ability to reason. The fight becomes more about being right and less about doing what is right. The majority of our schools were functioning well but the whole system has been upset over what to do with chronically low-performing schools. Stop. End the blame game and get on with school improvements where we desperately need them.

In politics, we have witnessed the detrimental impasse of rigid "ideologues" unable to legislate responsibly no matter how dire our needs. In the education wars, the "sides" are no different from our inflexible lawmakers—unwilling to compromise, leaving problems unsolved. But with education, this tug-of-war pulls down children, families, communities, and our country. The system has failed to maintain adequate public support for a reason—the educational establishment is no better at listening to the people than our representatives. Our crucial voices go unheard.

The exclusion of the voice of the people, the absence of the democratic process, in working through educational issues leads to frustration, decreased productivity, loss of liberty and freedom, and, in some cases, failure. The high level of frustration produced by "the education wars" has made easy pickings for those looking to make a buck off of us, the government of the people. We must acknowledge that our problems are real. Face the facts; not all schools are doing their best. Face "why" and answer "how" we can make them better. Fix what needs fixing and stop interfering with success.

In Idaho, our law governing schools ends by saying, "Fulfillment of the *expectations* of a thorough system of public schools will continue to depend upon the *vigilance* of district patrons, the *dedication* of school trustees and educators, the *responsiveness* of state rules, and the meaningful *oversight* by the legislature" (Idaho Code 33-1612). These words are good and just. But they ring of empty promises, needs go unfilled. There have been reasonable options offered by multiple organizations and individuals to replace the bad state and national legislation that oppresses us. Lawmakers have not acted. We have no other choice; we must act.

To fulfill our expectations of the system requires the vigilance and dedication *of the people* and responsiveness and oversight of *our "leaders."* It requires shared responsibility. As a parent in a "failing" school, I more than met my responsibility. It was the system that failed to meet its responsibility, while the community looked the other way. Vigilance by the people remains inconsistent and unpredictable. Equal opportunity under those circumstances remains a distant dream; quality education for all—out of reach.

Blame? What's the point? My children did not have access to the quality of education that others do because of where we live. But they did not fail; they didn't get left behind because of the caring, competent individuals in their lives and classrooms. It has always been *an educator* that makes the difference in classrooms—always will be.

It's not immediate investment in new assessments and accountability systems that we require. It is investment in "ensuring that teachers have the world's best training and preparation." It's not "incubators of innovation" , 2009) that we so desperately need; we need *caring individuals* with the ability to listen and personalize instruction (White House—Press Office Fact Sheet: Expanding the Promise of Education in America). We need ordinary Americans to get informed and get involved.

We have been subservient to wrongful federal and state education laws to the detriment of generations of children. There is no excuse for the calamity that has been created in classrooms and no excuse for the silence of our

inaction. We have reached the point where our government officials obviously believe we will not take action. They no longer have to answer to us.
Money has corrupted the lawmaking process.

We are obliged to take social actions. Equal educational opportunity is a
moral imperative. But the moral compass is missing. We are seriously lost
and we aren't looking to one another for support. "The inability to produce a
full-fledged mass movement can be, therefore, a grave handicap to a social
body" (Hoffer, 1951, 165).

Revolutionary change is necessary because the pressing issues in education need to be faced with a determination to make the change real and
lasting by changing the very core of our system so that we don't keep repeating a history not worth repeating. This time, let's not quit with the job
unfinished, the plan unfulfilled.

Dysfunctional districts create the clogs in the K–12 pipeline. Insulated
and insolent higher education officials stop the flow all together. The best
option for ordinary people is to climb up out of the dry stream bed and take
the high road. Stand tall, look back, and listen.

See William Penn. Hear his words, "a free government where the people
make their own laws." There is Frank Manley urging us to get the job done.
And John W. Gardner is telling us to "take the necessary social action" and
"institutionalize the process."

Then look forward and move in the direction of progress. No longer can
we continue to undereducate our people if we wish to survive in an economy
reliant on an educated workforce. Education is central to the solutions of all
our social ills because it is the essential infrastructure underlying all social
improvement. Our society needs to alter the structure of our public education
institutions and lay *new foundation based on principles* in which we believe.

Don't travel the low road. I've been there; it was not a worthwhile journey. It was crowded with others equally feeling excluded. The experience
would have been better had I been given the chance to participate in helping
plan my own children's education, as they do at the Met. I can only imagine
how it must feel to know your children are going to a school with a strong
sense of *cooperation* and *respect* for all, like at Central Park East.

More than anything, I wanted to see my schools consistently reinforce my
values. I wanted my schools to be places where people genuinely cared about
one another and every child's learning opportunities. Based on their individual interests, abilities, and desires, I wanted to see the young adults in my
community leave our schools with the confidence that they had been well
prepared to be successful with whatever career path they chose.

David Bensman stressed that schools are about more than just academic
development; they're about how "social and emotional development grows
out of *caring relationships*, relationships between one whole human being
and another" (2000, 127). Children want us to care. But on the low road,

caring people find that passion, knowledge, experience, common sense, and even wisdom is not enough to improve *their own school*. That is what is broken. Reforms have not overcome "dysfunctionality"; we have failed to use what we know, and we struggle to do as Muriel Lester has told us, be positive.

Think about the immeasurable results of *cooperation*. The productivity of people is improved in a positive work *environment*. The chance for positive self-fulfilling prophesies to become realities is increased. And when parents become welcomed into the equation for success and *share the vision* of their children's schools, what kind of multiplying effect does that have on positive student outcomes? It is our collective contributions that will fulfill the needs of children. We need all the ingredients of success to come together for every child, in every community, in every classroom, every day. The *conditions* for that to occur will be produced by ordinary Americans. Personal relationships build the "social capital" that makes progress possible.

Now think even bigger. We need to set the social machinery in motion to "create a *climate* of thought" (Keppel, 1966, 110) because as Seymour Sarason would remind us, it is crucial that we are *clear in our heads* before we proceed. And reflecting on the governing of schools and the need to tackle those problems, he provided this thought, "Governance issues are political and moral—political in the sense that they involve the *allocation of power* and moral in the sense that they rest on '*shoulds and oughts*'" (1993, 164). Education laws *should* represent our values, beliefs, goals, desires, and needs. We *ought* to be able to write proper legislation to guide our purposes and serve as a usable map.

As congress has already declared, it is the policy of our country that "a *high-quality* education for all individuals and a *fair and equal opportunity* to obtain that education are a *societal good*, are a *moral imperative*, and improve the life of every individual, because the *quality* of our individual lives ultimately *depends* on the quality of the *lives of others*" (ESEA, Sec.1001).

The 2001 Elementary and Secondary Education Act (ESEA) is not a good, desirable, or usable national directive. The 1965 ESEA *should* be our lawmakers' guide as we approach reauthorization of ESEA (No Child Left Behind). We *ought* to go back to using the 1965 version as a framework. Then, we *should* focus on the purposes of the U.S. Department of Education. That institution *ought* to become more supportive of and focused on school improvement efforts through their existing structure with the addition of an improved method of extension of information. We *should* be able to trust our public institutions to do their jobs. The people *ought* to push for their own enlightenment.

The education establishment lost my trust because it is not a publicly operated "system." In general, we can trust our public institutions; they are ours. But because we are not watching closely enough, our laws are allowing too many fingers in the pie making a mess of it. The "system" *should* become self-contained as much as possible because children *ought* to be insulated from the politics of how America does business. There is only one organization that *should* be trusted with the education of the masses and that is the institution of public education—it *ought* to be publicly funded, publicly operated, and publicly supported. With a healthy mistrust called "vigilance," our government can once more work for the people. It's up to us. The future is in our hands.

Ordinary Americans roll up their sleeves and get a job done, just like everyday people everywhere. With good reason, Muriel Lester dedicated *Dare You Face Facts?* "to the common people by whose sweat our grain is produced, our livestock tended, our houses built, our cloths made, our furnaces stoked, our factories manned, and who keep the world sane" (1940). I am asking fellow parents, educators, and all citizens of the United States to please stop the insanity of repeated failures and their detriment to our children. Don't allow the pendulum to swing again. Establish balance; establish common ground. The education system, and our country, is vulnerable and the very basis of democracy itself is our saving grace. The balance is in our hands.

When it comes to power issues in education, let there be no doubt, we've really lost our balance. Political power directing education policy and practices is the internal war most urgently in need of ending. Having rigid ideological agendas driving education law, or leaving renewal processes stalled, is unacceptable. The leverage needed to push policy is in forcing debate during elections; now is the time to create a thought-provoking *climate*. It's time for the people to rediscover their power. The *allocation of power* is not meant to be "them" allowing "us" some power; it is us granting them the privilege of representing our interests.

It is our duty to share the responsibility for student outcomes; we need our voices to carry the weight of that responsibility. Writing good law, though not easy, is just one step. Executing and implementing law is a *process* dependent on people—everyday people. We must have education law that we can, and willingly will, follow.

Simply put, instead of punishing schools and all school people, we need to assist "failing" schools in doing assessments of their school climate, governance issues, finances, student outcomes, unmet needs, and community resources. And we need to educate the people who will be assisting in the improvement efforts both in the schools and community, *building the capacity*, to enable them to go through a *school improvement process* successfully.

The improvement *process* goal is to identify problems, effective solutions, community resources, develop a plan that targets these elements, *and* develop the human and social capital to successfully carry the plan forward and monitor progress. This is the *process* for developing and maintaining the *community education concept*.

This process produces elements of effective schools in line with those revealed by Ratner and Neill in "Common Elements of Successful School Turnarounds: Research and Experience" (2010). Summarized in their words and mine, the *elements* that are *effective* in turning schools around:

1. Responsible and responsive leadership,
2. Instructional improvement,
3. A broad and challenging curriculum,
4. A school climate supportive of teaching and learning,
5. A system of educational support that is inclusive of family and community—a system that sees both as assets in a *partnership to support students*. (See Addendum 1: A National Approach to Effective Schools.)

Done successfully, *the school improvement process* produces children coming to school ready to learn, teachers ready to teach, and the material support to achieve the required "task" of properly educating all students. There is nothing new here. It has been done before and is being done successfully in our own country. This recipe doesn't have just one way of mixing it up and making it come out right. What it needs is *continuous monitoring* to ensure we don't miss an ingredient.

Proven practices will give proven results when selected carefully and applied properly to fit the circumstances of each school. This is why a dysfunctional bureaucracy unable to *disseminate best practices* is inexcusable. The "illusion" of a system, a pseudosystem, cannot be mobilized to support improvement when and where it is needed. We know what we need to do. There are no acceptable excuses for not doing it.

It is time for a revolution, but not one that tears down a government—rather, one that builds a strong education system with the *capacity* to supply the next generation of workers, scholars, and politicians prepared to take on the challenges of tomorrow, whatever they may be. Ordinary Americans have always met challenges with solutions based on a tried-and-true principle—quality matters.

Today, what matters in classrooms is the *climate* that our policies and practices produce. What matters is the teaching and learning *conditions* we create for our teachers and students. What matters is *personalized quality instruction*. Come hell or high water, those are the things we must fight for! Finish that fight.

Today, take aim at ending the pretense of education reform and beginning the effort to use a *proven process* of school improvement. Prepare to fight that good fight—to win. Arm yourself with knowledge; seek the truth. The foundation of progress is our *belief* in an informed citizenry.

Others have said we will need to teach our way out; I'd say we need to educate our way out. And that means the whole of the public. As we move forward, our quality of thought will matter. To "get it right" requires that research and common sense collide in the boundary waters of our school communities. Just like creating the climate for learning, only people can create *the climate for change* in our government institutions.

In the tradition of America, there has to be a balance. "The decision to work out a new federal, state, and local partnership, with checks against the danger of undue power in the hands of any one authority, was a characteristic American solution to the problem. The federal system, established after one revolution, needs constant revision and adaptation to meet new needs" (Keppel, 1966, 86). In a balanced American education system, we need a philosophically balanced curriculum (see Addendum 2) in addition to a *balance of power*. Political influence must be neutralized and *equal opportunity serve as our foundation.*

With mutual respect and understanding, the system can once again be based on *trust* in the fact that we will value the crucial voice of the people in our decisions. School improvement must be a *local responsibility* shared through the democratic governing of schools. States must ensure *accountability* of their system through shared knowledge of measurable results and financial accountings of adequacy and equity. The federal government must return to its role of oversight, support, guidance, research and development, and dissemination of information, and serve when needed to *protect and provide* for the national interest. A system such as this is not unreasonable.

To make progress in this country, we need to change our own *attitudes* before we can change our institutions. In *A Peacock in the Land of Penguins*, B. J. Gallagher and Warren H. Schmidt make the point that the "land of opportunity" "is more than a place. . . . It is *a state of mind . . . an attitude*. It is an openness to new ideas, a willingness to listen, an eagerness to learn, a desire to grow, and the flexibility to change."

Use what has been learned. Seek understanding of the change process so you can explain it to others. Be guided by the Theory of Action; use the Formula for Success as a compass. Demand a better map. Believe in the initiative, resourcefulness, and ability of the people of the United States to unite for the common good. It should be through the idea of "one kid at a time" that we provide educational opportunity. We just can't continue at the pace of one school at a time and expect that we'll ever float this stream to its fruition.

Let's make fixing our struggling schools a priority, for within them are children that need us doing that. Address the issues of the communities that have created those schools, for they are failing families and children in other ways. Make the focus our children, all our children. Use a guiding plan that defines *high expectations* for all the participants: "Ultimately, it is a collective responsibility to ensure that no one is abandoned . . . to a dead-end, dismal school" (Minow, 1999, 555). Kids don't get a second chance nearly often enough.

This edition of *Education's Missing Ingredient* is my second chance. Sahila C. expressed my feelings for me; "There comes a time when you realize that you have done more than your share, when you feel you have done enough and it's someone else's turn to pick up where you left off." Surly I have carried my load. What can I say about the journey? Ultimately, it's about happiness. It's about personal relationships; it's about accepting that things happen for a reason and searching for that reason. It's about, as Don P. would say, "finding our common spirit." It may be in people you meet; other times, you find those souls forged in the words of books, like Muriel Lester reminding us, "This is why you're on earth, to learn a lesson" (1940, 31). The lessons learned, that I chose to share, will sit on a shelf in the Library of Congress, across from the Halls of Congress, side-by-side with so many worthy and crucial voices. Your representative may choose to ignore the voices but you didn't. Now what will you do? Search further, or, if you have clarity, will you now share it?

Education is too important to only have a "brief" knowledge of its policies and practices. The right education battle is the one for clarity. We must clearly see the problems and the solutions. And we must educate each other through our personal interactions, *one person at a time*. As Stephan M. can tell you, you have to get on their level and connect before you can educate. *The public needs clarity*. They need to see the grave reality that our once public institutions are systematically being dismantled and sold. And they need to see that there is hope for the public regaining control and making them stronger and better, the fulfillment of which depends on us all—and our faith in each other.

I remain optimistic. But even optimists have moments of uncertainty. There is a heavy feeling looming over me like a huge, stormy cloud of doubt. It wasn't until the day I was permitted to attend my daughter's high school political philosophy class that the seed of this insecurity revealed itself.

I was stunned to speechlessness when I heard this young woman of mine state her thesis as "morality has gone from a universal idea to extremely relative." Young people get it. Their clear vision can see the culture of greed and selfishness, judging "rightness" as it relates to "me." The sad thing was, when the teacher asked the students what morals they had in common; they had no answers. I know these kids. I know their families. I know they share similar moral beliefs, but they didn't see their commonality. Our self-serving attitudes have blinded us to the value in our commonwealth. Our young need the advice and wisdom of older generations. Fill the wisdom gap. Give the next generation a working moral compass.

We are a nation at risk. Quality and equality in education is morally right for the common good. But do Americans care, enough about those values being applied to educating children, to act? This great uncertainty can only be answered by the people. Will we unite as a nation, this time not to support a war, but to support the American ideals of quality and equality? Will we make *the choice* to develop a system aimed at strengthening and improving all our schools? I know we can become better and better.

The promise of America will be fulfilled through her people. The urgency is the opportunity of this moment. I remain hopeful, hoping you better understand and see the power in understanding. I trust you can see that the answers have surfaced, again. I hope you are disturbed that the answers are within reach and uncomfortable with the fact that we haven't snatched them from the stream and clung to them like our lives depended on it. I hope, in your heart, that you know the answer. The answer to America's problems will always be found within her people; the answer is *us*.

My vision for the education of the citizens of the United States is to see us unite and finish the necessary and peaceful revolution that was started for us with equality and quality as our non-negotiable starting points. I see an awakening of the American spirit. I see us take aim. I see my stormy cloud of doubts bursting open, this time with kept promises that quickly send us down the turbulent stream to calmer waters.

> In the evolutionary stream we have to keep adjusting ourselves to changing environment. We have to be often disturbed, made uncomfortable: otherwise we should be content with second best.
>
> —Muriel Lester

# Addendum 1: Proclamation and Proposal for Excellent Education for All

## A DECLARATION OF DEVOTION TO EDUCATIONAL EXCELLENCE

We the People of the United States, in Order "to strengthen and improve educational quality and educational opportunity in this Nation's elementary and secondary schools" will act in accordance with the principles and practices that will guide and support our efforts to ensure excellent education for all.

Our goal is to achieve and maintain an education system that offers maximum opportunities for all students to learn while holding the highest expectations for the individual pupil and all those that are responsible for supporting the student. This system will continuously strive to improve its role in serving the needs of our free, fair, and democratic republic.

To accomplish our goal, the expectation set for the system is that all those governing, employed by, and voluntarily supporting our public schools will function based on mutual respect of each other and all stakeholders in an effort to earn and maintain the trust of the people in their institution of public education.

We:

1. Recognize that it is in the best interest of the nation to assure equal opportunity to be educated to the fullest of an individual's potential and that goal can best be realized by maintaining a strong and effective public education system.

Action: provide equitable and adequate resources with the knowledge, guidance, and oversight to use those resources wisely.

2. Recognize that to improve means we must consistently and accurately assess current conditions of our schools based on appropriate data that aligns with our national goals.

Action: establish a report card for the nation that uses indicators of what the public deems important and make the findings know in an annual State of the Nation's Schools with corresponding State of Our State schools reports.

3. Recognize that to ensure the strengthening and improvement of local schools requires a strong and capable Department of Education nationally and in every state.

Action: reaffirm the commitment of the U.S. Department of Education to its original purposes, identify the states seen as chronically low-performing, and support the training of those state department personnel in effective school improvement processes.

4. Support community organizing efforts to engage parents and the community in youth support activities, programs, and their schools.

Action: enlist Cooperative Extension System to train volunteers, disseminate proven practices, and assist in coordinating efforts to use locally available resources more efficiently and effectively.

5. Support research, development, and diffusion of effective practices.

Action: invest in our existing public institutions of higher education focusing on improving teacher, counselor, and leader education; and reinvest, reclaim, and refocus the function of regional educational laboratories to maintain integrity, relevance, and responsiveness in research aimed at seeking solutions for communities' education problems; and establish the outreach and extension of research findings to ensure their use in educational improvement practices.

6. Support those schools that have been identified as chronically low-performing by providing federal emergency assistance, immediately, in cooperation with state and local education agencies.

Action: provide a federal support team to help facilitate school and community members in a guided improvement process.

We will:

- Maintain local responsibility shared through the democratic governing of schools,
- Depend on state accountability with shared knowledge of measurable results and costs,
- And, rely on federal oversight, guidance, and support through the practices of the U.S. Department of Education and through responsive and responsible federal policy set by Congress and the president of the United States.

Federal education law will be written with the understanding that effective execution of the law depends on local education personnel with public participation and support. In order for all who wish to assist their schools in fulfilling the promise of maximum educational opportunities with the highest expectations, the Elementary and Secondary Education Act will be reduced, simplified, and made to once again address the needs of the educationally deprived children of this nation.

## EXCELLENT EDUCATION FOR ALL THROUGH THE ELEMENTARY AND SECONDARY EDUCATION ACT

The focus of the Elementary and Secondary Education Act is to provide the equal access to quality education that is not currently available to all children in the United States. The ultimate goal is to, someday in the near future, be able to change the focus of this law to preserving and protecting that equality. Until that day, we must recognize the issues that are barriers to equality in our schools and classrooms and fully address those problems directly.

To fulfill our duty to America's children, effective schools must be established in every community where they do not currently exist. Understanding that those communities with the highest concentrations of poverty have children at greatest risk of being educationally underserved, their needs will be our first priority. It is our responsibility as a nation to address the identified lowest performing schools throughout our land, as a short-term goal, while providing a long-term strategy to prevent the wide gaps in opportunities, and therefore educational achievement, that we have experienced in our past and that continue to plague our nation's children today.

In addition to providing the best in educational opportunities to every child, this plan views appropriation of funds as a national strategic educational investment and expects communities to make wise use of all education resources. It is acknowledged that the urgent need of children begs for some emergency measures.

Purposes:

- To establish equal access to quality education,
- To strengthen and improve all schools.

Title I—*Education of Children of Low Income Families* to provide formula-funded financial assistance to local education agencies in support of *children from low-income families* in order to *expand and improve* community efforts to meet their learning needs.

Execution: To address learning needs requires a "needs assessment." School staff (principals, counselors, aids, and teachers) and parents (or other adults involved in these high-needs children's lives) will be the first to collectively identify those needs. Those identified needs will then be brought to the attention of the larger group of community stakeholders (civic, nonprofit organizations, foundations, and concerned individuals) to be further defined, measures for success indicators established, and existing resources in the community identified. "Gaps" in resources will be identified and brought to the attention of state education officials so that no identified need goes unaddressed. State officials will be responsible for identifying their resources and establishing indicators of their success and to continually monitor and report on their ability to meet their responsibility. Needs assessments will be done using the existing government assessment tools.

Emergency measures: Those Title I schools now designated as chronically low-performing will be guided through the assessment and improvement processes with cooperative funding ("set aside" Title I money) and staff from the state and local districts with a "support team" provided through the U.S. Department of Education.

Schools identified as chronically low-performing need strong, effective, democratic leadership to take these schools through a successful school improvement process. A federal leadership program (Academy) will be "designed to enable people who are already experienced principals and other school leaders, knowledgeable about how schools work and the special problems they face, to learn how to turn around the expectations, beliefs and practices of school stakeholders in low-performing schools. The expected focus of the Academy would be on how to improve instruction and change schools' culture" (Ratner, The "Lead Act," H.R. 5495/S 3469: Briefing Paper).

Accountability: Using the indicators of success as designated for targeted results through the school improvement process, the "appropriate objective measurements" will be used to judge the "effectiveness of the programs in meeting the special educational needs of educationally deprived children." Local and state officials will have established the parameters (what and how often) of those measurements and will make those facts transparent to the community and state, respectively. An accounting of expenses and results of the uses of Title I money will be reported to federal officials for review.

National monitoring of achievement gaps through the random use of the National Assessment of Educational Progress (NAEP) will continue unchanged. Results of progress by the nation and cost/benefits will be reported annually to the president, Congress, and the nation.

Title II—*School Library Resources, Textbooks, and Other Instructional Materials* to be provided through grant-funding to offer access to educational materials *for all students* in the State recognizing the invaluable human and material resources that a library provides for a community.

Execution: To provide equal opportunity, the State will be required to assess the equity of resources in its districts, establish the communities that are priorities, establish the material priorities within those communities (using input from stakeholders), work cooperatively to use existing resources to provide the "materials gap," and, only where sources have been exhausted, work cooperatively with these communities to secure a federal grant through this title to supplement materials essential to offering equal-quality learning supports.

Title III—*Supplementary Educational Centers and Services*, available to the *entire community* through grant-funding, or formula funding where high-poverty rates and chronically low-performing schools exist, to provide services not currently offered but deemed vital to educational improvement in underserved areas. These centers and services are to have the "participation of persons broadly representative of the cultural and educational resources of the area" as a way to "utilize the best available talents and resources" to "substantially increase the educational opportunities."

Execution: Services deemed essential to children being "ready to learn," as determined by school and community needs assessments and demonstrated lack of existing resources, will be given priority. All communities will be encouraged to use their existing resources wisely by encouraging cooperative efforts with existing nonprofits and civic organizations.

Emergency measures: Where epidemiological studies show a disproportionate incidence of childhood disorders that affect learning, those areas will be designated a "disaster" and emergency measures implemented through the appropriate state and federal agencies, in cooperation with organizations and foundations. Examples being high levels of lead or high percentages of children affected by drugs such as methamphetamines. In addition, given that an adult advisor or mentor can greatly improve a student's chances for school success, if an "advisors corps" or mentorship program does not exist, one will be created immediately in an existing public institutional structure, if other resources are not available.

Title IV—*Educational Research and Training; Cooperative Research Act* to support educational research and training to enable the Department of Education to more effectively accomplish its purposes and to perform its duties including dissemination of information, funded directly for the Department with formula funding for the lowest-performing districts. The research, training, and dissemination of information will be targeted at improving the quality of teaching, counseling, advising, and parental and community engagement practices—to improve student achievement.

Execution: Regional Educational Research Laboratory facilities that were previously funded by federal dollars should be reclaimed and restructured to assist the research needs of the nation's chronically low-performing schools. The U.S. Department of Education will do an internal programs audit with an eye to potential duplications with regional laboratories that will be incorporated into their structure. In the short term, the department must "lead the states and localities to make the structural changes in teacher and administrator preparation and training, coupled with family support" (Ratner, 2007, 36).

Dissemination of research findings will, first, focus on the elements of developing effective schools, community education concepts, parent and family engagement and participation, with special focus on fostering understanding of the change process in people. Once the system of distribution is established, a free flow of information of best practices with practical applications will be available.

*Emergency measures*: Because chronically low-performing schools are in communities least likely to have the existing human capacity to overcome the obstacles of systemic school change, a community education organizer will facilitate the flow of information from the Department of Education to local school personnel and community members plus assist with the implementation of the other emergency measures previously mentioned. It is recommended that the feasibility of using the existing structure of the Cooperative Extension System to house this position be fully explored.

Title V—*State Departments of Education* formula-funding will be used "to stimulate and assist in strengthening the *leadership* resources of State educational agencies" to assist them in identifying "educational problems, issues, and needs in the State."

Execution: States that have a historical trend of low-performance or persistent and wide achievement gaps on NAEP scores will be required to assemble a state school improvement team to actively participate alongside the federal "support teams" in the communities that have emergency measures in place.

Knowing that our public schools will always have problems to solve, these measures are not proposed as a once-and-for-all answer. They should be seen as a necessary, temporary, first step in a transformation process aimed at providing equal educational opportunity of the highest quality. The first annual national report will simply and clearly provide the public with the measurements that we will be using as a nation. So, as a final proposal for this Act, it is recommended that a Presidential Commission on Indicators of Educational Quality be called to establish the quality indicators to which this nation will commit itself and its resources.

Final notes: The guidance required to write this addendum was provided by the past and present work of others. The framework for the national approach was provided by Francis (Frank) Keppel's summary of the work by the 88th and 89th Congresses (1966, 69). Keppel's writings also provided the general outline for the original titles of the Elementary and Secondary Education Act, which no longer correlate to what we now call No Child Left Behind.

In addition to Gary Ratner's work as quoted, there are so many other influential voices unheard by Congress over the years that it is an impossibility to mention them all. Their good work has been noticed and played a role in influencing the thought behind this proclamation and proposal. Here are a few examples: *Framework for Providing All Students an Opportunity to Learn through the Reauthorization of the Elementary and Secondary Education Act, A Broader-Bolder Approach, and Empowering Schools and Improving Learning: A Joint Organizational Statement on the Federal Role in Public Schooling.*

You will find very few qualifiers in this proposal in reference to race or special education status. That is because equality is equality; by its very definition, we are all the same. Once you understand how equality should be applied to school children and the practices we must hold in highest esteem in our classrooms, no qualifiers are necessary. What is necessary is that people now push policy that is fair and balanced, represents our expectations, and focuses on providing high-quality personalized learning opportunities. For America, this is what opportunity looks like.

# Addendum 2: Establishing Balanced Curriculum in Our Classrooms

*A NATION AT RISK* AND *THE STORY OF THE EIGHT-YEAR STUDY* ANSWER THE QUESTIONS, WHAT TO TEACH AND HOW TO TEACH

The history of these two commissioned research studies, *A Nation at Risk* and *The Eight-Year Study*, makes for good reading. But if you have a "side" in the curriculum wars, perhaps the history and the labels it would carry might add prejudice to your acceptance of the ideas. For those in the field of education, the titles may be enough to close your mind. Try harder.

Both studies focused on our secondary schools and their inadequacies in holding our students' interest in school, preparing students for college, and preparing them for life in general. Or as Aikin stated, we need "to consider ways by which the secondary schools of the United States might better serve all our young people" (1942, 1). These two studies addressed the same issue forty years apart.

Unfortunately, for the sake of correctness, I must identify the quotes I draw from the work of Wilford M. Aikin as he presented the findings of *The Eight-Year Study*. My preference would have been to mix them in with the recommendations of the National Commission on Excellence in Education and have no one be the wiser. I trust everyone will be open-minded enough to look at the findings of both studies through the lens of *what is best for our students*.

The following is a summary of *A Nation at Risk* with quotes from Aikin as indicated. Much of the summary is verbatim without editorial exclusion of ideas that are contrary to my own. Words have been put in italics to draw attention to the common ground of these two studies. Edits were made for ease of reading in hopes of making the advice more readily available for consideration and use.

## SUMMARY OF RECOMMENDATIONS
### (*A NATION AT RISK*, 1983, 23–33)

The recommendations are based on *the beliefs* that:

- Everyone can learn,
- Everyone is born with an urge to learn which can be nurtured,
- A solid high school education is within the reach of virtually all,
- Life-long learning will equip people with the skills required for new careers and for citizenship,
- The American people can begin to act now,
- These recommendations promise lasting reform,
- Schools, districts, and States plans may differ from our recommendations in some details,
- These recommendations apply to public, private, and parochial schools and colleges alike, all are valuable national resources,
- The variety of student aspirations, abilities, and preparation requires that appropriate content be available to satisfy diverse needs,
- Attention must be directed to both the nature of the content available and to the needs of particular learners, for example, gifted students may need a curriculum enriched and accelerated while educationally disadvantaged students may require special curriculum materials, smaller classes, or individual tutoring to help them master the material presented,
- We hold a common expectation, the best effort and performance from all students, whether they are gifted or less able, affluent or disadvantaged, whether destined for college, the farm, or industry.

*"The democratic way of life is based upon the assumption of respect for human personality" (Aikin, 31).

### Recommendation A: Content

We recommend that State and local high school graduation requirements be strengthened and that, at a minimum, all students seeking a diploma be required to lay the foundations in the Five New Basics by taking the following curriculum during their 4 years of high school: (a) 4 years of English; (b) 3 years of mathematics; (c) 3 years of science; (d) 3 years of social studies;

and (e) one-half year of computer science. For the college-bound, 2 years of foreign language in high school are strongly recommended in addition to those taken earlier.

These Basics, together with work in the fine and performing arts and foreign languages, constitute the mind and spirit of our culture. The following Implementing Recommendations are intended as illustrative descriptions to clarify what constitutes a strong curriculum.

## Implementing Recommendations

1. The teaching of English in high school should equip graduates to:
(a) Comprehend, interpret, evaluate, and use what they read;
(b) Write well-organized, effective papers;
(c) Listen effectively and discuss ideas intelligently;
(d) Know our literary heritage and how it enhances imagination and ethical understanding, and how it relates to the customs, ideas, and values of today's life and culture.

2. The teaching of mathematics in high school should equip graduates to:
(a) Understand geometric and algebraic concepts;
(b) Understand elementary probability and statistics;
(c) Apply mathematics in everyday situations;
(d) Estimate, approximate, measure, and test the accuracy of their calculations.

NOTE: In addition to the traditional sequence of studies available for college-bound students, new, equally demanding mathematics curricula need to be developed for those who do not plan to continue their formal education immediately.

*"Every student should achieve competence in the essential skills of communication—reading, writing, oral expression—and in the use of quantitative concepts and symbols" (Aikin, 138).

3. The teaching of science in high school should provide graduates with an introduction to:
(a) The concepts, laws, and processes of the physical and biological sciences;
(b) The methods of scientific inquiry and reasoning;
(c) The application of scientific knowledge to everyday life;
(d) The social and environmental implications of scientific and technological development.

NOTE: Science courses must be revised and updated for both the college-bound and those not intending to go to college. An example of such work is the American Chemical Society's Chemistry in the Community program.

*"The immediate purpose is satisfaction of the pupil's desire to know and understand; but the larger purpose may be to develop habits of critical thinking and intellectual honesty, to search for true cause and effect relationships" (Aikin, 50).

4. The teaching of social studies in high school should be designed to:
(a) Enable students to fix their places and possibilities within the larger social and cultural structure;
(b) Understand the broad sweep of both ancient and contemporary ideas that have shaped our world;
(c) Understand the fundamentals of how our economic system works and how our political system functions;
(d) Grasp the difference between free and repressive societies.

NOTE: An understanding of each of these areas is *requisite to the informed and committed exercise of citizenship in our free society*.

*"Inert subject matter should give way to content that is live and pertinent to the problems of youth and modern civilization" (Aikin, 138).

5. The teaching of computer science in high school should equip graduates to:
(a) Understand the computer as an information, computation, and communication device;
(b) Use the computer in the study of the other Basics and for personal and work-related purposes;
(c) Understand the world of computers, electronics, and related technologies.

In addition to the New Basics, other important curriculum matters must be addressed.

6. Achieving proficiency in a foreign language ordinarily requires from 4 to 6 years of study and should, therefore, be started in the elementary grades.
7. Provide students with programs that advance students' personal, educational, and occupational goals, such as the fine and performing arts and vocational education.
8. The curriculum leading to the high school years should provide a sound base in such areas as English language development and writing, computational and problem solving skills, science, social studies, foreign language, and the arts plus foster an enthusiasm for learning and the development of the individual's gifts and talents.

9. We encourage the continuation of efforts by groups to revise, update, improve, and make available new and more diverse curricular material and the consortia of educators and scientific, industrial, and scholarly societies that cooperate to improve the school curriculum.

*"No aspect of any school's work should be so firmly fixed in practice or tradition as to be immune from honest inquiry and possible improvement" (Aikin, 19).

## Recommendation B: Standards and Expectations

We recommend that schools, colleges, and universities adopt more rigorous and measurable standards, and higher expectations, for academic performance and student conduct, and that 4-year colleges and universities raise their requirements for admission. This will help students do their best educationally with challenging materials in an environment that supports learning and authentic accomplishment.

## Implementing Recommendations

1. Grades should be indicators of academic achievement so they can be relied on as evidence of a student's readiness for further study.
2. Four-year colleges and universities should raise their admissions requirements and advise all potential applicants of the standards for admission in terms of specific courses required, performance in these areas, and levels of achievement on standardized achievement tests in each of the five Basics and, where applicable, foreign languages.
3. Standardized tests of achievement (not to be confused with aptitude tests) should be administered at major transition points from one level of schooling to another and particularly from high school to college or work.

*The purposes of these tests would be to*:

(a) Certify the student's credentials;
(b) Identify the need for remedial intervention;
(c) Identify the opportunity for advanced or accelerated work.

NOTE: The tests should be administered as part of a nationwide (but not federal) system of State and local standardized tests. This system should include other diagnostic procedures that assist teachers and students to evaluate student progress.

4. Textbooks and other tools of learning and teaching should be upgraded and updated to assure more rigorous content.
5. In considering textbooks for adoption, States and school districts should:

(a) Evaluate texts and other materials on their ability to present rigorous and challenging material clearly;

(b) Require publishers to furnish evaluation data on the material's effectiveness.

6. Because no textbook in any subject can be geared to the needs of all students, funds should be made available to support text development in "thin-market" areas, such as those for disadvantaged students, the learning disabled, and the gifted and talented.

7. To assure quality, all publishers should furnish evidence of the quality and appropriateness of textbooks, based on results from field trials and credible evaluation. Widespread consumer information services for purchasers are badly needed.

8. New instructional materials should reflect the most current applications of technology in appropriate curriculum areas, the best scholarship in each discipline, and research in learning and teaching.

*"The Eight-Year Study has demonstrated beyond question that colleges can secure all the information they need for selection of candidates for admission without restricting the secondary school by prescribing the curriculum" (Aikin, 122).

## Recommendation C: Time

We recommend that significantly more time be devoted to learning the New Basics. This will require more effective use of the existing school day, a longer school day, or a lengthened school year.

## Implementing Recommendations

1. Students in high schools should be assigned far more homework than is now the case.

2. Instruction in effective study and work skills should be introduced in the early grades and continued throughout the student's schooling.

3. School districts and State legislatures should strongly consider 7-hour school days, as well as a 200- to 220-day school year.

4. The time available for learning should be expanded through better classroom management and organization of the school day. If necessary, additional time should be found to meet the special needs of slow learners, the gifted, and others who need more instructional diversity.

5. The burden on teachers for maintaining discipline should be reduced through the development of firm and fair codes of student conduct that are enforced consistently, and by considering alternative classrooms, programs, and schools to meet the needs of continually disruptive students.

6. Attendance policies with clear incentives and sanctions should be used to reduce the amount of time lost through student absenteeism and tardiness.

7. Administrative burdens on the teacher and related intrusions into the school day should be reduced to add time for teaching and learning.

8. Placement and grouping of students, as well as promotion and graduation policies, should be guided by the academic progress of students and their instructional needs, rather than by rigid adherence to age.

*"The Thirty Schools [in the Eight-Year Study] have tried to teach more important things in better ways" (85), "enriched content of traditional subjects" (47), recognized the "need of youth to do something useful in the adult world". . . in their community (Aikin, 64).

## Recommendation D: Teaching

This recommendation consists of seven parts. Each is intended to improve the preparation of teachers or to make teaching a more rewarding and respected profession. Each of the seven stands on its own and should not be considered solely as an implementing recommendation.

1. Persons preparing to teach should be required to meet high educational standards, to demonstrate an aptitude for teaching, and to demonstrate competence in an academic discipline. Colleges and universities offering teacher preparation programs should be judged by how well their graduates meet these criteria.

2. Salaries for the teaching profession should be increased and should be professionally competitive, market-sensitive, and performance-based. Salary, promotion, tenure, and retention decisions should be tied to an effective evaluation system that includes peer review so that superior teachers can be rewarded, average ones encouraged, and poor ones either improved or terminated.

3. School boards should adopt an 11-month contract for teachers. This would ensure time for curriculum and professional development, programs for students with special needs, and a more adequate level of teacher compensation.

4. School boards, administrators, and teachers should cooperate to develop career ladders for teachers that distinguish among the beginning instructor, the experienced teacher, and the master teacher.

5. Substantial nonschool personnel resources should be employed to help solve the immediate problem of the shortage of mathematics and science teachers. Qualified individuals, including recent graduates with mathematics and science degrees, graduate students, and industrial and retired scientists could, with appropriate preparation, immediately

begin teaching in these fields. A number of our leading science centers have the capacity to begin educating and retraining teachers immediately. Other areas of critical teacher need, such as English, must also be addressed.

6. Incentives, such as grants and loans, should be made available to attract outstanding students to the teaching profession, particularly in those areas of critical shortage.

7. Master teachers should be involved in designing teacher preparation programs and in supervising teachers during their probationary years.

*"The secondary school would be encouraged to know each student well and to provide experiences most suitable to his development . . . chief reason for confidence in the schools . . . the genuine sense of responsibility which most teachers feel" (Aikin, 124).

## Recommendation E: Leadership and Fiscal Support

We recommend that citizens across the Nation hold educators and elected officials responsible for providing the leadership necessary to achieve these reforms, and those citizens provide the fiscal support and stability required to bring about the reforms we propose.

## Implementing Recommendations

1. Principals and superintendents will play a crucial leadership role in developing school and community support for the reforms proposed, and school boards must provide them with the professional development and other support required in performing their leadership role effectively.

2. State and local officials, including school board members, governors, and legislators, have the primary responsibility for financing and governing the schools, and should incorporate the reforms we propose in their educational policies and fiscal planning.

3. The Federal Government, in cooperation with States and localities, should help meet the needs of key groups of students such as the gifted and talented, the socioeconomically disadvantaged, minority and language minority students, and the handicapped. In combination these groups include both national resources and the Nation's youth who are most at risk.

4. In addition, we believe the Federal Government's role includes several functions of national consequence that States and localities alone are unlikely to be able to meet:

   (a) Protecting constitutional and civil rights for students and school personnel;

(b) Collecting data, statistics, and information about education generally;

(c) Supporting curriculum improvement and research on teaching, learning, and the management of schools;

(d) Supporting teacher training in areas of critical shortage or key national needs;

(e) Providing student financial assistance and research and graduate training.

NOTE: We believe the assistance of the Federal Government should be provided with a minimum of administrative burden and intrusiveness.

5. The Federal Government has the primary responsibility to identify the national interest in education. It should also help fund and support efforts to protect and promote that interest. It must provide the national leadership to ensure that the Nation's public and private resources are marshaled to address the issues discussed in this report.

6. This Commission calls upon educators, parents, and public officials at all levels to assist in bringing about the educational reform proposed in this report. We also call upon citizens to provide the financial support necessary to accomplish these purposes.

*"The Thirty Schools [in the Eight-Year Study] have learned that effective democratic leadership is essential" (Aikin, 134).

## A Final Word (p. 36)

"This is not the first or only commission on education, and some of our findings are surely not new, but old business that now at last must be done. For no one can doubt that the United States is under challenge from many quarters. . . . It is by our willingness to take up the challenge, and our resolve to see it through, that America's place in the world will be either secured or forfeited. Americans have succeeded before and so we shall again."

"We are determined that the earth they [boys and girls now in high schools] inherit shall not be in chains. Theirs will be the task that only free men can perform in a world of freedom. It will be an even greater task than ours. To prepare them for it is the supreme opportunity of the schools of our democracy" (Aikin, 139).

# Addendum 3: Noteworthy People

Throughout this book each quotation used at chapter and section beginnings was carefully chosen to convey a thought. Many of the people quoted may not be familiar to you at all or as contributors to educational improvement. Many have gone to their graves with unfulfilled dreams for improved educational opportunity. They all deserve another look and merit another listen.

As with any attempt at giving a reader a historical perspective, the following brief descriptions are skewed based on my perspective and what I would like the reader to take away from this section. I encourage all to explore further and read their work or what others have written about them. Their individual and combined contributions to education and the world in general are truly inspiring.

The majority of facts were gathered from the 2002 *World Book Encyclopedia* published by World Book, Inc., out of Chicago, Illinois. Other quotes, additional facts, and updates for this second edition are as indicated.

I encourage the reader to take the time to refer back in the book to the quotes before reading about each person. It adds depth to the understanding of their words.

## John Adams (1735–1826)

See quotation on page 107.

John Adams was a Harvard College graduate who taught school briefly before going on to practice law. He bravely and openly opposed the Stamp Act and was said to have become "enraged" about the British tax on tea, thus becoming infamous for his role in adoption of the Declaration of Independence. As a delegate to the Second Continental Congress in 1776, he urged Thomas Jefferson to be the one to draft that document for us.

About education, he wrote, "Laws for the liberal education of youth, especially of the lower class of people, are so extremely wise and useful, that, to a humane and generous mind, no expense for this purpose would be thought extravagant" (www.liberty1.org/JohnAdamsThoughtsonGovernment.htm).

## Francis Bacon (1561–1626)

See quotation on page 59.

Francis Bacon was born in London, entered Trinity College, Cambridge, at the age of twelve, and held several government positions. He believed that, to discover truths, the mind must be rid of four prejudices: (1) tribe—the tendency to generalize (uncritical perception cannot be trusted); (2) cave—the tendency to base knowledge on experiences, education, and tastes (failing to see the variables in these things); (3) marketplace—the tendency to depend on language to communicate (words may be misinterpreted); and (4) theater—the tendency to be influenced by previous philosophies and laws of reasoning that are merely products of imagination.

His greatest contribution to education and science in particular was the development of the scientific method of solving problems: "He argued that a clear system of scientific inquiry would assure man's mastery over the world" (www.blupete.com).

## Nicholas Murray Butler (1862–1947)

See quotation on page 72.

Butler is known as an educational administrator, national Republican leader, advisor to seven presidents, and university president. He received his bachelor's, master's, and doctoral degrees from Columbia College (University).

He established the institution known as Teachers College, became president of Columbia University in 1902, founded the *Educational Review*, served on the New Jersey Board of Education, and was instrumental in the development of the College Entrance Examination Board. Theodore Roosevelt referred to him as Nicholas Miraculous Butler.

Butler "sought to unite the world of education and that of politics in a struggle to achieve world peace through international cooperation." He won the Nobel Peace Prize along with Jane Addams in 1931 (Nobelprize.org).

## S. (Silas) Douglass Cater Jr. (1923–1995)

See quotation on page 136.

Douglass Cater, close advisor and speechwriter for President Johnson, understood both the concepts behind educational improvement and those of the politics of problem solving. Prior to his work in the White House, he worked as an author and journalist covering national affairs. He was considered Johnson's "resident education specialist."

His wife said, in reference to the Elementary and Secondary Education Act (ESEA), "It was one of his proudest achievements" (http://www.nytimes.com/1995/09/16/obituaries/douglass-cater-is-dead-at-72-educator-and-presidential-aide.html?src=pm).

Francis Keppel (credited as the architect of ESEA, author of *The Necessary Revolution in American Education*) seemed to concur in an inscription of his book: To Doug Cater, who would have written this book far better if his life allowed—and who has made a devoted admirer of . . . Frank Keppel, May, 3 1966.

## Calvin Coolidge (1872–1933)

See quotation on page 99.

Calvin Coolidge served as vice president under Warren Harding and became our thirtieth president on Harding's death. Coolidge then won the following election and was viewed as very popular with the people of that time.

He felt education was "primarily a means of establishing ideals" and that its "first great duty is the formation of character, which is the result of heredity and training." In his view, "the whole question at issue is, what does the public welfare require for the purpose of education? What are the fundamental things that young Americans should be taught? What is necessary for society to come to a larger comprehension of life?" (community.middlebury.edu).

## John Dewey (1859–1952)

See quotations on pages 104 and 146.

A graduate of the University of Vermont, with a PhD from Johns Hopkins, John Dewey left his mark on the world as an educator, philosopher, and leader of the pragmatism movement. During his career, he lectured throughout the world and here at home on various issues from education to political and social movements, including women's suffrage.

His own philosophy has been labeled as instrumentalism, in that he believed we must use intelligence as an instrument for overcoming obstacles. A focus of his writings was often on the problem of how to close the gap between thought and action. He thought children coming to school should be considered in the context that they are "to do things and live in a community which gave them real, guided experiences which fostered their capacity to contribute to society" (wildercom.com).

### Christopher Dock (late 1690s–1771)

See quotation on page 60.

Christopher Dock immigrated to the American colonies around 1714. He was seen as a deeply religious person and served as a schoolmaster for Mennonite schools in Skippack and Philadelphia. He is credited with writing what is considered the first American book of teaching (pedagogy) and also one on etiquette, *A Hundred Rules of Conduct for Children.*

Here is an excerpt from that book: "Toward your fellows act lovingly and peacefully; do not quarrel with them, hit them, dirty their clothes with your shoes or ink, nor give them nicknames. Act toward them always as you would have them act towards you" (www.skippack.org).

### Ronald Edmonds (1935–1983)

See quotation on page 144.

Edmonds was born and raised in Ypsilanti, Michigan, was educated in Michigan, and pursued advanced studies at Harvard. He worked at every level of the education system starting by teaching school in three states, working for Michigan's State Department of Education, and working as a professor and researcher.

His innovative work with Effective Schools is a great contribution he left behind for us to use. He "fostered the belief that improving education for poor children with management and discipline would improve education for all children,believing that every child can learn. (http://www.lib.lfc.edu/archives/Ronald_R._Edmonds.html)

### Ralph Waldo Emerson (1803–1882)

See quotations on pages 41 and 80.

Emerson is remembered as a philosopher and literary artist. Thanks to his family history and social position, Emerson entered Harvard at the age of fourteen. He taught school briefly before returning to school himself to study theology. He was ordained a Unitarian pastor and served as such for several years.

In 1833, he began his career as a lecturer, which included time on the Chautauqua Circuit of which the American Lyceum was the forerunner. In a speech at Harvard in 1837, Emerson "challenged his audience to cease imitating Europe and to ground their ideas in American resources, sincerity and realism." "Self-Reliance" was one of his more noteworthy themes and, in his terms, "to be self-reliant was to listen to and heed the still, small voice of God within" (www.25.uua.org).

## Abraham Flexner (1866–1959)

See quotation on page 123.

Flexner is best known as a leading authority on higher education. His contributions led to major changes in curriculum and teaching in medical schools. He started his own college career at Johns Hopkins University then founded an experimental school, which had no formal curriculum, exams, or grades, but excelled at preparing students for prestigious colleges. He did his master's at Harvard in psychology before pursuing his career in higher education research. He was the founding director of the Institute for Advanced Study

He firmly believed "in offering opportunities to all individuals" (http://www.ias.edu/people/flexner).

## John W. Gardner (1912–2002)

See quotations on pages 128 and 132.

Gardner began his career as a teacher before moving on to work for the Carnegie Corporation. His writing covered topics including "excellence" and the rejection of "shoddiness" in every field, making the case for "the common good" without sacrificing individuality, in addition to the topics of social reform, moral values, and leadership. Gardner felt that "America's future will seek to restore *faith in government* as a critical partner in community problem solving" (1994).

He was a Republican who served presidents of both parties. After leaving public office, he continued to foster volunteerism and the idea that cities should and can "tackle their own problems." He was the founder of Common Cause (http://www.bookrags.com/biography/john-w-gardner/).

## H. G. Good (1880–1971)

See quotations on pages 64, 71, and 84.

In an article published in *School and Society* ("The Approach to the History of Education," vol. 20, no. 504, August 23, 1924, 231–37), Good talks about approaching the history of education in relation to teacher preparation. He states, "Probably, as is now widely believed, young persons preparing to become teachers should first be introduced to some of the concrete problems of their profession."

He felt we were approaching teacher training by teaching "them their trade." And he suggested "if our purpose were—as it should be—the stimulation of professional intelligence we should undertake the task of cultivating a seriously critical attitude toward education." He advised that "[w]hat we ought to do depends upon what we mean to accomplish through the means at our command."

## Eric Hoffer (1902–1983)

See quotation on page 140.

Eric Hoffer was longshoreman with a thirst for reading. He had little formal education yet had eleven books successfully published. His first, *The True Believer*, is concerned with the main ingredient of mass movements, the frustrated individual. He carries the theme of "the nature of man" in his writings and provides insights that perhaps can only be provided by those living life with their eyes and ears open. He writes, "It is the individual alone who is timeless" http://www.erichoffer.net/).

## Harold Howe II (1918–2002)

See quotation on page 137.

Howe was a school teacher, principal, superintendent, public servant, and professor emeritus at Harvard. He "was in the forefront of efforts to combat social ills at the school level. Among his targets were poverty and racial segregation" (http://www.nytimes.com/2002/12/03/us/harold-howe-ii-84-fighter-against-segregated-schools.html).

He was most directly responsible for putting ESEA into practice, and in his reflections on the law he pointed to elements of it that should not be done away with such as its focus on disadvantaged students. One emphasis in his writings was on the responsibility and role of schools, families, and communities in instilling a cooperative ethic in young children believing that "education comes not just from schooling, but from all kinds of things" (http://www.thecrimson.com/article/2002/12/3/johnson-era-education-leader-former-lecturer-dies/).

### John Jensen (1935–)

See quotation on page 141.

Dr. Jensen is a clinical psychologist, education consultant, and former Catholic priest. He earned a master's degree in counseling, and a PhD in human development. His research focused on how classroom methods impact children. His "sustaining interest has been helping people prosper, which he has pursued through spirituality, education, and social change" (http://www.tokenrock.com/bio-John-Jensen-PhD-24.html).

Jensen is the author of several books; and in a series of articles, "Demystifying Social Change," he makes this point:"Awareness of the world these days means seeing needs unmet and wishing one could do something about them—education, for example. We can wish and hope for change, or we can set causes in motion" (http://www.educationnews.org/blogs/59469.html).

### Lyndon B. Johnson (1908–1973)

See quotation on page 142.

Commonly known as LBJ, he became president of the United States on November 22, 1963, following the assassination of President Kennedy. In May of 1964, he is quoted as saying, "We have the opportunity to move not only toward the rich society and the powerful society, but upward to the Great Society." The term "Great Society" is associated with him still, and the programs it represents include the "war on poverty," improving the education system, providing for the elder citizens, and aiding urban areas.

The list of his legislative accomplishments is long, but his legacy of them being realized was jeopardized by the Vietnam War. One of his programs was the Volunteers in Service to America (VISTA) where schools in impoverished American regions would "receive volunteer teaching attention" (http://www.ushistory.org/us/56e.asp).

### John F. Kennedy (1917–1963)

See quotations on pages 79 and 134.

John F. Kennedy was elected as our thirty-fifth president with the campaign pledge to "get America moving again." He launched economic programs to do just that while also responding to the demand for equal rights in the United States, the need for human rights throughout the world, and the call for stopping the spread of nuclear weapons.

On June 11, 1963, with the Alabama National Guard ready if needed, two young black men were peacefully admitted on the University of Alabama campus. In an address to the nation that night, Kennedy wisely stated that "law alone cannot make men see right." He went on to say, "A great change is at hand, and our task, our obligation, is to make that revolution, that change, peaceful and constructive for all." He asked for our help "to give a chance for every child to be educated to the limit of his talents" (www.americanrhetoric.com).

## Francis (Frank) Keppel (1916–1990)

See quotations on pages 121, 127, and 162.

Keppel received a bachelor's degree from Harvard and returned there to eventually become the dean of the Graduate School of Education. He never held a graduate degree himself. He served as dean until being asked to join the Kennedy administration. He was "often referred to as the 'Pied Piper of American Education'" (http://www.kdp.org/meetourlaureates/laureates/franciskeppel.php).

In a short article, "Voices from the Past," Keppel answers Robert Kennedy's inquiry about "measuring those damned educators" and about "investing money where it is really going to accomplish very little if any good." Keppel responded that there was "an assumption behind your statement, which is that the school systems are not prepared to change their habits. It seems to me that . . . there is a change going on in all school systems, both urban and rural, recognizing that children who have the special deprivation in terms of homes and schools need special help" (http://www.aypconsulting.org/Why_AYP_files/RFKComments.pdf).

## Martin Luther King Jr. (1929–1968)

See quotation on page 78.

Dr. King was a Baptist minister and credited for being the main leader of the civil rights movement during the 1950s and 1960s. His "March on Washington" in 1963 was organized to urge Congress to pass John F. Kennedy's civil rights bill calling for equal opportunity in employment and education.

He left us many words worth contemplating, including from his Nobel Peace Prize acceptance speech in 1964: "I refuse to accept the idea that man is mere flotsam and jetsam in the river of life unable to influence the unfolding of events which surround him"; and from his sermon on April 3, 1968, "Let us move on in these powerful days, these days of challenge to make America what it ought to be. We have an opportunity to make America a better nation" (www.thekingcenter.org).

### Muriel Lester (1883–1968)

See quotation on page 172.

Muriel Lester has been labeled a social reformer, pacifist, and nonconformist (www.en.wikipedia.org). She devoted her life to social justice by attempting to impact the structures of society through her Christian beliefs.

Lester seemed driven by the belief that we should take the teachings of Jesus Christ and apply them to daily life, especially in their application to the problems of the poor. In one poverty-stricken area of London, she and her sister Doris founded a community center that provided various services to the people including nondenominational spiritual guidance.

In the face of World War I and the call for patriotism of the English, Lester clung to her pacifist beliefs and joined the Fellowship of Reconciliation in 1914. She continued her work through politics and community organizing efforts and developed a following as a writer.

As World War II was mounting, she was "detained" but on release returned to her work in organizing food and medical aid for Europeans on both sides of the issue. In his paper "A Random Chapter in the History of Nonviolence," Michael L. Westmoreland-White wrote, "We can take strength from the way she faced her challenges as we face ours" (www.ecapc.org).

### Frank Manley (1904–1972)

See quotation on page 125.

Frank Manley's story is the story of an ordinary American with extraordinary leadership abilities described as "an almost indefinable combination of conviction and personality." He was a high school dropout drawn back into education through his interest in sports. In 1927, he became a physical education teacher in Flint, Michigan, and there he laid the foundation for the "modern community schools movement."

His daughter noted that "his children and family were his biggest priority and he wanted to make sure they were doing well and were happy in what they were doing." And he had what she described as this "missionary zeal. . . . He just simply thought they [community members] would want to help if they just knew what the problem was" (Decker, 1999).

## Horace Mann (1796–1859)

See quotation on page 105.

The "Father of American Public School Education," Horace Mann is credited with helping to establish a state-supervised, state-funded, mandatory-attendance school system in the United States. It has been said that one belief that motivated him to pursue that course was the idea that too much local control would result in improper schooling for some.

Mann also emphasized teacher training and established the first state-supported normal school (teacher training school) in 1839. Horace Mann understood the importance of money in making improvements to education and believed, among other things, that compensated school committees were needed to supervise teaching improvements and that it was in the best interest of businesses to pay taxation for education since they would most benefit.

In 1853 he became president of Antioch College in Ohio. In an address to graduates of that college a few weeks before he died, he said, "Be ashamed to die before you have won some battle for humanity" (www.cals.ncsu.edu).

## Ernest O. Melby (1891–1972)

See quotation on page 130.

Dr. Melby had a long history as an educator (teacher, principal, professor, and college dean). He left behind some short essays that are more than worth the time it takes to read them. From *The True Teacher Accepts All Students*, "it is in relation to students who are difficult that the teacher's true qualities are demonstrated" (http://www2.honolulu.hawaii.edu/facdev/guidebk/teachtip/m-files/m-trutea.htm).

And in *This I Believe* he said, "The great teacher is, thus, one who has faith in his pupils, affection for them, understanding of them, and wisdom enough to permit each pupil to be himself. What is true of the teacher is true of leadership in every area of human relationship. . . . Since I believe we can build a society in America and in the world which is based on freedom, faith, love, understanding, and human brotherhood, I have confidence in the ultimate triumph of the human spirit" (http://thisibelieve.org/essay/16813/).

## Thomas Paine (1737–1809)

See quotation on page 147.

Paine held a variety of jobs including one as a schoolteacher in London. As luck would have it, he met Benjamin Franklin, who helped him make his way to America, where he began a new career as a journalist in Philadelphia. He published *Common Sense*, the pamphlet that earned him the description as an agitator or revolutionary propagandist. He did not participate in reform measures themselves. His writings were his greatest accomplishments.

Paine left for Europe in 1787 and spent his time in France and Britain. It is said that his greatest work was *Rights of Man*, in which he "argued rationally that all men had an equal claim to political rights and that government must rest on the ultimate sovereignty of the people" (www.thehistoryguide.org).

## William Penn (1644–1718)

See quotation on page 1.

William Penn was expelled from England's Oxford University for rebelling against the rule that all enrolled students would attend the Church of England. He was later imprisoned several times for his preaching of Quakerism, but was granted permission to govern an area of America because his father was an admiral in good standing.

In his colony, he framed a government where the people could follow their religious beliefs without fear. Penn modeled the behavior he felt we should demonstrate toward each other, as evident by the way he got along with the Indians and honored any agreement he made with them. He did return to England, and it is said that two of his greatest works were a plan for a league of nations and an explanation of the principles for proper living.

## Theodore Roosevelt

See quotation on page 73.

Theodore Roosevelt, at forty-two, became the youngest president in the nation's history following the assassination of President McKinley. He is remembered for being a steward of the land, while he viewed the position of president as a "steward of the people" he fought to uphold "the ideal that the Government should be the great arbiter of the conflicting economic forces in the Nation, especially between capital and labor, guaranteeing justice to each and dispensing favors to none." He liked to quote a favorite proverb, "Speak softly and carry a big stick" (http://www.whitehouse.gov/about/presidents/theodoreroosevelt).

His view of curriculum matters is expressed in this quote: "To educate a person in mind and not morals is to educate a menace to society."

## Seymour B. Sarason (1919–2010)

See quotations on pages xiii, 77, 119, 121, 163.

Dr. Sarason received his PhD in psychology in 1942 and spent most of his career serving at Yale University in the fields of psychology and education. His many publications cover a wide range of topics. Particularly notable are his views on the multitude of "superficial" educational reforms and their failures.

Among his many awards is the Kappa Delta Pi Laureate in the field of education. During that society's 1999 convocation, Dr. Sarason was interviewed by Grant E. Mabie. In that interview, he once again demonstrated his courage and bluntness with words deserving of our reverence.

In talking about educators being treated with distain within the professional community, he said, "I'm being blunt, because people in positions to change this situation are not listening." He went on to say, "We need to move beyond predicting change to making it happen." He predicted that "only through shared knowledge of measurable results do we have any chance of truly making a difference, and, so far, no one is really trying to do that" (www.kdp.org).

## Edward Austin Sheldon (1823–1897)

See quotation on page 68.

While working as an evangelical missionary, Sheldon became interested in the education of the poor of Oswego. It's believed he had a genuine desire to make free education available to all children, even though his work was later viewed as having significant underlying religious motivations to convert Catholic children to Protestantism. He proposed taxation of the public to form citywide free schooling for Oswego; unsuccessful the first time, he returned to that battle and eventually prevailed.

In a June 7, 2001, independent study done by Michael Ruddy while at the University at Buffalo, the philosophies of Thomas Jefferson and the actions of Sheldon are discussed with respect to the ideals of democracy and education and the separation of church and state. Ruddy states that "Jefferson's ideals of a public school system serving the democratic needs of the republic would eventually evolve into being, it would happen only by a means Jefferson would not have likely approved" (Oswego.edu/~ruddy/BuffaloPapers/OswegoinEducation/SheldonPaper.pdf).

## Edwin E. Slosson (1865–1929)

See quotation on page 101.

Edwin Emery Slosson received his BS and MS from the University of Kansas and his PhD from the University of Chicago. He taught chemistry at the University of Wyoming and was a chemist at the Wyoming Agricultural Experiment Station. He became an editor for *The Independent* and a published author of books and articles in both the field of science and literature (www.en.wikipedia.org).

In an introduction he wrote for *The Life Stories of Undistinguished Americans*, you get a sense for the way he combines science with literature and an understanding of how children learn when he states that "the hardest part of the training of the scientist is to get back the clear sight of his childhood." He goes on to talk about "the discovery of the importance of the average man" and how "it is the undistinguished people who move the world, or who prevent it from moving" (www.brocku.ca).

## George Washington (1732–1799)

See quotation on page 96.

George Washington earned the title of "Father of the Country" by serving as the commander of the Continental Army that won our independence, the presiding president of the convention that produced our constitution, and the first president of the United States. He believed in a strong national government and governed with a fairness and integrity that set the standard for all presidents to follow. He felt that he was dispensable and asserted that liberty was larger than any individual.

He did not attend college or learn a foreign language as was common among the "learned" men of that time. On his own, he read and studied, and it is said that his library was quite extensive. It has been speculated that, because he felt his own education had been lacking, he "strongly believed in the value of a good education and left money in his will for establishing a school in Alexandria, Virginia as well as for establishing a national university."

According to an article by Jack D. Warren Jr., George Washington wrote, "It should be the highest ambition of every American to extend his views beyond himself and to bear in mind that his conduct will not only affect himself, his country, and his immediate posterity; but that its influence may be co-extensive with the world, and stamp political happiness or misery on ages yet unborn" (www.mountvernon.org).

# References

Aikin, Wilford M. "The Story of the Eight-Year Study: With Conclusions and Recommendations." *Adventure in American Education, Vol.1.* New York and London: Harper & Brothers, 1942.

Barr, Robert D., and William H. Parrett. *Hope Fulfilled for At-Risk and Violent Youth: K–12 Programs That Work,* 2nd ed. Needham Heights, MA: Allyn & Bacon, 2001.

Bensman, David. *Central Park East and Its Graduates: "Learning by Heart."* New York: Teachers College Press, 2000.

Bosch, Carl. *Schools Under Siege: Guns, Gangs, and Hidden Dangers.* Springfield, NJ: Enslow, 1997.

Bowler, Mike. "Professor's Work Was Misinterpreted." *Baltimore Sun,* April 4, 1995. http://articles.baltimoresun.com/keyword/busing/featured/2

Bradbury, Ray. *Fahrenheit 451,* 2nd ed. New York: Del Rey Books, 1953.

Bullough, Robert V. "Professional Learning Communities and the Eight-Year Study." *Educational Horizons* (Spring 2007): 168–80.

Bushaw, William J., and Shane J. Lopez. "A Time for Change: 42nd Annual Phi Delta Kappa/Gallup Poll of the Public's Attitude Toward the Public Schools." *Phi Delta Kappan,* September, 2010.

———. "Betting on Teachers: 43rd Annual Phi Delta Kappa/Gallup Poll of the Public's Attitude Toward the Public Schools." *Phi Delta Kappan,* September, 2011.

Cater, Douglass. Interview IV, April 24, 1981, Joe B. Frantz, p. 15, LBJ Library. http://www.lbjlib.utexas.edu/johnson/archives.hom/oralhistory.hom/cater/cater04.pdf

*Code of Fair Testing Practices in Education,* 2nd ed. Washington, DC: Joint Committee on Testing Practices, 2004.

Coleman, James. *Equality of Educational Opportunity: Summary.* U.S. Department of Health, Education, and Welfare, July 2, 1966. http://www.eric.ed.gov/PDFS/ED015953.pdf

Congressional Quarterly. *Congress and the Nation: A Review of the Government and Politics During the Johnson Years, Vol. II, 1965–1968.* Washington, DC: Congressional Quarterly, 1969.

Cooperative Study of Secondary School Standards. *Evaluation of Secondary Schools: General Report on the Methods, Activities, and Results of the Cooperative Study of Secondary School Standards.* Washington, DC: Author, 1939.

Darling-Hammond, Linda. *The Flat World and Education: How America's Commitment to Equity Will Determine Our Future.* New York: Teachers College Press, 2010.

Decker, Larry E. *The Evolution of the Community School Concept: The Leadership of Frank J. Manley.* National Community Education Association, 1999. http://www.eric.ed.gov/PDFS/ED440178.pdf

Edmonds, Ronald R. "Programs of School Improvement: An Overview." *Educational Leadership*, December 1982. http://www.ascd.org/ASCD/pdf/journals/ed_lead/el_198212_edmonds.pdf

Elementary and Secondary Education Act (ESEA) (P.L. 89-10). *United States Statutes at Large* 79 (April 11, 1965): 27–58. http://www.ncticl1p.org/files/40646763.pdf

Emery, Kathy, and Susan Ohanian. *Why Is Corporate America Bashing Our Public Schools?* Portsmouth, NH: Heinemann, 2004.

*Encyclopedia Americana International Edition, Vol. 17*. Danbury, CT: Grolier, 1999.

Engel, Angela. *Seeds of Tomorrow: Solutions for Improving Our Children's Education*. Boulder, CO: Paradigm, 2009.

Foley, Ellen, et al. *Beyond Test Scores: Leading Indicators for Education*. Annenberg Institute for School Reform, Brown University. http://annenberginstitute.org/pdf/LeadingIndicators.pdf

Gallagher, B.J., and Warren H. Schmidt. *A Peacock in the Land of Penguins: A Story about Courage in Creating a Land of Opportunity*. Naperville, IL: Simple-Truths, 2008.

Gamoran, A., and D. A. Long. *Equality of Educational Opportunity: A 40-Year Retrospective*. Wisconsin Center for Education Research, December, 2006. http://www.wcer.wisc.edu/publications/workingpapers/Working_Paper_No_2006_09.pdf

Gardner, John W. *There Is More Than a Ray of Hope for America's Future . . . Rebuilding America's Sense of Community*. Common Cause, 1994. http://www.worldtrans.org/qual/americancommunity.html

Gatto, John Taylor. *Dumbing Us Down: The Hidden Curriculum of Compulsory Schooling*. Gabriola Island, BC: New Society, 2005.

Good, H. G. *A History of American Education*, 1st ed. New York: Ohio State University, Macmillan, 1956.

Hanna, Julia. *The Elementary and Secondary Education Act: 40 Years Later*. Harvard Graduate School of Education, 2005. http://www.gse.harvard.edu/news/2005/0819_esea.html

Hamilton, Alexander, James Madison, and John Jay. *The Federalist Papers, 1787–1788*. Introduction by Garry Wills, 1982. New York: Bantam Dell, 2003.

Hoffer, Eric. *The True Believer: Thoughts on the Nature of Mass Movements*. New York: Harper & Row, 1951.

Hofstadter, Richard. *The Age of Reform: From Bryan to F.D.R.* New York: Vintage Books, 1955.

Hubbard, L. Ron. *Learning How to Learn*. Los Angeles: Bridge, 1992.

Idaho Code Commission. *Idaho Code containing the General Laws of Idaho Annotated, Titles 33-34*. Charlottesville, VA: Michie, 2008.

Johnson, Lyndon B. *Special Message to Congress: "Toward Full Educational Opportunity,"* January 12, 1965. http://www.presidency.ucsb.edu/ws/index.php?pid=27448#axzz1dobIpZIL

Johnston, Howard. "Advisory Programs to Restructured Adult-Student Relationships: Restoring Purpose to the Guidance Function of the Middle Level School." *Schools in the Middle*. National Association of Secondary Schools Principals, March, 1997.

Kennedy, John F. *Special Message to the Congress on Education*, January 29, 1963. http://www2.ed.gov/policy/elsec/leg/esea02/107-110.pdf

Keppel, Francis. *The Necessary Revolution in American Education*. New York and London: Harper & Row, 1966.

Lawrence-Lightfoot, Sara. *The Essential Conversation: What Parents and Teachers Can Learn from Each Other*. New York: Random House, 2003.

Lester, Muriel. *Dare You Face Facts?*, 3rd ed. New York: Harper & Brothers, 1940.

Levine, Eliot. *One Kid at a Time: Big Lessons from a Small School*. New York: Teachers College Press, 2002.

Lewis, James, Jr. *Achieving Excellence in Our Schools . . . by Taking Lessons from America's Best-Run Companies*. Westbury, NY: Wilkerson, 1986.

Loucks-Horsley, Susan. *The Concerns-Based Adoption Model (CBAM): A Model for Change in Individuals*. Dubuque, IA: Kendall/Hunt, 1996.

Marden, Peter V. "The Sociology of James S. Coleman." *Annual Review of Sociology* 31 (2005): 1–24. http://www.annualreviews.org/doi/pdf/10.1146/annu-rev.soc.31.041304.122209

Marzano, Robert J., and Jon S. Kendall. *The Fall and Rise of Standards-Based Education.* September 26, 1997. http://www.mcrel.org/pdf/standards/5962ir_fallandrise.pdf

Mathers, Carrie, et al. *Improving Instruction Through Effective Teacher Evaluation: Options for States and Districts.* National Comprehensive Center for Teacher Quality, February 2008.

McKinsey & Company. *How the World's Best-Performing School Systems Come Out on Top.* September, 2007. http://mckinseyonsociety.com/how-the-worlds-best-performing-schools-come-out-on-top/

Meier, Deborah, Monty Neill, et al. The Forum for Education and Democracy. *Many Children Left Behind: How the No Child Left Behind Act Is Damaging Our Children and Our Schools.* Boston, MA: Beacon Press, 2004.

Minow, Martha. "Choice or Commonality: Welfare and Schooling After the End of Welfare as We Knew It." *Duke Law Journal* 49 (1999): 493–559.

Minzey, Jack D., and Clyde E. LeTarte. *Reforming Public Schools Through Community Education.* Dubuque, IA: Kendall/Hunt, 1994.

National Advisory Council on the Education of Disadvantaged Children. *Report of the National Advisory Council on the Education of Disadvantaged Children.* Washington, DC: Author, March 31, 1966. http://www.eric.ed.gov/PDFS/ED030688.pdf

National Commission on Excellence in Education. *A Nation at Risk: The Imperative for Educational Reform.* Washington, DC: United States Department of Education, 1983.

No Child Left Behind (NCLB) Act of 2002, (P.L. 107-110), January 8, 2002. http://www2.ed.gov/policy/elsec/leg/esea02/107-110.pdf

Noguera, Pedro A. *City Schools and the American Dream: Reclaiming the Promise of Public Education.* New York: Teachers College Press, 2003.

Payne, Ruby K. *Working with Parents: Building Relationships for Student Success*, 2nd ed. Highlands, TX: aha! Process, 2005.

Phillips, Kevin. *Arrogant Capital: Washington, Wall Street, and the Frustration of American Politics.* New York: Little, Brown, 1994.

Price-Mitchell, Marilyn. "Boundary Dynamics: Implications for Building Parent-School Partnerships." *Community Journal* 19, no. 2 (2009): 9–26.

Ratner, Gershon (Gary) M. "Why the No Child Left Behind Act Needs to Be Restructured to Accomplish Its Goals and How to Do It." *University of the District of Columbia Law Review* 9, no. 1 (Winter 2007).

Ratner, Gary, and Monty Neill. *Common Elements of Successful School Turnarounds: Research and Experience.* May 14, 2010. www.citizenseffectiveschools.org/successfulschool-turnarounds.pdf

Ravitch, Diane. *The Death and Life of the Great American School System: How Testing and Choice Are Undermining Education.* New York: Basic Books, 2010.

Reeves, Douglas B. *101 Questions & Answers about Standards, Assessment, and Accountability.* Denver, CO: Advanced Learning Press, 2001.

Reigeluth, Charles M. "Educational Standards: To Standardize or to Customize Learning?" *Phi Delta Kappan*, November 1997. www.indiana.edu/~syschang/decatur/documents/72_Standards_to_Customize.pdf

Sacks, Peter. *Standardized Minds: The High Price of America's Testing Culture and What We Can Do to Change It.* Cambridge, MA: Perseus Books, 1999.

Sarason, Seymour. *The Case for Change: Rethinking the Preparation of Educators.* San Francisco: Jossey-Bass, 1993.

———. *Parental Involvement and the Political Principle: Why the Existing Governance Structure of Schools Should Be Abolished.* San Francisco: Jossey-Bass, 1995.

Slosson, Edwin E. *The American Spirit in Education.* New Haven, CT: Yale University Press, 1921.

"Smith-Towner Bill." *The Elementary School Journal* (April 1920): 575–83.

208       *References*

United States Advisory Commission on Intergovernmental Relations. *Intergovernmentalizing the Classroom: Federal Involvement in Elementary and Secondary Education.* Washington, DC: UNT Digital Library. http://digital.library.unt.edu/ark:/67531/metadc1334/m1/50/

Valverde, G., and W. Schmidt. "Refocusing U.S. Math and Science Education." *Issues in Science and Technology* (Winter 1997–1998): 60–66.

*Webster's New World Dictionary*, 2nd college ed. Cleveland, OH: William Collins and World Publishing, 1976.

Weinstein, Rhona. *Reaching Higher: The Power of Expectations in Schooling.* Cambridge, MA: Harvard University Press, 2002.

White House. "Press Office Fact Sheet: Expanding the Promise of Education in America." March 10, 2009. www.whitehouse.gov/the_press_office/Fact-Sheet-Expanding-the-Promise-of-Education-in-America/.

Zhao, Yong. *Catching Up or Leading the Way: American Education in the Age of Globalization.* Alexandria, VA: ASCD, 2009.

# Index

# About the Author

**Victoria M. Young** earned both her bachelor of science in animal husbandry and doctorate of veterinary medicine from Michigan State University. She enjoys working with animals and their people, playing tennis, skiing, and returning home to canoe on the Kalamazoo River and visit family. She is married and a mother of two, both of whom graduated from high school and successfully pursued college degrees.

Dr. Young served in her children's schools for eleven years, in her district for eighteen, and received a Friend of Caldwell Schools Award in recognition of her support in the pursuit of excellence education. Residing in Idaho, she has continued her educational advocacy by developing a better understanding of the issues facing our country with the objective of helping people get back their voices and take back their schools. She was the ad hoc secretary for the Save Our Schools March in the summer of 2011 and continues to believe, like the original core group of the movement, that the country will benefit by establishing a National Support Public Education Day to promote transparency and discourse. She believes informed citizens will choose wisely.